FUNDAMENTALS OF

ENGLISH GRAMMAR

Third Edition

Volume B

Longman

Betty Schrampfer Azar

Fundamentals of English Grammar, Third Edition
Volume B

Azar Associates
Shelley Hartle, Editor
Susan Van Etten, Manager

Pearson Education, 10 Bank Street, White Plains, NY 10606

Vice president, director of publishing: Allen Ascher
Editorial manager: Pam Fishman
Project manager: Margo Grant
Development editor: Janet Johnston
Vice president, director of design and production: Rhea Banker
Director of electronic production: Aliza Greenblatt
Executive managing editor: Linda Moser
Production manager: Ray Keating
Production editor: Robert Ruvo
Director of manufacturing: Patrice Fraccio
Senior manufacturing buyer: Edie Pullman
Cover design: Monika Popowitz
Illustrations: Don Martinetti
Text composition: Carlisle Communications, Ltd.
Text font: 10.5/12 Plantin

ISBN: 0-13-013652-2

Printed in the United States of America
4 5 6 7 8 9 10–CRK–06 05

W is for White Dodo. Almost everyone knows that Dodo birds are extinct. They used to live peacefully on islands in the Indian Ocean. They had no natural predators until sailors arrived with pigs, monkeys, cats, and rats. Eventually, the Dodo birds vanished.

Legend has it that people could walk right up to a Dodo and step on it. Apparently, Dodos were not very smart.

W w

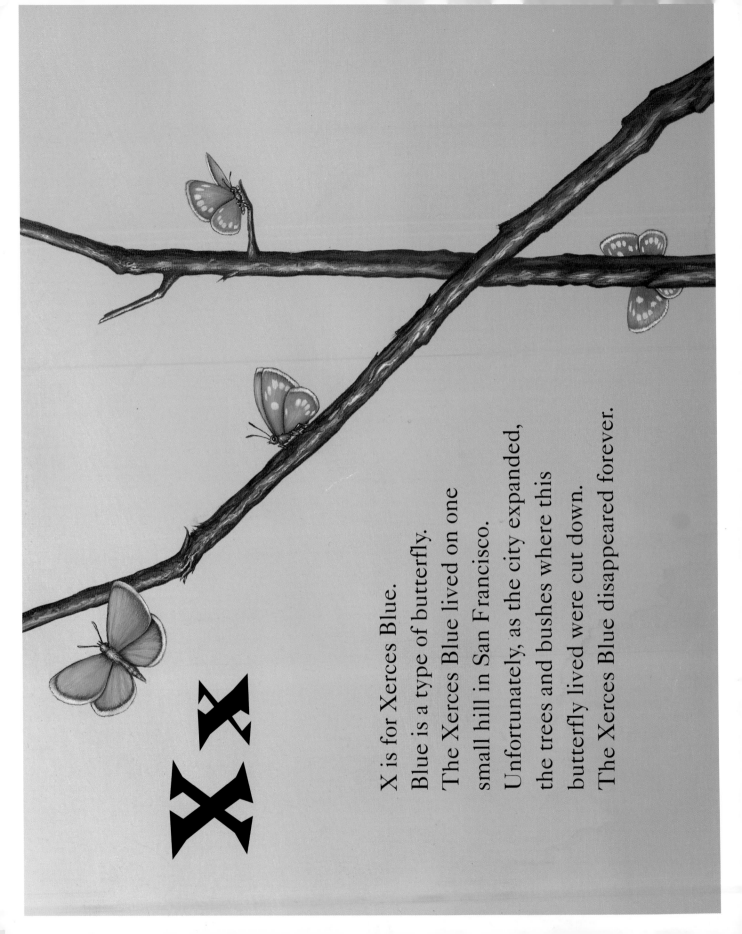

X x

X is for Xerces Blue.
Blue is a type of butterfly.
The Xerces Blue lived on one
small hill in San Francisco.
Unfortunately, as the city expanded,
the trees and bushes where this
butterfly lived were cut down.
The Xerces Blue disappeared forever.

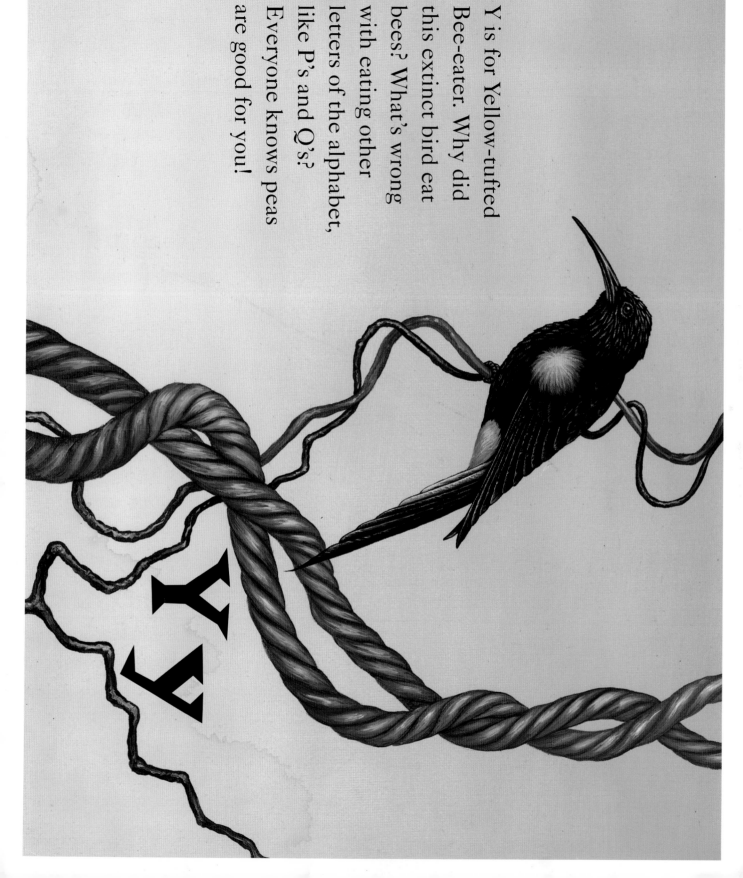

Y is for Yellow-tufted
Bee-eater. Why did
this extinct bird eat
bees? What's wrong
with eating other
letters of the alphabet,
like P's and Q's?
Everyone knows peas
are good for you!

Z is for Zygorhiza. Notice that this sea mammal had a neck. Today, dolphins, porpoises, and whales are beautifully streamlined so that they can swim faster.

Zillions of plants and animals lived on Earth and then became extinct over the last four billion years. Imagine how many other species will be extinct in the future. Let's hope human beings never become extinct.

CONTENTS

Preface to the Third Edition

Fundamentals of English Grammar is a developmental skills text for lower-intermediate and intermediate students of English as a second or foreign language. It combines clear and understandable grammar information with a variety of exercises and activities.

Fundamentals of English Grammar is the second in a series of three texts: *Basic English Grammar* (red cover), *Fundamentals of English Grammar* (black cover), and *Understanding and Using English Grammar* (blue cover).

The principal aims of all three texts in this series are to present clear, cogent information about English grammar and usage, to provide extensive and varied practice that encourages growth in all areas of language use, and to be interesting, useful, and fun for student and teacher alike. The approach is eclectic, with the texts seeking to balance form-focused language-learning activities with abundant opportunities for engaged and purposeful communicative interaction.

The new editions of the texts in the Azar Grammar Series include these changes:

- The communicative aspects are more fully developed and explicit in the third editions. This edition of *Fundamentals of English Grammar* includes a greatly increased number of "real communication" opportunites for the teacher to exploit. The text often uses the students' own life experiences as context and regularly introduces topics of interest to stimulate the free expression of ideas in structured as well as open discussions.

  The Azar Grammar Series texts support the view of many experienced teachers that grammar-based and communicative approaches are not mutually exclusive, but rather mutually supportive, and can advantageously co-exist in the same language program, even in the same class, even in the same lesson.

- Similarly, the interactive aspects of the texts receive greater emphasis in the third editions. Many of the exercises formerly designated ORAL or ORAL (BOOKS CLOSED) are now reformatted to be more clearly available for pair work or group work, in addition to still being viable as class work led by a teacher. This edition of *Fundamentals of English Grammar* encourages interactivity but leaves it open for the users to decide what degree of interactivity best suits their needs.

- There is now an even wider variety of exercise types. This edition has a much larger number of free-response exercises and open-ended communicative tasks, while still providing ample controlled-response exercises to aid initial understanding of the form, meaning, and usage of the target structures. It also includes more writing topics, more speaking activities, new error-analysis exercises in every chapter, and additional extended-context exercises. Classroom teaching materials formerly found in the *Workbook* are now included in this student text, with the *Workbook* devoted solely to self-study exercises. The *Workbook* has a variety of practice approaches for independent study.

- A specific change in this edition of *Fundamentals of English Grammar* is the two Appendices, one with phrasal verbs and one with preposition combinations. Rather than asking students to study a whole chapter of these phrases at one time, the text uses appendices to present them in smaller groupings for teachers to intersperse throughout the teaching term. Another specific change is the omission of conditional sentences, which are presented in *Understanding and Using English Grammar.*

- The accompanying *Teacher's Guide* is written for both experienced and inexperienced teachers. It contains amplified grammar notes the teacher might want to present to the class or will find useful as background information. It outlines various ways of approaching the materials in the classroom and frequently suggests fresh teaching ideas for individual exercises beyond the directions in the text. It seeks to share with the teacher an understanding of the rationale behind the text's content and approaches. Its principal purpose is to make the busy teacher's job easier.

Fundamentals of English Grammar consists of
  - a *Student Book* without an answer key
  - a *Student Book* with an answer key
  - a *Workbook,* consisting of self-study exercises for independent work
  - a *Chartbook,* a reference book consisting of only the grammar charts
  - a *Teacher's Guide,* with teaching suggestions and additional notes on grammar, as well as the answers to the exercises
  - a *Test Bank*

ACKNOWLEDGMENTS

The third edition of *FEG* was reviewed by nine ESL/EFL professionals. I wish to express my thanks to these colleagues for their exceedingly helpful insights and suggestions. They are Stephanie La Qua, International Center for American English; Diane Mahin, University of Miami; Amy Parker, Embassy CES Intensive English Program; Gary Pietsch, Green River Community College; Thomas Pinkerton, North Miami Senior High School; Haydée Alvarado Santos, University of Puerto Rico; Hye-Young Um, Myongji University, Seoul, Korea; Lyn Waldie, Helenic-American Union, Athens, Greece; Aida Zic, Montgomery College.

My wholehearted thanks go to Shelley Hartle, who makes my job easy, and Editor Janet Johnston, who guides and assists us in so very many ways. Editor Margo Grant is simply super to work with, as are the many other skilled professionals at Pearson Education who have contributed to the publication of this work; in particular, Joanne Dresner, Anne Boynton-Trigg, Allen Ascher, Pam Fishman, Rhea Banker, Linda Moser, Aliza Greenblatt, Ray Keating, Barry Katzen, Kate McLoughlin, Sylvia Herrera-Alaniz, Bruno Paul, Hugo Loyola, Mike Bennett, Stacy Whitis, Monika Popowicz, Julie Hammond, and Amy Durfy.

A special thank you is reserved for Production Editor Robert Ruvo, who stayed on top of everything and remained unflappable.

I'd like to thank Carlisle Communications, Ltd., whose staff so excellently turned our disks into print pages. Without a doubt, they are the most skilled and reliable compositors I've worked with in twenty years.

I also once again thank Don Martinetti, the illustrator, whose touches of whimsy are so delightful. My appreciation also goes to graphic designer Christine Shrader, creator of the swallow that heralds this third edition.

My great appreciation goes to Stacy Hagen, an experienced ESL author,* who created new materials for the revised *Fundamentals of English Grammar Workbook*, bringing fresh approaches and ideas. Working with her was a very good experience.

I wish to express special acknowledgment of the contributing writers for the previous edition of the *Workbook:* Rachel Spack Koch, Susan Jamieson, Barbara Andrews, and Jeanie Francis. Some of the exercise material originally created for that workbook has been woven into this third edition of the student book, and I thank them for the ways in which this material has enriched the text. I am additionally very grateful to Rachel Spack Koch for her devotion and expertise in answering grammar and usage questions from teachers on the current Azar Companion Web Site.

I am indebted especially and always to my many students through the years; I learned so much from them. I also am indebted to my fellow ESL/EFL materials writers, past and present; we learn much from each other. I would like to make special mention of Thomas Crowell and Irene Schoenberg.

In addition, my thanks go to Donna Cowan, University of Washington, Patti Gulledge-White, Sue Van Etten, Joy Edwards, my great girls Chelsea and Rachel, and my wonderfully supportive husband, Larry Harris.

---

*Sound Advice: A Basis for Listening, 2000, Pearson Education; Better Writing Through Editing, 1999, McGraw-Hill (co-author Jan Peterson); and Sound Advantage: A Pronunciation Book, 1992, Pearson Education (co-author Pat Grogan).

CHAPTER 8
Connecting Ideas

CONTENTS

☐ EXERCISE 1. Preview. (Chapter 8)

Directions: Add punctuation (commas and periods) and capital letters if necessary. Do not change or add any words.

1. Butterflies are insects all insects have six legs.
   → *Butterflies are insects. All insects have six legs.*

2. Ants and butterflies are insects. OK *(no change)*

3. Ants, butterflies, cockroaches, bees, and flies are insects.

4. Butterflies and bees are insects, spiders are different from insects.

5. Spiders have eight legs, so they are not called insects.

6. Most insects have wings, but spiders do not.

7. Bees are valuable to us, they pollinate crops and provide us with honey.

8. Some insects bite us and carry diseases.

Free flower pollination with each purchase

Honey for SALE

9. Insects can cause us trouble. They bite us carry diseases and eat our food.

10. Insects are essential to life on earth. The plants and animals on earth could not live

without them. Insects may bother us, but we have to share this planet with them.

11. We have to share the earth with insects because they are essential to plant and

animal life. *no change*

12. Because insects are necessary to life on earth, it is important to know about them.

8-1 CONNECTING IDEAS WITH *AND*

CONNECTING ITEMS WITHIN A SENTENCE	When *and* connects only **two** words (or phrases) within a sentence, NO COMMA is used, as in (a).
(a) NO COMMA: I saw a cat *and* a mouse. (b) COMMAS: I saw a cat**,** a mouse**,** *and* a dog.	When *and* connects **three or more** items within a sentence, COMMAS are used, as in (b).★
CONNECTING TWO SENTENCES	When *and* connects two complete sentences (also called independent clauses), a comma is usually used, as in (c).
(c) COMMA: I saw a cat**,** *and* you saw a mouse.	
(d) PERIOD: I saw a cat**.** You saw a mouse. (e) *INCORRECT: I saw a cat, you saw a mouse.*	Without **and**, two complete sentences are separated by a period, as in (d), NOT a comma.★★ A complete sentence begins with a capital letter; note that *You* is capitalized in (d).

 ★In a series of three or more items, the comma before *and* is optional.
   ALSO CORRECT: *I saw a cat**,** a mouse and a dog.*
 ★★A "period" (the dot used at the end of a sentence) is called a "full stop" in British English.

☐ EXERCISE 2. Connecting ideas with AND. (Chart 8-1)
   Directions: Underline and label the words (noun, verb, adjective) connected by **and**. Add commas as necessary.

   noun + noun
1. My aunt puts milk and sugar in her tea. → *no commas needed*

   noun + noun + noun
2. My aunt puts milk**,**   sugar**,** and lemon in her tea. → *commas needed*

   n v adj   adj
3. The river is wide and deep. no comma

4. The river is wide deep and dangerous. no comma

5. Goats and horses are farm animals.

6. Giraffes anteaters tigers and kangaroos are wild animals.

7. The children played games sang songs and ate birthday cake.

8. The children played games and sang songs.

9. My mother father and grandfather went to the airport to pick up my brother and

   sister.

10. When he wants to entertain the children, my husband moos like a cow roars like a lion

   and barks like a dog.

☐ **EXERCISE 3. Connecting ideas with AND. (Chart 8-1)**
   Directions: Write sentences for some or all of the topics below. Use ***and*** in your sentences.

   Example: three things you are afraid of
   → *I'm afraid of heights, poisonous snakes, and guns.*

   1. your three favorite sports
   2. three adjectives that describe a person whom you admire
   3. four cities that you would like to visit
   4. two characteristics that describe *(name of this city)*
   5. three or more separate things you did this morning
   6. the five most important people in your life
   7. two or more things that make you happy
   8. three or more adjectives that describe the people in your country

☐ **EXERCISE 4. Punctuating with commas and periods. (Chart 8-1)**
   Directions: Add commas and periods where appropriate. Capitalize as necessary.

   1. The rain fell the wind blew.
      → *The rain fell.* ***T****he wind blew.*

   2. The rain fell and the wind blew.
      → *The rain fell**,** and the wind blew.*★

                He
   3. I talked, ̶h̶e listened.

   4. I talked to Ryan about his school grades,and he listened to me carefully.

★Sometimes the comma is omitted when ***and*** connects two very short independent clauses.
   ALSO CORRECT: *The rain fell* ***and*** *the wind blew.* (NO COMMA)
In longer sentences, the comma is helpful and usual.

5. The man asked a question. ~~the~~ The woman answered it.

6. The man asked a question, and the woman answered it.

7. People and animals must share the earth and its resources. no

8. Rome is an Italian city. ~~it~~ It has a mild climate and many interesting attractions.

9. You should visit Rome. ~~its~~ Its climate is mild, and there are many interesting attractions.

10. The United States is bounded by two oceans and two countries. ~~the~~ The oceans are the

    Pacific to the west and the Atlantic to the east, and the countries are Canada to the

    north and Mexico to the south.

11. The twenty-five most common words in English are: *the, and, a, to, of, I, in, was, that, it, he*

    you, for, had, is, with, she, has, on, at, have, but, me, my, and *not*.

8-2 CONNECTING IDEAS WITH *BUT* AND *OR*

(a) I *went to bed **but** couldn't sleep.* (b) Is a lemon *sweet **or** sour?* (c) Did you order *coffee**,** tea**,** or milk?*	***And, but,*** and ***or*** are called "conjunctions."★ Like ***and, but*** and ***or*** can connect items within a sentence. Commas are used with a series of three or more items, as in (c).
I dropped the vase. = a sentence *It didn't break.* = a sentence (d) I dropped the vase**,** *but* it didn't break. (e) Do we have class on Monday**,** *or* is Monday a holiday?	A comma is usually used when ***but*** or ***or*** combines two complete (independent) sentences into one sentence, as in (d) and (e).★★

  ★More specifically, *and, but,* and *or* are called "coordinating conjunctions."
  ★★Except in very formal writing, a conjunction can also come at the beginning of a sentence.
       ALSO CORRECT: *I dropped the vase.* ***B****ut it didn't break.*
           I saw a cat. ***A****nd you saw a mouse.*

☐ EXERCISE 5. Connecting ideas with AND, BUT, and OR. (Charts 8-1 and 8-2)
   Directions: Add ***and, but,*** or ***or.*** Add commas if necessary.

   1. I washed my shirt __, but__ it didn't get clean.

   2. Would you like some water ____or____ some fruit juice?

   3. I bought some paper, a greeting card __, and__ some envelopes.

   4. The flight attendants served dinner __, but__ I didn't eat.

5. I was hungry ____but____ didn't eat on the plane. The food didn't look appetizing.

6. I washed my face, brushed my teeth ₉ _and_ combed my hair.

7. Golf __and__ tennis (are) popular sports.

8. Sara is a good tennis player ₉ _but_ she's never played golf.

9. Which would you prefer? Would you like to play tennis ____or____ golf Saturday morning?

10. Who called whom? Did Bob call you ₉ _or_ did you call Bob?

☐ EXERCISE 6. Punctuating with commas and periods. (Charts 8-1 and 8-2)
   Directions: Add commas, periods, and capital letters as appropriate.

1. Cats are mammals turtles are reptiles.
   → *Cats are mammals.* **T**urtles are reptiles.

2. Cats are mammals₉but turtles are reptiles.

3. Cows and horses are farm animals₉but zebras and giraffes are wild animals.

4. Cows and horses are farm animals,~~z~~ebras₉giraffes₉ and lions are wild animals.
   Zebras

5. Cars use roads,~~t~~rains run on tracks.
   Trains

6. Cars₉buses₉and trucks use roads₉but trains run on tracks.

7. Most vegetables grow above the ground₉but some are roots and grow under the ground₉.corn₉beans₉and cabbage grow above the ground₉but carrots and onions grow under the ground.
   Corn

8. Why do people with different ethnic backgrounds sometimes fear and distrust each other? *no*

9. Nothing in nature stays the same forever₉today's land₉sea₉climate₉plants₉and animals are all part of a relentless process of change continuing through millions of years.
   To

10. Mozart was a great composer, but he had a short and difficult life. At the end of his life, he was penniless, sick, and unable to find work, but he wrote music of lasting beauty and joy.

8-3 CONNECTING IDEAS WITH *SO*

(a) The room was dark, *so* I turned on a light.	*So* can be used as a conjunction. It is preceded by a comma. It connects the ideas in two independent clauses. *So* expresses **results**: cause: *The room was dark.* result: *I turned on a light.*
(b) COMPARE: The room was dark, *but* I didn't turn on a light.	*But* often expresses an unexpected result, as in (b).

☐ EXERCISE 7. SO vs. BUT. (Charts 8-2 and 8-3)
   Directions: Add *so* or *but*.

1. It began to rain, _____so_____ I opened my umbrella.

2. It began to rain, _____but_____ I didn't open my umbrella.

3. I didn't have an umbrella, _____so_____ I got wet.

4. I didn't have an umbrella, _____but_____ I didn't get wet because I was wearing my raincoat.

5. The water was cold, _____so_____ I didn't go swimming.

6. The water was cold, _____but_____ I went swimming anyway.

7. Scott's directions to his apartment weren't clear, _____so_____ George got lost.

8. The directions weren't clear, _____but_____ I found Scott's apartment anyway.

9. My friend lied to me, _____but_____ I still like and trust her.

10. My friend lied to me, _____so_____ I don't trust her anymore.

☐ **EXERCISE 8. Punctuating with commas and periods. (Charts 8-1 → 8-3)**
   Directions: Add commas, periods, and capital letters as necessary.

1. African elephants are larger than Asiatic elephants. **E** elephants native to Asia are easier to train and have gentler natures than African elephants.

2. Asiatic elephants are native to the jungles and forests in India Indonesia Malaysia Thailand India China and other countries in southeastern and southern Asia.

3. Elephants spend a lot of time in water and are good swimmers they take baths in rivers and lakes they like to give themselves showers by shooting water from their trunks.

4. After a bath, they often cover themselves with dirt the dirt protects their skin from the sun and insects.

5. A female elephant is pregnant for approximately twenty months and almost always has only one baby a young elephant stays close to its mother for the first ten years of its life.

6. Elephants live peacefully together in herds but some elephants (called *rogues)* leave the herd and become mean these elephants usually are in pain from decayed teeth a disease or a wound.

□ **EXERCISE 9. Punctuating with commas and periods. (Charts 8-1 → 8-3)**
    Directions: Add commas, periods, and capital letters as necessary.

(1)   **A** a few days ago, a friend and I were driving from Benton Harbor to Chicago.

(2)   **W** we didn't experience any delays for the first hour but near Chicago we ran into

(3)   some highway construction the traffic wasn't moving at all my friend and I sat in the

(4)   car and waited we talked about our jobs our families and the terrible traffic slowly the

(5)   traffic started to move

(6)   we noticed a black sports car at the side of the road the right blinker was blinking

(7)   the driver obviously wanted to get back into the line of traffic car after car passed

(8)   without letting the black sports car get in line I decided to do a good deed so I

(9)   motioned for the black car to get in line ahead of me the driver of the black car waved

(10)   thanks to me and I waved back at him

(11)   all cars had to stop at a toll booth a short way down the road I held out my

(12)   money to pay my toll but the tolltaker just smiled and waved me on she told me that the

(13)   man in the black sports car had already paid my toll wasn't that a nice way of saying

(14)   thank you?

8-4 USING AUXILIARY VERBS AFTER *BUT* AND *AND*

(a) I **don't like** coffee, **but** my husband **does**. (b) I **like** tea, **but** my husband **doesn't**. (c) I **won't be** here tomorrow, **but** Sue **will**. (d) I**'ve seen** that movie, **but** Joe **hasn't**. (e) He **isn't** here, **but** she **is**.★	In (a): **does** = *likes coffee*. After **but** and **and**, often only an auxiliary verb is used. It has the same tense or modal as the main verb.

(f) I **don't like** coffee, **and** Ed **doesn't** either.
 (g) I **like** tea, **and** Kate **does** too.
 (h) I **won't be** here, **and** he **won't** either.
 (i) I**'ve seen** that movie, **and** Pat **has** too.
 (j) He **isn't** here, **and** Anna **isn't** either.
	Notice in the examples:
	      negative + *but* + affirmative
	      affirmative + *but* + negative
	
	      negative + *and* + negative
	      affirmative + *and* + affirmative

★A verb is not contracted with a pronoun at the end of a sentence after *but* and *and*:

     CORRECT: . . . *but she is.*
     INCORRECT: . . . *but she's.*

☐ EXERCISE 10. Using auxiliary verbs after BUT. (Chart 8-4)
     Directions: Complete the sentences with auxiliary verbs.

1. Debra **reads** a lot of books, but her brothers _____ *don't* _____.

2. Sam **isn't** in the school play this year, but Adam _____ *is* _____.

3. I **will be** at home this evening, but my roommate _____.

4. Ducks **like** to swim, but chickens _____.

5. That phone **doesn't work**, but this one _____.

6. Joe **isn't** at home, but his parents _____.

7. Carl **can touch** his nose with his tongue, but most people _____.

8. Jack **has visited** my home, but Linda _____.

9. I**'m not going** to graduate this year, but my best friend _____.

10. My dog **crawls** under the bed when it thunders, but my cat _____.

☐ EXERCISE 11. Using auxiliary verbs after BUT. (Chart 8-4)
　　Directions: Complete the sentences by using the names of your classmates and appropriate auxiliary verbs.

1. _____Maria_____ has long hair, but _____Kutaiba doesn't_____.

2. _____Kunio_____ doesn't live in an apartment, but _____Boris does_____.

3. _____ isn't in class today, but _____.

4. _____ is here today, but _____.

5. _____ can speak (*a language*), but _____.

6. _____ doesn't have brown eyes, but _____.

7. _____ didn't come to class yesterday, but _____.

8. _____ will be at home tonight, but _____.

9. _____ has a mustache, but _____.

10. _____ has lived here for a long time, but _____.

☐ EXERCISE 12. Using auxiliary verbs after AND and BUT. (Chart 8-4)
　　Directions: Complete the sentences by adding appropriate auxiliary verbs. Add **too** and **either** as appropriate.

1. Alex goes to college, and his sisters _____do too_____.

2. Anna goes to college, but her cousin _____doesn't_____.

3. Hugo doesn't go to college, and his brother _____doesn't either_____.

4. Horses are domesticated animals, and camels _____.

5. Lions aren't domesticated animals, and tigers _____.

6. Horses are domesticated animals, but lions _____.

7. Paula didn't go to the picnic, and Jack _____.

8. I work at an airplane factory, and my brother _____.

9. Gray is a dull color, but orange _____.

10. Rita won't be at the party, and Jean _____.

11. Olga was in class yesterday, but Antonio _____.

12. Fatima is in class today, and Pedro _____.

13. I can't sing very well, but my wife _____.

8-5 USING *AND* + *TOO, SO, EITHER, NEITHER*

(a) Sue works, *and* **Tom** does too. $\quad$ S $\quad+\quad$ *aux* $\quad+\quad$ TOO (b) Sue works, *and* **so** does Tom. $\quad$ SO $\quad+\quad$ *aux* $\quad+\quad$ S	(a) and (b) have the same meaning. Word order: $\quad$ *subject* + *auxiliary* + ***too*** $\quad\quad$ ***so*** + *auxiliary* + *subject*
(c) Ann doesn't work, *and* **Joe** doesn't either. $\quad$ S $\quad+\quad$ *aux* $\quad+\quad$ EITHER (d) Ann doesn't work, *and* **neither** does Joe. NEITHER $+$ *aux* $+$ S	(c) and (d) have the same meaning. Word order: $\quad$ *subject* + *auxiliary* + ***either*** $\quad$ ***neither*** + *auxiliary* + *subject* Note: An affirmative auxiliary is used with *neither*.
(e) A: I'm hungry. $\quad$ B: ***I am too.*** (g) A: I don't eat meat. $\quad$ B: ***I don't either.*** $\qquad$ (f) A: I'm hungry. $\qquad$ B: ***So am I.*** (h) A: I don't eat meat. $\qquad$ B: ***Neither do I.***	***And*** is usually not used when there are two speakers. (e) and (f) have the same meaning. (g) and (h) have the same meaning.
(i) A: I'm hungry. $\quad$ B: ***Me too.*** *(informal)* $\qquad$ (j) A: I don't eat meat. $\qquad$ B: ***Me neither.*** *(informal)*	***Me too*** and ***me neither*** are often used in informal spoken English.

☐ **EXERCISE 13. AND + TOO, SO, EITHER, NEITHER. (Chart 8-5)**

Directions: Complete the sentences using the given words. Pay special attention to word order.

Omar $\qquad$ James $\qquad$ Marco $\qquad$ Ivan

1. a. *too* $\qquad$ Marco has a mustache, and ___James does too___ .

$\quad$ b. *so* $\qquad$ Marco has a mustache, and _____ .

2. a. *either* $\qquad$ Omar doesn't have a mustache, and _____ .

$\quad$ b. *neither* $\qquad$ Omar doesn't have a mustache, and _____ .

3. a. *too* $\qquad$ Marco is wearing a hat, and _____ .

$\quad$ b. *so* $\qquad$ Marco is wearing a hat, and _____ .

4. a. *either* $\qquad$ Ivan isn't wearing a hat, and _____ .

$\quad$ b. *neither* $\qquad$ Ivan isn't wearing a hat, and _____ .

☐ EXERCISE 14. AND + TOO, SO, EITHER, NEITHER. (Chart 8-5)
    Directions: Complete the sentences by using *too, so, either,* or *neither*. Use the names of your classmates and appropriate auxiliaries.

1. _____Maria_____ is in class today, and _____so is Po / Po is too_____ .

2. _____ lives in an apartment, and _____ .

3. _____ can't speak Chinese, and _____ .

4. _____ wasn't in class yesterday, and _____ .

5. _____ stayed home and studied last night, and _____ .

6. _____ doesn't have a mustache, and _____ .

7. _____ will be in class tomorrow, and _____ .

8. _____ isn't married, and _____ .

9. _____ has dimples, and _____ .

10. _____ has been in class all week, and _____ .

☐ EXERCISE 15. AND + TOO, SO, EITHER, NEITHER. (Chart 8-5)
    Directions: Complete by using *too, so, either,* or *neither* and the given words.

1. *clouds*   Snow is white, and _____clouds are too / so are clouds_____ .

2. *salt*   Sugar isn't expensive, and _____ .

3. *cats*   Monkeys have long tails, and _____ .

4. *gorillas*   Human beings don't have tails, and _____ .

5. *the teacher*   I forgot to bring my book to class, and _____ .

6. *the teacher*   I was late for class today, and _____ .

7. *I*   You've never* been in Nepal, and _____ .

8. *penguins*   Ostriches can't fly, and

    _____

    _____ .

    I WONDER HOW THEY DO THAT?

    SO DO I!

_____
*****Never** makes a sentence negative:
    *The teacher is **never** late, and **neither** am I.* OR *I'm **not either.***

□ EXERCISE 16. AND + TOO, SO, EITHER, NEITHER. (Chart 8-5)
Directions: Complete the dialogues by agreeing with Speaker A's idea. Use **so** or **neither**. Use **I**.

1. A: I'm tired.
   B: ___So am I___ .

2. A: I didn't enjoy the movie last night.
   B: ___Neither did I___ .

3. A: I always have coffee in the morning.
   B: _____ .

4. A: I don't feel like going to class today.
   B: _____ .

5. A: I didn't eat breakfast this morning.
   B: _____ .

6. A: I've never been in Peru.
   B: _____ .

7. A: I studied last night.
   B: _____ .

8. A: I should study tonight.
   B: _____ .

9. A: I can't speak Hungarian.
   B: _____ .

10. A: But I can speak English.
    B: _____ .

□ EXERCISE 17. SO and NEITHER. (Chart 8-5)
Directions: Work in pairs.
Speaker A: Say the given sentence. Complete the sentence with your own words if necessary. Your book is open.
Speaker B: Respond to Speaker A's statement by using **so** or **neither**. Your book is closed.

Example: I'm confused.
SPEAKER A *(book open):* I'm confused.
SPEAKER B *(book closed):* So am I.*

Example: Frogs don't have tails.
SPEAKER A *(book open):* Frogs don't have tails.
SPEAKER B *(book closed):* Neither do human beings.

Example: (Name of a restaurant) is a good place to eat in (this city).
SPEAKER A *(book open):* Ivar's Seafood Restaurant is a good place to eat in Seattle.
SPEAKER B *(book closed):* So is Hong Kong Gardens.

_____

*This exercise is designed to practice the use of **so** and **neither** in conversational responses. If, however, Speaker B doesn't want to agree, echo, or support Speaker A's statement, there are alternative responses. For example:
SPEAKER A: I'm confused.
SPEAKER B: **You are? What's the matter?**
SPEAKER A: Frogs don't have tails.
SPEAKER B: **Really? Is that so? Hmmm. I didn't know that. Are you sure?**
SPEAKER A: Ivar's Seafood Restaurant is a good place to eat in Seattle.
SPEAKER B: **Oh? I've never eaten there.**

Switch roles.

1. I studied last night.
2. I study grammar every day.
3. I'm thirsty.
4. I'd like *(a kind of drink)*.
5. I've never been in *(name of a country)*.
6. I don't like *(a kind of food)*.
7. ... is a *(big/small)* country.
8. Paper burns.
9. Snakes don't have legs.
10. I've never seen an iceberg.

11. San Francisco is a seaport.
12. Chickens lay eggs.
13. I *(like/don't like)* the weather today.
14. Swimming is an Olympic sport.
15. Coffee contains caffeine.
16. Elephants can swim.
17. *(Name of a country)* is in Africa.
18. I've never had caviar* for breakfast.
19. Denmark has no volcanoes.
20. I'd rather go to *(name of a place)* than *(name of a place)*.

□ EXERCISE 18. TOO, SO, EITHER, NEITHER. (Chart 8-5)
Directions: Create dialogues (either with a partner or in writing).
Speaker A: Use the given verb to make a statement (not a question). Your book is open.
Speaker B: React to Speaker A's idea by using *too, so, either,* or *neither* in a response. Your book is closed.

Example: would like
SPEAKER A *(book open):* I'd like to sail around the world someday.
SPEAKER B *(book closed):* So would I. OR I would too.**

Example: didn't want
SPEAKER A *(book open):* Toshi didn't want to give a speech in front of the class.
SPEAKER B *(book closed):* Neither did Ingrid. OR Ingrid didn't either.**

Switch roles.

1. don't have
2. can't speak
3. enjoy
4. isn't going to be
5. haven't ever seen
6. will be
7. can fly
8. would like
9. didn't go
10. are
11. is sitting
12. wasn't

---

*Caviar = fish eggs (an expensive delicacy in some cultures).

**This exercise asks you to use *too, so, either,* or *neither* in conversational responses. Other responses are, of course, possible. For example:
SPEAKER A: I'd like to sail around the world someday.
SPEAKER B: **Really? Why?**

SPEAKER A: Toshi didn't want to give a speech in front of the class.
SPEAKER B: **Oh? Why not?**

8-6 CONNECTING IDEAS WITH *BECAUSE*

(a) He drank water *because* he was thirsty.	*Because* expresses a cause; it gives a reason. Why did he drink water? Reason: he was thirsty.
(b) MAIN CLAUSE: *He drank water.*	A main clause is a complete sentence: *He drank water* = a complete sentence.
(c) ADVERB CLAUSE: *because he was thirsty*	An adverb clause is NOT a complete sentence: *because he was thirsty* = NOT a complete sentence. **Because** introduces an adverb clause: **because** + *subject* + *verb* = *an adverb clause.*
MAIN CLAUSE ADVERB CLAUSE (d) He drank water because he was thirsty. (no comma) ADVERB CLAUSE MAIN CLAUSE (e) Because he was thirsty, he drank water. (comma)	An adverb clause is connected to a main clause, as in (d) and (e).* In (d): **main clause** + **no comma** + **adverb clause** In (e): **adverb clause** + **comma** + **main clause** (d) and (e) have exactly the same meaning.
(f) *INCORRECT IN WRITING:* *He drank water.* **Because he was thirsty.**	(f) is incorrect in written English: *because he was thirsty* cannot stand alone as a sentence that starts with a capital letter and ends with a period. It has to be connected to a main clause, as in (d) and (e).
(g) CORRECT IN SPEAKING: A: Why did he drink some water? B: **Because he was thirsty.**	In spoken English, an adverb clause can be used as the short answer to a question, as in (g).

*See Chart 2-10, p. 48, for a discussion of other adverb clauses. "Time clauses" are adverb clauses that are introduced by *when, after, before, while, until,* and *as soon as.*

☐ EXERCISE 19. Adverb clauses with BECAUSE. (Chart 8-6)

Directions: Combine each pair of sentences in two different orders. Use *because*. Punctuate carefully.

1. We didn't have class.
   The teacher was absent.
   → *We didn't have class because the teacher was absent.*
   → *Because the teacher was absent, we didn't have class.*

2. The children were hungry.
   There was no food in the house.

3. The bridge is closed.
   We can't drive to the other side of the river.

4. My car didn't start.
   The battery was dead.

5. Larry and Patti laughed hard.
   The joke was very funny.

☐ EXERCISE 20. Adverb clauses with BECAUSE. (Chart 8-6)
Directions: Add periods, commas, and capital letters as necessary.

1. Jimmy is very young because he is afraid of the dark he likes to have a light on in his

   bedroom at night.
   → *Jimmy is very young.* ***B****ecause he is afraid of the dark,* *he likes to have a light on in his*
   bedroom at night.

2. Mr. El-Sayed had a bad cold because he was not feeling well he stayed home from the

   office.

3. Judy went to bed early because she was tired she likes to get at least eight hours of

   sleep a night.

4. Frank put his head in his hands he was angry and upset because he had lost a lot of

   work on his computer.

☐ EXERCISE 21. BECAUSE and SO. (Charts 8-3 and 8-6)
Directions: Create sentences with the same meaning. Use commas as appropriate.

PART I. Restate the sentence, using ***so***.
1. Jack lost his job because he never showed up for work on time.
   → *Jack never showed up for work on time,* *so he lost his job.*

2. I opened the window because the room was hot.

3. Because it was raining, I stayed indoors.

PART II. Restate the sentence, using ***because***.
4. Jason was hungry, so he ate.
   → *Because Jason was hungry, he ate.* OR *Jason ate because he was hungry.*

5. The water in the river is polluted, so we can't go swimming.

6. My watch is broken, so I was late for my job interview.

☐ EXERCISE 22. Review: conjunctions and adverb clauses. (Charts 8-1 → 8-6)
Directions: Add commas, periods, and capital letters as appropriate. Don't change any of
the words or the order of the words.

1. Jim was hot he sat in the shade.
   → *Jim was hot.* ***H****e sat in the shade.*

2. Jim was hot and tired so he sat in the shade.

3. Jim was hot tired and thirsty.

4. Because he was hot Jim sat in the shade.

5. Because they were hot and thirsty Jim and Susan sat in the shade and drank tea.

6. Jim and Susan sat in the shade and drank tea because they were hot and thirsty.

7. Jim sat in the shade drank tea and fanned himself because he was hot tired and thirsty.

8. Because Jim was hot he stayed under the shade of the tree but Susan went back to work.

9. Mules are domestic animals they are the offspring of a horse and a donkey mules are called "beasts of burden" because they can work hard and carry heavy loads.

10. Because mules are strong they can work under harsh conditions but they need proper care.

11. Ann had been looking for an apartment for two weeks yesterday she went to look at an apartment on Fifth Avenue she rented it because it was in good condition and had a nice view of the city she was glad to find a new apartment.

12. The word "matter" is a chemical term matter is anything that has weight this book your finger water a rock air and the moon are all examples of matter radio waves and heat are not matter because they do not have weight happiness daydreams and fear have no weight and are not matter.

8-7 CONNECTING IDEAS WITH *EVEN THOUGH / ALTHOUGH*

(a) **Even though** *I was hungry,* I did not eat.
    I did not eat **even though** *I was hungry.*
(b) **Although** *I was hungry,* I did not eat.
    I did not eat **although** *I was hungry.*
	Even though and **although** introduce an adverb clause.
	(a) and (b) have the same meaning. They mean:
	I was hungry, but I did not eat.

COMPARE (c) *Because* I was hungry, *I ate.* (d) *Even though* I was hungry, *I did not eat.*	*Because* expresses an expected result. *Even though/although* expresses an unexpected or opposite result.

☐ EXERCISE 23. EVEN THOUGH vs. BECAUSE. (Chart 8-7)
Directions: Complete the sentences by using *even though* or *because*.

1. _____Even though_____ the weather is cold, Rick isn't wearing a coat.

2. _____Because_____ the weather is cold, Ben is wearing a coat.

3. _____ Jane was sad, she smiled.

4. _____ Jane was sad, she cried.

5. _____ it was cold outside, we went swimming in the lake.

6. _____ I like to swim, I joined my friends in the lake.

7. People ask Tony to sing at weddings _____ he has a good voice.

8. George sings loudly _____ he can't carry a tune.

9. _____ our friends live on an island, it is easy to get there by car

   _____ there is a bridge from the mainland.

☐ EXERCISE 24. EVEN THOUGH/ALTHOUGH and BECAUSE. (Charts 8-6 and 8-7)
Directions: Choose the best completion.

1. Even though ostriches have wings, ___C___ .
   A. their feathers are large
   B. they are big birds
   C. they can't fly

2. My brother came to my graduation ceremony although _____ .
   A. he was sick
   B. he was eager to see everyone
   C. he was happy for me

3. Even though I looked in every pocket and every drawer, _____ .
   A. my keys were under the bed
   B. my roommate helped me look for my keys
   C. I never found my keys

4. Jack hadn't heard or read about the murder even though _____ .
   A. he was the murderer
   B. it was on the front page of every newspaper
   C. he was out of town when it occurred

5. We can see the light from an airplane high in the sky at night before we hear the plane
   because _____ .
   A. light travels faster than sound
   B. airplanes travel at high speeds
   C. our eyes work better than our ears at night

6. Although _____ , he finished the race in first place.
   A. John was full of energy and strength
   B. John was leading all the way
   C. John was far behind in the beginning

7. My partner and I worked late into the evening. Even though _____ , we stopped at our favorite restaurant before we went home.
   A. we were very hungry
   B. we had finished our report
   C. we were very tired

8. Snakes don't have ears, but they are very sensitive to vibrations that result from noise. Snakes can sense the presence of a moving object even though _____ .
   A. they have ears
   B. they feel vibrations
   C. they can't hear

9. In mountainous areas, melting snow in the spring runs downhill into streams and rivers. The water carries with it sediment, that is, small particles of soil and rock. In the spring, mountain rivers become cloudy rather than clear because _____ .
   A. mountain tops are covered with snow
   B. the water from melting snow brings sediment to the river
   C. ice is frozen water

10. Even though it was a hot summer night, we went inside and shut the windows because _____ .
    A. the rain stopped
    B. we were enjoying the cool breeze
    C. a storm was coming

☐ EXERCISE 25. EVEN THOUGH vs. BECAUSE. (Charts 8-6 and 8-7)
   Directions: Answer "yes" or "no," as you wish. Answer in a complete sentence using either ***because*** or ***even though***. Change the wording as you wish. Only the teacher's book is open.

   Example: Last night you were tired. Did you go to bed early?
   → *Yes, I went to bed early because I was tired.* OR
      Yes, because I was tired, I went to bed before nine. OR
      No, I didn't go to bed early even though I was really sleepy. OR
      No, even though I was really tired, I didn't go to bed until after midnight.

   1. Last night you were tired. Did you stay up late?

   2. You are thirsty. Do you want (a glass of water)?

   3. You're hungry. Do you want (a candy bar)?

   4. Vegetables are good for you. Do you eat a lot of them?

   5. Space exploration is exciting. Would you like to be an astronaut?

6. Guns are dangerous. Do you want to own one?

7. *(A local restaurant)* is expensive/inexpensive. Do you eat there?

8. *(A local delicacy)* is/are expensive. Do you buy it/them?

9. The *(name of a local)* river is/isn't polluted. Do you want to swim in it?

10. Who (in this room) can't swim? Do you want to go to (the beach/the swimming pool) with (. . .) and me this afternoon?

11. Who loves to go swimming? Do you want to go to (the beach/the swimming pool) with (. . .) and me this afternoon?

12. What are the winters like here? Do you like living here in winter?

13. *(A recent movie)* has had good reviews. Do you want to see it?

14. Are you a good artist? Do you want to draw a picture of me on the board?

15. Where does your family live? Are you going to go there (over the next holiday)?

☐ EXERCISE 26. EVEN THOUGH and BECAUSE. (Chart 8-7)
Directions: Complete the sentences with your own words. Pay attention to proper punctuation.

1. I like our classroom even though . . . .
2. I like my home because . . . .
3. . . . even though I don't . . . . .
4. . . . because I don't . . . .
5. Because we . . . , we . . . .
6. Even though . . . , we . . . .
7. Even though . . . , . . . because . . . .
8. Because . . . , I . . . , but . . . because . . . .

☐ EXERCISE 27. Error analysis. (Charts 8-1 → 8-7)
Directions: Correct the errors in these sentences. Pay special attention to punctuation.

1. Even though I was sick, but I went to work.
   → *Even though I was sick, I went to work.*
   → *I was sick, but I went to work.*

2. Gold silver and copper. They are metals.

3. The students crowded around the bulletin board. Because their grades were posted there.

4. I had a cup of coffee, and so does my friend.

5. My roommate didn't go. Neither I went either.

6. Even I am very exhausted, I didn't stop working until after midnight last night.

7. The teacher went too the meeting, and too of the students did to.

8. Although I like chocolate, but I can't eat it because I'm allergic to it.

9. Many tourists visit my country. Warm weather all year. Many interesting landmarks.

10. Because the weather in my country is warm and comfortable all year so many tourists visit it in the winter.

11. I like to eat raw eggs for breakfast and everybody else in my family too.

12. A hardware store sells tools and nails and plumbing supplies and paint and etc.*

13. Because the war broke out in late September we had to cancel our October trip even though we already had our passports visas airplane tickets and hotel reservations.

14. Many of us experience stress on our jobs my job is stressful because my workplace is not pleasant or comfortable it is noisy hot and dirty even though I try to do my best my boss is unhappy with my work and always gives me bad performance reports I need to find another job.

15. I like animals I have a little dog at home her name is Linda she is brown and white.

☐ EXERCISE 28. Punctuating with commas and periods. (Chapter 8)
Directions: Add commas, periods, and capital letters as necessary. (There are four adverb clauses in the following passage. Can you find and <u>underline</u> them?)

(1)   What is the most common substance on earth? I it isn't wood, iron, or sand. T the most common substance on earth is water it occupies more than seventy percent of the earth's surface it is in lakes rivers and oceans it is in the ground and in the air it is practically everywhere.

---

*Etc. is an abbreviation of the Latin *et cetera.* It means "and other things of a similar nature." The word ***and*** is NOT used in front of ***etc.***
    INCORRECT: The farmer raises cows, sheep, goats, ***chickens, and etc.***
    INCORRECT: The farmer raises cows, sheep, goats, ***and chickens, etc.***
    CORRECT: The farmer raises cows, sheep, goats, chickens, ***etc.***
Also, notice the spelling: *etc.,* NOT *ect.*

(2)   Water is vital because life on earth could not exist without it people animals and plants all need water in order to exist every living thing is mostly water a person's body is about sixty-seven percent water a bird is about seventy-five percent water most fruit is about ninety percent water.

(3)   Most of the water in the world is saltwater ninety-seven percent of the water on earth is in the oceans because seawater is salty people cannot drink it or use it to grow plants for food only three percent of the earth's water is fresh only one percent of the water in the world is easily available for human use.

(4)   Even though water is essential to life human beings often poison it with chemicals from industry and agriculture when people foul water with pollution the quality of all life—plant life animal life and human life—diminishes life cannot exist without fresh water so it is essential for people to take care of this important natural resource.

CHAPTER 9
Comparisons

CONTENTS

☐ EXERCISE 1. Preview of comparisons. (Chapter 9)
   Directions: Use the given words to make comparisons.

   1. short/long lines (Compare the lengths of the lines.)

   line A _____

   line B _____

   line C _____

   line D _____

   line E _____

   → *Line C is shorter than lines A and B.*
   → *B is the longest line of all.*   line D is as long as line E
   → *C isn't as long as A.*
   → *(continue to make comparisons)*
         line D is shorter than lines A, B and C

   2. happy/sad look on his face

DAVID   MIKE   RICK   JIM

3. large/small country (in total land area)

> Brazil: 3,286,488 sq. mi. (8,511,965 sq km)
> Egypt: 385,229 sq. mi. (997,739 sq km)
> Spain: 194,897 sq. mi. (504,782 sq km)
> Canada: 3,553,303 sq. mi. (9,203,054 sq km)

4. easy/difficult questions

> FIRST QUESTION: What's 2 plus 2?
> SECOND QUESTION: What's the square root of 937 divided by 16?
> THIRD QUESTION: What's 3 times 127?
> FOURTH QUESTION: What's 2 plus 3?

5. good/bad handwriting

> EXAMPLE A: *The meeting starts at eight!*
> EXAMPLE B: *The meeting starts at eight*
> EXAMPLE C: *The meeting starts at eight!*

9-1 MAKING COMPARISONS WITH *AS...AS*

(a) Tina is 21 years old. Sam is also 21. Tina is *as old as* Sam (is). (b) Mike came *as quickly as* he could.	*As...as* is used to say that the two parts of a comparison are equal or the same in some way. In (a): *as* + *adjective* + *as* In (b): *as* + *adverb* + *as*
(c) Ted is 20. Tina is 21. Ted is *not as* old *as* Tina. (d) Ted is*n't quite as* old *as* Tina. (e) Amy is 5. She is*n't nearly as* old *as* Tina.	Negative form: *not as...as.*★ *Quite* and *nearly* are often used with the negative. In (d): *not quite as...as* = a small difference. In (e): *not nearly as...as* = a big difference.
(f) Sam is *just as* old *as* Tina. (g) Ted is *nearly/almost as* old *as* Tina.	Common modifiers of *as...as* are *just* (meaning "exactly") and *nearly/almost*.

★Also possible: *not so...as: Ted is not so old as Tina.*

TINA
age 21

SAM
age 21

TED
age 20

AMY
age 5

☐ **EXERCISE 2. Comparisons with AS . . . AS. (Chart 9-1)**

Directions: Complete the sentences with one of the following:
- *just as*
- *almost as/not quite as*
- *not nearly as*

PART I. Compare the fullness of the glasses.

1. Glass 4 is ___almost as/not quite as___ full as glass 2.
2. Glass 3 is ___not nearly as___ full as glass 2.
3. Glass 1 is ___just as___ full as glass 2.

PART II. Compare the boxes.

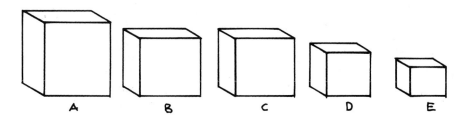

4. Box B is ___not quite as___ big as Box A.
5. Box E is ___not nearly as___ big as Box A.
6. Box C is ___just as___ big as Box B.
7. Box E is ___not quite as___ big as Box D.

☐ **EXERCISE 3. Comparisons with AS . . . AS. (Chart 9-1)**

Directions: Using the given words, complete the sentences with ***as . . . as***. Use a negative verb if appropriate.

1. a housefly and an ant

   ___An ant isn't (quite) as___ big as ___a housefly___.

2. a lion and a tiger

   ___A lion is just as___ dangerous and wild as ___a tiger___.

3. a lake and an ocean

   A lake is not nearly as _____ big as __an ocean__ .

4. honey and sugar

   Honey is just as _____ sweet as __sugar__ .

5. good health and money

   Good health is just as _____ important as __money__ .

6. adults and children/usually

   Children are usually not nearly as patient as __Adults__ .

7. a galaxy and a solar system

   A galaxy is not quite as _____ large as __a solar system__ .

8. monkeys and people

   People is not nearly as _____ agile in climbing trees as __Monkeys__ .

9. reading a novel and listening to music

   In my opinion, reading a novel is not nearly as _____ relaxing as _____ .

☐ **EXERCISE 4. Comparisons with AS . . . AS. (Chart 9-1)**
   Directions: Complete the sentences by using **as . . . as** and your own words.

1. I need you right away! Please come . . . .
   → *Please come as soon as possible.*

2. We can't go any farther. This is . . . .
   → *This is as far as we can go.*

3. I can't work any faster. I'm working . as . fast as I can

4. An orange is sweeter than a lemon. In other words, an orange is not nearly as sweet as lemon

5. A stream is usually much narrower than a river. In other words, a stream isn't . . . .

6. I had expected the test to be difficult, and it was. In other words, the test was
   just . . . .

7. It's important to use your English every day. You should practice speaking
   English . as .

8. You're only old if you feel old. You are . as . young . as . .

9. You might think it's easy to do, but it's not quite . . . .

10. It takes an hour to drive to the airport. It takes an hour to fly to Chicago. In other
    words, it takes . . . .

□ **EXERCISE 5. Comparisons with AS . . . AS. (Chart 9-1)**

   Directions: ***As . . . as*** is used in many traditional phrases. These phrases are generally spoken rather than written. See how many of these phrases you're familiar with by completing the sentences with the given words.

✓*a bear*	*a feather* ขนนก, สิ่งเบา	*a mule*
a bird	*the hills*	*a rock*
a bull/an ox	*a kite*	*a wet hen*
a cat		

1. When will dinner be ready? I'm as hungry as _____**a bear**_____!

2. Did Bill really lift that heavy box all by himself? He must be as strong as _____*a rock*_____.

3. It was a lovely summer day. School was out, and there was nothing in particular that I had to do. I felt as free as _____*a kite*_____.

4. Marco won't change his mind. He's as stubborn as _____*a bull*_____.

5. How can anyone expect me to sleep in this bed? It's as hard as _____*the hills*_____.

6. Of course I've heard that joke before! It's as old as _____*a mule*_____.

7. Why are you pacing? What's the matter? You're as nervous as _____*a cat*_____.

8. Thanks for offering the help, but I can carry the box alone. It looks heavy, but it isn't. It's as light as _____*a feather*_____.

9. When Erica received the good news, she felt as high as _____*a bird*_____.

10. Was she angry? You'd better believe it! She was as mad as _____*a wet hen*_____.

□ EXERCISE 6. Comparisons with AS . . . AS. (Chart 9-1)
Directions: Complete the sentences with your own words.

Example: . . . not as sharp as . . . .
→ *A pencil point isn't as sharp as a needle.*
A kitchen knife isn't as sharp as a razor blade.
My mind isn't as sharp in the afternoon as it is in the morning.

1. . . . just as important as . . . .
2. . . . not as comfortable as . . . .
3. . . . not nearly as interesting as . . . .
4. . . . just as good as . . . .
5. . . . not quite as difficult as . . . .
6. . . . not as quiet as . . . .
7. . . . almost as good as . . . .
8. . . . not as friendly as . . . .
9. . . . not as heavy as . . . .
10. . . . just as nutritious as . . . .
11. . . . as often as I can.
12. . . . as often as I used to.
13. . . . as soon as possible.
14. . . . not as easy as it looks.
15. . . . as much as possible.

9-2 COMPARATIVE AND SUPERLATIVE

(a) "A" is *older than* "B."	The comparative compares *this* to *that* or *these* to *those.*
(b) "A" and "B" are *older than* "C" and "D."	Form: *-er* or *more.* (See Chart 9-3.)
(c) Ed is *more generous than* his brother.	Notice: A comparative is followed by *than.*
(d) "A," "B," "C," and "D" are sisters. "A" is *the oldest* of all four sisters.	The superlative compares one part of a whole group to all the rest of the group. Form: *-est* or *most.* (See Chart 9-3 for forms.)
(e) A woman in Turkey claims to be *the oldest person* in the world.	Notice: A superlative begins with *the.*
(f) Ed is *the most generous person* in his family.	

□ EXERCISE 7. Error analysis: comparative and superlative. (Chart 9-2)
Directions: Correct the errors.

1. Alaska is large than Texas.
   → *Alaska is larger than Texas.*

2. Alaska is largest state in the United States.

3. Texas is the larger from France in land area.

4. Old shoes are usually more comfortable to new shoes.

5. I like Chinese food more better than French food.

6. A pillow is more soft from a rock.

7. My brother is 22. I am 20. My sister is 18. I am the youngest than my brother. My

   sister is the younger person in our family.

□ EXERCISE 8. Comparative and superlative. (Chart 9-2)
　　　Directions: Choose five to ten moveable objects (in this room or in the possession of anyone in this room) and put them in a central place. Compare the items using the given words and your own words. Use both the comparative (*-er/more*) and the superlative (*-est/most*).

Example: big/small
SPEAKER A: Omar's pen is bigger than Anya's ring.
SPEAKER B: Sergio's calculator is smaller than Kim's briefcase.
SPEAKER C: The biggest thing on the table is the briefcase.
SPEAKER D: Etc.

　　1. big/small　　　　4. cheap/expensive
　　2. soft/hard　　　　5. etc.
　　3. light/heavy

9-3 COMPARATIVE AND SUPERLATIVE FORMS OF ADJECTIVES AND ADVERBS

		COMPARATIVE	SUPERLATIVE	
ONE-SYLLABLE ADJECTIVES	old wise	older wiser	the oldest the wisest	For most one-syllable adjectives, *-er* and *-est* are added.
TWO-SYLLABLE ADJECTIVES	famous pleasant	more famous more pleasant	the most famous the most pleasant	For most two-syllable adjectives, *more* and *most* are used.
	busy pretty	busier prettier	the busiest the prettiest	*-Er* and *-est* are used with two-syllable adjectives that end in *-y*. The *-y* is changed to *-i*.
	clever gentle friendly	cleverer more clever gentler more gentle friendlier more friendly	the cleverest the most clever the gentlest the most gentle the friendliest the most friendly	Some two-syllable adjectives use either *-er/-est* or *more/most*: *able, angry, clever, common, cruel, friendly, gentle, handsome, narrow, pleasant, polite, quiet, simple, sour.*
ADJECTIVES WITH THREE OR MORE SYLLABLES	important fascinating	more important more fascinating	the most important the most fascinating	*More* and *most* are used with long adjectives.
IRREGULAR ADJECTIVES	good bad	better worse	the best the worst	*Good* and *bad* have irregular comparative and superlative forms.
-LY ADVERBS	carefully slowly	more carefully more slowly	the most carefully the most slowly	*More* and *most* are used with adverbs that end in *-ly.*★
ONE-SYLLABLE ADVERBS	fast hard	faster harder	the fastest the hardest	The *-er* and *-est* forms are used with one-syllable adverbs.
IRREGULAR ADVERBS	well badly far	better worse farther/further★★	the best the worst the farthest/furthest	

　★Exception: *early* is both an adjective and an adverb. Forms: *earlier, earliest.*

　★★Both *farther* and *further* are used to compare physical distances: *I walked farther/further than my friend did.* **Further** (but not *farther*) can also mean "additional": *I need further information.*

□ EXERCISE 9. Comparative and superlative forms. (Charts 9-2 and 9-3)
Directions: Give the comparative and superlative forms of the following adjectives and adverbs.

1. high   _higher, the highest_

2. good   _____

3. lazy   _____

4. hot*   _____

5. neat*   _____

6. late*   _____

7. happy   _____

8. dangerous   _____

9. slowly   _____

10. common   _____

11. friendly   _____

12. careful   _____

13. bad   _____

14. far   _____

□ EXERCISE 10. Comparatives. (Charts 9-2 and 9-3)
Directions: Complete the sentences with the correct comparative form (*more/-er*) of the given adjectives.

clean	dangerous	funny	✓ sweet
confusing	dark	pretty	wet

1. Oranges are _____sweeter_____ than lemons.

2. I heard a little polite laughter when I told my jokes, but everyone laughed loudly when Janet told hers. Her jokes are always much _____ than mine.

3. Many more people die in car accidents than in plane accidents. Statistics show that driving your own car is _____ than flying in an airplane.

4. Professor Sato speaks clearly, but I have trouble understanding Professor Larson's lectures. Her lectures are much _____ than Professor Sato's.

5. Bobby! How did you get all covered with mud? Hurry and take a bath. Even the floor is _____ than you are.

_____

*Spelling notes:
- When a one-syllable adjective ends in **one vowel** + **a consonant**, double the consonant and add *-er/-est*. Example: *sad, sadder, saddest*.
- When an adjective ends in **two vowels** + **a consonant**, do NOT double the consonant: *cool, cooler, coolest*.
- When an adjective ends in *-e*, do NOT double the consonant: *wide, wider, widest*.

6. A: Why does wet sand look _____ than dry sand?

   B: Because wet sand reflects less light.

7. A: The moon is full tonight. There's not a cloud in the sky. Look at the moonlight on the lake. It makes the water sparkle. Have you ever seen a _____ sight than this?

   B: No. It's beautiful.

8. If a cat and a duck are out in the rain, the cat will get much _____ than the duck. The water will simply roll off the duck's feathers but will soak into the cat's hair.

□ EXERCISE 11. FARTHER and FURTHER. (Chart 9-3)
   Directions: Complete the sentences with *farther* and/or *further*. Use both if possible.

1. Ron and his friend went jogging. Ron ran two miles, but his friend got tired after one mile. Ron ran ____farther/further____ than his friend did.

2. If you have any ____further____ questions, don't hesitate to ask.

3. Paris is _____ north than Tokyo.

4. I gave my old computer to my younger sister because I had no _____ use for it.

5. I like my new apartment, but it is _____ away from school than my old apartment was.

6. Thank you for your help, but I'll be fine now. I don't want to cause you any _____ trouble.

☐ **EXERCISE 12. Comparatives.** (Charts 9-2 and 9-3)

Directions: Choose any appropriate adjective from the list (or any adjective of your own choosing) to make comparisons between the given items. Use the comparative form (***more/-er***).

bright	*flexible*	*short*
easy	*heavy*	*thick*
enjoyable	*relaxing*	*thin*
fast	*shallow*	*wide and deep*

1. traveling by air \ traveling by bus
   → *Traveling by air is faster than traveling by bus.*
   Traveling by air is easier than traveling by bus.
   Etc.

2. a pool \ a lake

3. an elephant's neck \ a giraffe's neck

4. sunlight \ moonlight

5. iron \ wood

6. walking \ running

7. a river \ a stream

8. rubber \ wood

9. nothing \ sitting in a garden on a quiet summer day

10. a butterfly's wing \ a blade of grass

☐ **EXERCISE 13. Comparatives.** (Charts 9-2 and 9-3)

Directions: Work in pairs.
Speaker A: Ask the given question. Your book is open.
Speaker B: Answer the question. Begin your response with "**Not really, but at least** . . . ." Your book is closed.

Example:
SPEAKER A *(book open):* Is the mayor of this city famous?
SPEAKER B *(book closed):* Not really, but at least he/she is more famous than I am.

Switch roles.

1. Is a mouse big?
2. Is this room large?
3. Is your desk comfortable?
4. Is an elephant intelligent?
5. Was the last exercise easy?

7. Is the floor clean?
8. Is a pen expensive?
9. Is this book heavy?
10. Is blue a bright color?
11. Is *(name of a city)* close to *(name of this city)?*

9-4 COMPLETING A COMPARATIVE

(a) I'm older *than **my brother** (is)*. (b) I'm older *than **he** is*. (c) I'm older *than **him**. (informal)*	In formal English, a subject pronoun (e.g., *he*) follows ***than***, as in (b). In everyday, informal spoken English, an object pronoun (e.g., *him*) often follows ***than***, as in (c).
(d) He works harder *than **I do***. (e) I arrived earlier *than they **did***.	Frequently an auxiliary verb follows the subject after ***than***. In (d): *than I do = than I work*.
(f) *Ann's* hair is longer *than **Kate's***. (g) *Jack's* apartment is smaller *than **mine***.	A possessive noun (e.g., *Kate's*) or pronoun (e.g., *mine*) may follow ***than***.

☐ **EXERCISE 14. Completing a comparative. (Chart 9-4)**
Directions: Complete the sentences. Use pronouns in the completions.

1. My sister is only six. She's much younger than _____ I am OR *(informally)* me _____ .

2. Peggy is thirteen, and she feels sad. She thinks most of the other girls in school are far more popular than _____ .

3. The children can't lift that heavy box, but Mr. Ford can. He's stronger than

    _____ .

4. Jim isn't a very good speller. I can spell much better than _____ .

5. I was on time. Jack was late. I got there earlier than _____ .

6. Ted is out of shape. I can run a lot faster and farther than _____ .

7. Isabel's classes are difficult, but my classes are easy. Isabel's classes are more difficult than _____ . My classes are easier than _____ .

8. Our neighbor's house is very large. Our house is much smaller than

    _____ . Their house is larger than _____ .

☐ EXERCISE 15. Comparative and superlative forms. (Charts 9-3 and 9-4)

Directions: As a class or in smaller groups, divide into two teams. Each team will try to score points.

SCORING:
    (1) One point for the correct *meaning* of the given adjective.
    (2) One point for the correct *comparative* and *superlative forms* of that adjective.
    (3) One point for a clear *sentence* with the comparative or superlative form.

The teams should prepare for the contest by discussing the words in the list, looking them up in the dictionary if necessary, and making up possible sentences.

Example: dependable

LEADER: What does "dependable" mean?

TEAM: "Dependable" means "responsible, reliable, trustworthy." For example, it describes people who do their jobs well every day.

LEADER: Yes. That's one point. Now, comparative and superlative forms?

TEAM: *more dependable than, the most dependable of all*

LEADER: Correct. That's another point. And a sentence with one of those forms?

TEAM: Vegetables are more dependable than fruit.

LEADER: What? That doesn't make any sense. No point.

TEAM: Adults are more dependable than children.

LEADER: Good. One point. Your total points as a team: three.

List of adjectives for the leader to choose from:

1. absent-minded	8. confusing	15. fresh	22. pleasant
2. active	9. cute	16. friendly	23. polite
3. attractive	10. dangerous	17. heavy	24. soft
4. bright	11. delightful	18. hectic	25. sour
5. calm	12. dim	19. high	26. straight
6. clever	13. easy	20. humid	27. wild
7. common	14. flexible	21. intelligent	28. wonderful

9-5   MODIFYING COMPARATIVES

(a) Tom is **very** old. (b) Ann drives **very** carefully.	**Very** often modifies adjectives, as in (a), and adverbs, as in (b).

(c) INCORRECT: Tom is very older than I am.
     INCORRECT: Ann drives very more carefully
             than she used to.
	Very is NOT used to modify comparative adjectives and adverbs.

(d) Tom is **much/a lot/far** older than I am. (e) Ann drives **much/a lot/ far** more carefully than she used to.	Instead, **much, a lot,** or **far** are used to modify comparative adjectives and adverbs, as in (d) and (e).
(f) Ben is **a little (bit)** older than I am / OR (*informally*) me.	Another common modifier is **a little/a little bit,** as in (f).

□ **EXERCISE 16. Modifying comparatives. (Chart 9-5)**
   Directions: Add ***very, much, a lot,*** or ***far*** to these sentences.

1. It's hot today. → It's ***very*** *hot today.*

2. It's hotter today than yesterday. → It's ***much/a lot/far*** *hotter today than yesterday.*

3. An airplane is fast.

4. Taking an airplane is faster than hitchhiking.

5. Learning a second language is difficult for many people.

6. Learning a second language is more difficult than learning chemistry formulas.

7. You can live more inexpensively in student housing than in a rented apartment.

8. You can live inexpensively in student housing.

9-6 COMPARISONS WITH *LESS . . . THAN* AND *NOT AS . . . AS*

MORE THAN ONE SYLLABLE (a) A pen is ***less*** *expensive* ***than*** a book. (b) A pen is ***not as*** *expensive* ***as*** a book.	The opposite of ***-er/more*** is expressed by ***less*** or ***not as . . . as***. (a) and (b) have the same meaning. ***Less*** and ***not as . . . as*** are used with adjectives and adverbs of **more than one syllable**.
ONE SYLLABLE (c) A pen is ***not as*** *large* ***as*** a book. (d) *INCORRECT: A pen is less large than a book.*	Only ***not as . . . as*** (NOT ***less***) is used with one-syllable adjectives or adverbs, as in (c).

□ **EXERCISE 17. LESS . . . THAN and NOT AS . . . AS. (Chart 9-6)**
   Directions: Circle the correct answer or answers.

1. My nephew is _____ ambitious _____ my niece.
   Ⓐ less . . . than   Ⓑ not as . . . as

2. My nephew is _____ old _____ my niece.
   A. less . . . than   Ⓑ not as . . . as

3. A bee is _____ big _____ a bird.
   A. less . . . than   B. not as . . . as

4. My brother is _____ interested in planning for the future _____ I am.
   A. less . . . than   B. not as . . . as

5. I am _____ good at repairing things _____ Diane is.
   A. less . . . than   B. not as . . . as

6. Some students are _____ serious about their schoolwork _____ others.
   A. less . . . than   B. not as . . . as

☐ EXERCISE 18. MORE/-ER, LESS, and NOT AS . . . AS. (Charts 9-1 → 9-6)
Directions: Use the words in the given order to make comparisons using one of the following:
- *more/-er . . . than*
- *less . . . than*
- *not as . . . as*

1. France \ large \ Brazil
   → *France isn't as large as Brazil.*
2. a river \ big \ a stream
   → *A river is bigger than a stream.*
3. metal \ flexible \ rubber
   → *Metal is less flexible than rubber.* OR *Metal isn't as flexible as rubber.*
4. a sidewalk \ wide \ a road
5. arithmetic \ difficult \ advanced algebra
6. a hill \ high \ a mountain
7. bottled water \ clear and clean \ river water
8. cold, wet weather \ pleasant \ warm weather
9. sitting in an easy chair \ comfortable \ sitting on a park bench
10. hiking along a path \ dangerous \ climbing a mountain peak
11. toes \ long \ fingers
12. toes \ useful \ fingers
13. toes \ long or useful \ fingers
14. fingers \ long and useful \ toes

☐ EXERCISE 19. MORE/-ER, LESS, and AS . . . AS. (Charts 9-1 → 9-6)
Directions: Compare the following. Use *(not) as . . . as, less,* and *more/-er.* How many points of comparison can you think of? Work in pairs, on teams, or as a class.

Example: trees and flowers *(big, colorful, useful, etc.)*
   → *Trees are bigger than flowers.*
   Trees are rarely as colorful as flowers.
   Flowers are less useful than trees.
   Flowers aren't as sturdy as trees.
   Trees are more important to clean air quality than flowers.

1. the sun and the moon
2. children and adults
3. two restaurants in this city
4. two famous people in the world

9-7 UNCLEAR COMPARISONS

UNCLEAR (a) Ann likes her dog better than her husband.	Sometimes it is necessary to complete the idea following ***than*** in order to make a comparison clear.
CLEAR (b) Ann likes her dog better than her husband does. (c) Ann likes her dog better than she does her husband.	In (b): *does* means "likes the dog." In (c): *does* means "likes."

□ EXERCISE 20. Unclear comparisons. (Chart 9-7)
    Directions: The following are unclear comparisons. Discuss the possible meanings by creating clear comparisons.

1. UNCLEAR: I know John better than Mary.
   → *I know John better than Mary does.* OR *I know John better than I do Mary.*
2. UNCLEAR: Sam likes football better than his wife.
3. UNCLEAR: Frank helps me more than Debra.
4. UNCLEAR: I pay my plumber more than my dentist.

9-8 USING *MORE* WITH NOUNS

(a) Would you like some ***more coffee***? (b) Not everyone is here. I expect ***more people*** to come later.	In (a): *coffee* is a noun. When ***more*** is used with nouns, it often has the meaning of *additional*. It is not necessary to use ***than***.
(c) There are ***more people*** in China ***than*** there are in the United States.	***More*** is also used with nouns to make complete comparisons by adding ***than***.
(d) Do you have enough coffee, or would you like some ***more***?	When the meaning is clear, the noun may be omitted and ***more*** used by itself.

□ EXERCISE 21. Comparatives with nouns, adjectives, and adverbs.
        (Charts 9-2, 9-3, and 9-8)
    Directions: Use *-er* or ***more*** and the words in the list to complete the sentences. Discuss whether the words are nouns, adjectives, or adverbs, and review how comparatives are formed. When do you use *-er,* and when do you use ***more***?

✓bright	happily	information	responsibilities	salt
✓brightly	happiness	mistakes	responsible	✓traffic
doctors	happy	quick	responsibly	

1. A city has _____more traffic_____ than a small town.

2. Sunlight is much _____brighter_____ than moonlight.

3. Did you know that a laser burns billions of times _____more brightly_____ than the light at the sun's surface?

4. There is _____ about geography in an encyclopedia than (there is) in a dictionary.

5. I used to be sad, but now I'm a lot _____ about my life (than I used to be).

6. Unhappy roommates or spouses can live together _____ if they learn to respect each other's differences.

7. She's had a miserable life. I hope she finds _____ in the future.

8. I made _____ on the last test than (I did) on the first one, so I got a worse grade.

9. My daughter Annie is trustworthy and mature. She behaves much _____ than my nephew Louie.

10. A twelve-year-old has _____ at home and in school than a nine-year-old.

11. My son is _____ about doing his homework than his older sister is.

12. A rabbit is _____ than a turtle.

13. This soup doesn't taste quite right. I think it needs just a little _____ .

14. Health care in rural areas is poor. We need _____ to treat people in rural areas.

9-9 REPEATING A COMPARATIVE

(a) Because he was afraid, he walked *faster and faster*. (b) Life in the modern world is becoming *more and more complex*.	Repeating a comparative gives the idea that something becomes progressively greater, i.e., it increases in intensity, quality, or quantity.

☐ **EXERCISE 22. Repeating a comparative. (Chart 9-9)**
   Directions: Complete the answers by repeating a comparative. Use the words in the list.

angry	discouraged	hard	weak
big	✓fast	long	wet
cold/warm	good	loud	

1. When I get excited, my heart beats _____ faster and faster _____ .

2. When you blow up a balloon, it gets _____ .

3. My English is improving. It is getting _____ every day.

4. As the ambulance came closer to us, the siren became _____.

5. She sat there quietly, but during all that time she was getting _____
_____ . Finally she exploded.

6. The line of people waiting to get into the theater got _____.

7. I've been looking for a job for a month and still haven't been able to find one. I'm
getting _____ .

8. The weather is getting _____ with each passing day.

9. As I continued walking in miserable weather, it rained _____.
I got _____ . By the time I got home, I was
completely soaked.

10. As I continued to row the boat, my arms got _____
until I had almost no strength left in them at all.

9-10 USING DOUBLE COMPARATIVES

(a) ***The harder*** you study, ***the more*** you will learn. (b) ***The more*** she studied, ***the more*** she learned. (c) ***The warmer*** the weather (is), ***the better*** I like it.	A double comparative has two parts; both parts begin with ***the,*** as in the examples. The second part of the comparison is the **result** of the first part. In (a): If you study harder, the result will be that you will learn more.

(d) A: Should we ask Jenny and Jim to the party too?
     B: Why not? ***The more, the merrier.***
 (e) A: When should we leave?
     B: ***The sooner, the better.***
	The more, the merrier and ***the sooner, the better*** are two common expressions.
	 In (d): It is good to have more people at the party.
	 In (e): It is good if we leave as soon as we can.

☐ **EXERCISE 23. Double comparatives.** (Chart 9-10)
Directions: Complete the sentences with double comparatives (*the more/-er . . . the more/-er*).

1. If the fruit is *fresh*, it tastes *good*.

   → _____The fresher_____ the fruit (is), _____the better_____ it tastes.

2. We got *close* to the fire. We felt *warm*.

   → _____ we got to the fire, _____ we felt.

3. If a knife is *sharp*, it is *easy* to cut something with.

   → _____ a knife (is), _____ it is to cut something.

4. The party got *noisy* next door. I got *angry*.

   → I had a terrible time getting to sleep last night. My neighbors were having a loud party. _____ it got, _____ I got. Finally, I banged on the wall and told them to be quiet.

5. If a flamingo eats a lot of *shrimp*, it becomes very *pink*.

   → The _____ a flamingo eats, the _____ it gets.

   SHRIMP, ALL YOU CAN EAT.

6. She drove *fast*. I became *nervous*.
   → Erica offered to take me to the airport, and I was grateful. But we got a late start, so on the way she stepped on the accelerator. I got more than a little uncomfortable. The . . . .

7. He *thought* about his family. He became *homesick*.
   → Pierre tried to concentrate on his studying, but his mind would drift to his family and his home. The . . . .

8. We ran *fast* to reach the house. The sky grew *dark*.
   → A storm was threatening. The . . . .

9-11 USING SUPERLATIVES

(a) Tokyo is one of **the largest cities in the world**. (b) David is **the most generous person I have ever known**. (c) I have three books. These two are quite good, but this one is the **best** (book) **of all**.	Typical completions when a superlative is used: In (a): superlative + *in* a place *(the world, this class, my family, the corporation, etc.)*. In (b): superlative + adjective clause.* In (c): superlative + *of all*.
(d) I took four final exams. The final in accounting was **the least difficult** of all.	*The least* has the opposite meaning of *the most*.
(e) Ali is **one of** the best **students** in this class. (f) **One of** the best **students** in this class **is** Ali.	Notice the pattern with **one of**: **one of** + PLURAL **noun** (+ SINGULAR **verb**)

*See Chapter 12 for more information about adjective clauses.

☐ EXERCISE 24. Superlatives. (Chart 9-11)

Directions: Complete the sentences with superlatives and the appropriate preposition, *in* or *of*.

1. Jack is *lazy*. He is _____the laziest_____ student ____in____ the class.

2. Mike and Julie were *nervous*, but Amanda was __the most nervous of__ all.

3. Costa Rica is *beautiful*. It is one of _____

   countries _____ the world.

4. Scott got a *bad* score on the test. It was one of _____ scores

   _____ the whole school.

5. Pluto is *far* from the sun. In fact, it is _____ planet from the

   sun _____ our solar system.

6. There are a lot of *good* cooks in my family, but my mom is _____ cook

   _____ all.

7. Alaska is *big*. It is _____ state _____ the United States.

8. My grandfather is very *old*. He is _____ person _____ the

   town where he lives.

9. That chair in the corner is *comfortable*. It is _____

   chair _____ the room.

10. Everyone who ran in the race was *exhausted*, but I was _____

    _____ all.

☐ **EXERCISE 25. Superlatives. (Chart 9-11)**

Directions: Use the given phrases to complete the sentences with superlatives.

big bird	long river in South America
clean air	popular forms of entertainment
✓deep ocean	three common street names
high mountains on earth	two great natural dangers

1. The Pacific is ___the deepest ocean___ in the world.

2. There is almost no air pollution at the South Pole. The South Pole has _____
   _____ in the world.

3. _____ are in
   the Himalayan Range in Asia.

4. Most birds are small, but not the flightless North African ostrich. It is _____
   _____ in the world.

5. _____ to
   ships are fog and icebergs.

6. One of _____ throughout
   the world is the motion picture.

7. _____ in the United
   States are Park, Washington, and Maple.

8. _____ is the Amazon.

☐ **EXERCISE 26. Completing superlatives with adjective clauses. (Chart 9-11)**

Directions: Complete the sentences with an appropriate superlative followed by an adjective clause.

1. I have had many *good experiences.* Of those, my vacation to Honduras was one of . . . .
   → *the best experiences I have ever had.*

2. Sally has had many *nice times,* but her birthday party was one of . . . .

3. I've taken many *difficult courses,* but statistics is one of . . . .

4. I've made some *bad mistakes* in my life, but lending my cousin money was one of . . . .

5. We've seen many *beautiful buildings* in the world, but the Taj Mahal is one of . . . .

6. A: How do you think you did on the exam this morning?
   B: I think I did pretty well. It was an *easy test.* In fact, it was one of . . . .

☐ **EXERCISE 27. Using ONE OF with superlatives. (Chart 9-11)**

Directions: Work in pairs.

Speaker A: Give the cues. (Listen carefully to Speaker B's answer, making sure s/he is using a plural noun following *one of.*) Your book is open.

Speaker B: Answer the questions in complete sentences, using *one of* plus a superlative. Your book is closed.

Example:

SPEAKER A *(book open):* You have known many interesting people. Who is one of them?

SPEAKER B *(book closed):* **One of the most interesting people** I've ever known **is** (Ms. Lee). OR (Ms. Lee) **is one of the most interesting people** I've ever known.

1. There are many beautiful countries in the world. What is one of them?
2. There are many famous people in the world. Who is one of them?
3. What is one of the best movies you've seen recently? And have you seen any bad movies? What is one of them?
4. What is one of the most exciting things you've ever done?
5. You know many wonderful people. Who is one of them?

Switch roles.

6. Think of some happy days in your life. What was one of them?
7. There are a lot of interesting animals in the world. What is one of them?
8. Who is one of the most important people in the history of your country?
9. You have had many good experiences. What is one of them?
10. There are many important people in your life among your family, friends, teachers, co-workers, and others. Who is one of these people?

☐ **EXERCISE 28. Superlatives. (Chart 9-11)**

Directions: Use superlatives of the given words and your own words to complete the sentences.

1. *bad*   . . . is the . . . movie I . . . .
   → *"Sea Monsters" is the worst movie I've ever seen.*

2. *popular*   The . . . sport in . . . is . . . .

3. *large*   The . . . city in . . . is . . . .

4. *good*   . . . is the . . . restaurant in . . . .

5. *interesting*   . . . is one of the . . . people I . . . .

6. *valuable*   The . . . thing I . . . is . . . .

7. *important*   The three . . . things in life are . . . .

8. *serious*   The . . . problems in . . . today are . . . .

☐ **EXERCISE 29. Review: comparatives and superlatives.** (Charts 9-1 → 9-11)

Directions: Work in pairs.
Speaker A: Ask a question that uses either a comparative or a superlative.
Speaker B: Answer the question. Use complete sentences.

Example: what . . . sweet
SPEAKER A: What is sweeter than sugar?
SPEAKER B: Nothing is sweeter than sugar.

Example: who is . . . wonderful
SPEAKER A: Who is the most wonderful person you've ever known?
SPEAKER B: That's a hard question. Probably my mother is the most wonderful person I've ever known.

Switch roles.

1. what is . . . important
2. who is . . . famous
3. what is . . . good
4. what is . . . bad
5. whose hair is . . . long
6. what is . . . interesting
7. which car is . . . expensive
8. what country is . . . near
9. what is . . . dangerous
10. who is . . . old
11. what is . . . beautiful
12. who is . . . kind

☐ **EXERCISE 30. Review: comparatives and superlatives.** (Charts 9-1 → 9-11)

Directions: Compare the items in each list using the given words. Use **as . . . as,** the comparative **(-er/more)**, and the superlative **(-est/most)**. Discuss the topics orally or in writing.

Example: streets in this city: *wide \ narrow \ busy \ dangerous*
→ *First Avenue is* **wider** *than Market Street.*
Second Avenue is **nearly as wide as** *First Avenue.*
First Avenue is **narrower** *than Interstate Highway 70.*
The busiest *street is Main Street.*
Main Street is **busier** *than Market Street.*
The most dangerous street *in the city is Olive Boulevard.*

1. a lemon, a grapefruit, and an orange:
   sweet \ sour \ large \ small

2. three different books in the classroom:
   thin \ fat \ interesting \ useful \ good \ bad

3. a kitten, a cheetah, and a lion:
   weak \ powerful \ wild \ gentle \ fast

4. air, water, and wood:
   heavy \ light \ important to human life

5. boxing, soccer, and golf:
   dangerous \ safe \ exciting \ boring

6. the food at *(three places in this city where you have eaten):*
   delicious \ appetizing \ inexpensive \ good \ bad

□ EXERCISE 31. Review of comparatives and superlatives. (Charts 9-1 → 9-11)
Directions: Complete the sentences. Use any appropriate form of the words in parentheses and add any other necessary words. There may be more than one possible completion.

1. Lead is a very heavy metal. It is (heavy) ____heavier than____ gold or silver.
   It is one of (heavy) ____the heaviest____ metals ___of___ all.

2. Dogs are usually (friendly) _____ cats.

3. One of (famous) _____ volcanoes _____ the world is Mount Etna in Sicily.

4. A car has two (wheels) _____ a bicycle.

5. Mrs. Cook didn't ask the children to clean up the kitchen. It was (easy) _____ for her to do it herself _____ to nag them to do it.

6. Duck eggs and chicken eggs are different. Duck eggs are (large) _____ chicken eggs. Also, the yolk of a duck egg is (dark) _____ yellow _____ the yolk of a chicken egg.

7. The volcanic explosion of Krakatoa near Java in 1883 may have been (loud) _____ noise _____ recorded history. It was heard 2,760 miles (4,441 kilometers) away.

8. (important) _____ piece of equipment for birdwatching is a pair of binoculars.

9. Although both jobs are important, being a teacher requires (education) _____ _____ being a bus driver.

10. The Great Wall of China is (long) _____ structure that has ever been built.

11. Howard Anderson is one of *(delightful)* _____ people I've ever met.

12. *(hard)* _____ I tried, *(impossible)* _____ _____ it seemed to solve the math problem.

13. Perhaps *(common)* _____ topic of everyday conversation _____ the world is the weather.

14. World Cup Soccer is *(big)* _____ sporting event _____ the world. It is viewed on TV by *(people)* _____ any other event in sports.

15. Human beings must compete with other species for the food of the land. *(great)* _____ competitors we have for food are insects.

16. When the temperature stays below freezing for a long period of time, the Eiffel Tower becomes six inches (fifteen centimeters) *(short)* _____ .

17. Have you ever been bothered by a fly buzzing around you? *(easy)* _____ _____ way to get a fly out of a room is to darken the room and turn on a light somewhere else.

18. Young people have *(high)* _____ rate of automobile accidents _____ all drivers.

19. The wall of a soap bubble is very, very thin. A human hair is approximately ten thousand times *(thick)* _____ _____ the wall of a soap bubble.

20. English has approximately 600,000 words. Because of the explosion of scientific discoveries and new technologies, there are *(words)* _____ in English _____ in any other language.

21. You'd better buy the tickets for the show soon. *(long)* _____ you wait, *(difficult)* _____ it will be for you to get good seats.

22. No animals can travel (fast) _____ birds. Birds are (fast) _____ animals _____ all.

23. Most birds have small eyes, but not ostriches. Indeed, the eye of an ostrich is (large) _____ its brain.

24. (great) _____ variety of birds _____ a single area can be found in the rainforests of Southeast Asia and India.

25. It's easy to drown a houseplant. (houseplants) _____ die from too much water _____ not enough water.

9-12 USING *THE SAME, SIMILAR, DIFFERENT, LIKE, ALIKE*

(a) John and Mary have **the same books**. (b) John and Mary have **similar books**. (c) John and Mary have **different books**. (d) Their books are **the same**. (e) Their books are **similar**. (f) Their books are **different**.	**The same, similar,** and **different** are used as adjectives. Notice: **the** always precedes **same**.
(g) This book is **the same as** that one. (h) This book is **similar to** that one. (i) This book is **different from** that one.	Notice: **the same** is followed by **as;** **similar** is followed by **to;** **different** is followed by **from.**★
(j) She is **the same age as** my mother. My shoes are **the same size as** yours.	A noun may come between **the same** and **as**, as in (j).
(k) My pen **is like** your pen. (l) My pen and your pen **are alike**.	Notice in (k) and (l): *noun* + **be like** + *noun* *noun* and *noun* + **be alike**
(m) She **looks like** her sister. It **looks like** rain. It **sounds like** thunder. This material **feels like** silk. That **smells like** gas. This chemical **tastes like** salt. Stop **acting like** a fool. He **seems like** a nice fellow.	In addition to following **be**, **like** also follows certain verbs, primarily those dealing with the senses. Notice the examples in (m).
(n) The twins **look alike**. We **think alike**. Most four-year-olds **act alike**. My sister and I **talk alike**. The little boys are **dressed alike**.	**Alike** may follow a few verbs other than **be**. Notice the examples in (n).

★In informal speech, native speakers might use **than** instead of **from** after **different**. **From** is considered correct in formal English, unless the comparison is completed by a clause: *I have a different attitude now than I used to have.*

□ **EXERCISE 32. THE SAME, SIMILAR, DIFFERENT, LIKE, and ALIKE. (Chart 9-12)**
  Directions: Complete the sentences with *as, to, from,* or **Ø** if no word is necessary.

1. Geese are similar _____to_____ ducks. They are both large water birds.

2. But geese are not the same _____as_____ ducks. Geese are usually larger and have longer necks.

3. Geese are different _____from_____ ducks.

4. Geese are like _____Ø_____ ducks in some ways, but geese and ducks are not exactly alike _____Ø_____ .

5. An orange is similar _____ a grapefruit. They are both citrus fruits.

6. But an orange is not the same _____ a grapefruit. A grapefruit is usually larger and sourer.

7. An orange is different _____ a grapefruit.

8. An orange is like _____ a grapefruit in some ways, but they are not exactly alike _____ .

9. Gold is similar _____ silver. They are both valuable metals that people use for jewelry. But they aren't the same _____ . Gold is not the same color _____ silver. Gold is also different _____ silver in cost. Gold is more expensive than silver.

10. Look at the two zebras. Their names are Zee and Bee. Zee looks like _____ Bee. Is Zee exactly the same _____ Bee? The pattern of the stripes on each zebra in the world is unique. No two zebras are exactly alike _____ . Even though Zee and Bee are similar _____ each other, they are different _____ each other in the exact pattern of their stripes.

☐ EXERCISE 33. THE SAME, SIMILAR, DIFFERENT, LIKE, and ALIKE. (Chart 9-12)

Directions: Compare the figures. Complete the sentences using ***the same (as)***, ***similar (to)***, ***different (from)***, ***like***, and ***alike***.

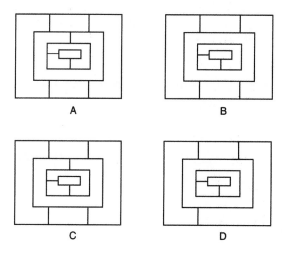

1. All of the figures are _____ *similar to* _____ each other.

2. Figure A is _____ Figure B.

3. Figure A and Figure B are _____ .

4. A and C are _____ .

5. A and C are _____ D.

6. C is _____ A.

7. B isn't _____ D.

☐ EXERCISE 34. THE SAME, SIMILAR, DIFFERENT, LIKE, and ALIKE. (Chart 9-12)

Directions: Compare the figures. Work in pairs or groups.

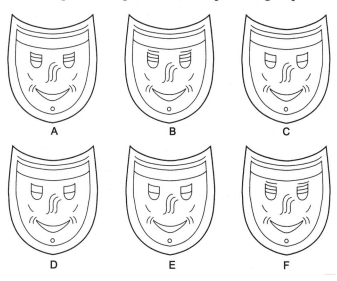

□ EXERCISE 35. THE SAME, SIMILAR, DIFFERENT, LIKE, and ALIKE. (Chart 9-12)
   Directions: Use **the same (as)**, **similar (to)**, **different (from)**, **like**, and **alike** in the
   sentences. There may be more than one possible response in some of them. Use whatever
   response sounds best to you.

1. Jennifer and Jack both come from Rapid City. In other words, they come from
   _____the same_____ town.

2. This city is __the same as / similar to / like__ my hometown. Both are quiet
   and conservative.

3. You and I don't agree. Your ideas are _____ mine.

4. Eric never wears _____ clothes two days in a row.

5. Ants are fascinating. An ant colony is _____ a
   well-disciplined army.

6. In terms of shape, cabbage looks _____ lettuce. But cabbage and
   lettuce don't taste _____ .

7. A male mosquito is not _____ size _____ a female
   mosquito. The female is larger.

8. I'm used to strong coffee. I think the coffee Americans drink tastes _____
   dishwater!

9. "Meet" and "meat" are homonyms; i.e., they have _____
   pronunciation.

10. The pronunciation of "caught" is _____ the pronunciation of
    "cot."

11. "Flower" has _____ pronunciation _____ "flour."

12. My dictionary is _____ yours.

13. Trying to get through school without
    studying is _____ trying to
    go swimming without getting wet.

14. A crocodile and an alligator are
    _____ in appearance.

15. If it looks _____ a duck,
    quacks _____ a duck, and
    walks _____ a duck, it is a duck.
    (*a humorous saying*)

□ EXERCISE 36. Making comparisons. (Chapter 9)
Directions: Do you have sayings in your language that are similar to or the same as the following English proverbs?

1. Don't count your chickens before they hatch.
2. The early bird gets the worm.
3. Too many cooks spoil the broth.
4. A bird in the hand is worth two in the bush.
5. A stitch in time saves nine.
6. When in Rome, do as the Romans do.
7. Birds of a feather flock together.
8. A rolling stone gathers no moss.

□ EXERCISE 37. Making comparisons. (Chapter 9)
Directions: Write a composition based on one of the following topics.

Compare and contrast:
1. being single and being married.
2. cities you have lived in or have visited.
3. different schools you have attended.
4. your way of life before and after you became a parent.
5. yourself now to yourself ten years ago.
6. your country now to your country 100 years ago.
7. life today to life 100 years from now.
8. two sports.
9. the seasons of the year.
10. food in two countries.

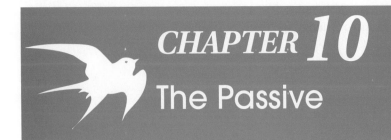

CHAPTER 10
The Passive

CONTENTS

10-1 ACTIVE SENTENCES AND PASSIVE SENTENCES

(a) **ACTIVE:** The mouse *ate* the cheese. (b) **PASSIVE:** The cheese *was eaten* by the mouse.	(a) and (b) have the same meaning.

ACTIVE	PASSIVE

ACTIVE: 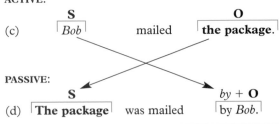 S O (c) *Bob* mailed **the package**. **PASSIVE:** S *by* + **O** (d) **The package** was mailed by *Bob*.	In (c): The object in an active sentence becomes the subject in a passive sentence. In (d): The subject in an active sentence is the object of *by* in the *by*-phrase in a passive sentence.

10-2 FORM OF THE PASSIVE

	BE	+	PAST PARTICIPLE		Form of all passive verbs: **be** + past participle
(a) Corn	**is**		**grown**	by farmers.	**Be** can be in any of its forms: *am, is, are, was, were,*
(b) Sara	**was**		**surprised**	by the news.	*has been, have been, will be, etc.*
(c) The report	**will be**		**written**	by Mary.	

	ACTIVE	PASSIVE
SIMPLE PRESENT	Farmers **grow** corn. ⟶	Corn **is grown** by farmers.
SIMPLE PAST	The news **surprised** Sara. ⟶	Sara **was surprised** by the news.
PRESENT PERFECT	Jack **has mailed** the letter. ⟶	The letter **has been mailed** by Jack.
FUTURE	Mr. Lee **will plan** the meeting. ⟶ Sue **is going to write** the report. ⟶	The meeting **will be planned** by Mr. Lee. The report **is going to be written** by Sue.

☐ EXERCISE 1. Active vs. passive. (Charts 10-1 and 10-2)
Directions: Change the active verbs to passive verbs. Write the subject of the passive sentence.

1. SIMPLE PRESENT

    (a) The teacher *helps* **me**.
        (a) ____I____ ____am helped____ by the teacher.

    (b) The teacher *helps* **Jane**.
        (b) __Jane__ ____is helped____ by the teacher.

    (c) The teacher *helps* **us**.
        (c) _____ _____ by the teacher.

2. SIMPLE PAST

    (a) The teacher *helped* **me**.
        (a) _____ _____ by the teacher.

    (b) The teacher *helped* **them**.
        (b) _____ _____ by the teacher.

3. PRESENT PERFECT

    (a) The teacher *has helped* **Joe**.
        (a) _____ _____ by the teacher.

    (b) The teacher *has helped* **us**.
        (b) _____ _____ by the teacher.

4. FUTURE

    (a) The teacher *will help* **me**.
        (a) _____ _____ by the teacher.

    (b) The teacher *is going to help* **Tim**.
        (b) _____ _____ by the teacher.

☐ **EXERCISE 2. Form of the passive. (Charts 10-1 and 10-2)**
　　Directions: Change the verbs to the passive. Do not change the tense.

		BE +	PAST PARTICIPLE	
1. Bob *mailed* the package.	The package	was	mailed	by Bob.
2. That company *employs* many people.	Many people	_____	_____	by that company.
3. That company *has hired* Sue.	Sue	_____	_____	by that company.
4. The secretary *is going to fax* the letters.	The letters	_____	_____	by the secretary.
5. A college student *bought* my old car.	My old car	_____	_____	by a college student.
6. Mrs. Adams *will do* the work.	The work	_____	_____	by Mrs. Adams.
7. Mr. Fox *washed* the windows.	The windows	_____	_____	by Mr. Fox.

☐ **EXERCISE 3. Active vs. passive. (Charts 10-1 and 10-2)**
　　Directions: Change the sentences from active to passive.

　　1. Ms. Hopkins invited me to dinner.
　　　→ *I was invited to dinner by Ms. Hopkins.*

　　2. Thomas Edison invented the phonograph.

　　3. Water surrounds an island.

　　4. A plumber is going to fix the leaky faucet.

　　5. A doctor has examined the sick child.

　　6. A large number of people speak Spanish.

　　7. Helicopters fascinate children.

　　8. Shakespeare wrote *Hamlet*.

　　9. This news will amaze you.

☐ EXERCISE 4. Active vs. passive: question forms. (Charts 10-1 and 10-2)
　　　Directions: Change the active sentences to passive sentences that have the same meaning and tense.

	ACTIVE	PASSIVE	
1.	(a) The news surprised John.	John was surprised	by the news.
	(b) Did the news surprise you?	Were you surprised	by the news?
2.	(a) The news surprises Erin.	_____	by the news.
	(b) Does the news surprise you?	_____	by the news?
3.	(a) The news will shock Steve.	_____	by the news.
	(b) Will the news shock Pat?	_____	by the news?
4.	(a) Liz signed the petition.	_____	by Liz.
	(b) Did Ryan sign it?	_____	by Ryan?

PETITION

We, the undersigned, believe that the house at 3205 Tree Street is an historic building. We believe that it should not be destroyed in order to build a fast-food restaurant at that location.

Robert E. Miller　　　　　　　Wm. H. Brock

Elizabeth J. Wilson　　　　　Ms. Catherine Ann Jackson

James Walsh　　　　　　　　An Binh Nguyen

Alicia Alvarez

5.	(a) Bob has signed the petition.	_____	by Bob.
	(b) Has Jim signed it yet?	_____	by Jim yet?
6.	(a) Sue is going to sign it.	_____	by Sue.
	(b) Is Carol going to sign it?	_____	by Carol?

☐ EXERCISE 5. Active vs. passive. (Charts 10-1 and 10-2)
　　　Directions: Change the sentences from active to passive.

1. A thief stole Ann's purse. → *Ann's purse was stolen by a thief.*
2. Did a cat kill the bird?
3. My cat didn't kill the bird.
4. Do a large number of people speak French?
5. Is the janitor going to fix the window?
6. Will a maid clean our hotel room?
7. Does the hotel provide clean towels?
8. Sometimes my inability to understand spoken English frustrates me.

□ **EXERCISE 6. Active vs. passive. (Charts 10-1 and 10-2)**
Directions: Change the passive sentences to active. Keep the same tense. Some of the sentences are questions.

1. Was the riot stopped by the police?
   → *Did the police stop the riot?*

2. My suitcase was inspected by a customs officer.

3. Love and understanding are needed by all children.

4. Were you taught to read by your parents?

5. I was taught to read by my parents.

6. Are we going to be met at the train station by your cousin?

7. Have the plans for the new hospital already been drawn by
   the architect?

8. The bear was chased up a tree by a dog.

10-3 TRANSITIVE AND INTRANSITIVE VERBS

(a) **TRANSITIVE**			A *transitive* verb is a verb that is followed by an object. An object is a noun or a pronoun.

	S	**V**	**O**
	Bob	*mailed*	*the letter.*
	Mr. Lee	*signed*	*the check.*
	A cat	*killed*	*the bird.*

(b) **INTRANSITIVE** — An *intransitive* verb is a verb that is not followed by an object.

	S	**V**	
	An accident	*happened.*	
	Kate	*came*	to our house.
	I	*slept*	well last night.

COMMON INTRANSITIVE VERBS*

agree	die	happen	rise	stand
appear	exist	laugh	seem	stay
arrive	fall	live	sit	talk
become	flow	occur	sleep	wait
come	go	rain	sneeze	walk

(c) **TRANSITIVE VERBS** ACTIVE: Bob *mailed* the letter. PASSIVE: The letter *was mailed* by Bob.	Only transitive verbs can be used in the passive.
(d) **INTRANSITIVE VERBS** ACTIVE: An accident *happened.* PASSIVE: *(not possible)*	An intransitive verb is NOT used in the passive.
(e) *INCORRECT: An accident was happened.*	

*To find out if a verb is transitive or intransitive, look in your dictionary. The usual abbreviations are v.t. (transitive) and v.i. (intransitive). Some verbs have both transitive and intransitive uses. For example:
   transitive: *Students study books.*
   intransitive: *Students study.*

□ **EXERCISE 7. Transitive vs. intransitive verbs. (Chart 10-3)**

Directions: <u>Underline</u> the verbs and identify them as transitive (**v.t.**) or intransitive (**v.i.**). Change the sentences to the passive if possible.

        v.i.
1. Jack <u>walked</u> to school yesterday. *(no change)*

        v.t.
2. Susie <u>broke</u> the window.
   → *The window was broken by Susie.*

3. We stayed in a hotel.

4. The leaves fell to the ground.

5. I slept at my friend's house last night.

6. An accident happened at the corner of Third and Main.

7. Many people saw the accident.

8. Dinosaurs existed millions of years ago.

9. I usually agree with my sister.

10. Many people die during a war.

11. The /*th*/ sound doesn't occur in my native language.

12. Research scientists will discover a cure for AIDS★ someday.

13. A cloud of migrating butterflies appeared out of nowhere.

14. Did the Koreans invent gunpowder?

15. In the fairy tale, a princess kissed a frog.

———————
★AIDS = a disease (**A**uto **I**mmune **D**eficiency **S**yndrome).

10-4 USING THE *BY*-PHRASE

(a) This sweater *was made* **by my aunt**.	The *by*-phrase is used in passive sentences when it is important to know who performs an action. In (a): *by my aunt* is important information.
(b) My sweater *was made* in Korea. (c) Spanish *is spoken* in Colombia. (d) That house *was built* in 1940. (e) Rice *is grown* in many countries.	Usually there is no *by*-phrase in a passive sentence. The passive is used when it is **not known or not important to know exactly who performs an action**. In (b): The exact person (or people) who made the sweater is not known and is not important to know, so there is no *by*-phrase in the passive sentence.
(f) **My aunt** is very skillful. **She** *made* this sweater. (g) — I like your sweaters. — Thanks. **This sweater** *was made by* my aunt. **That sweater** *was made by* my mother.	Usually the active is used when the speaker knows who performed the action, as in (f), where the focus of attention is on *my aunt*. In (g), the speaker uses the passive WITH a *by*-phrase because he wants to focus attention on the subjects of the sentences. The focus of attention is on the two sweaters. The *by*-phrases add important information.

☐ **EXERCISE 8. The BY-phrase. (Chart 10-4)**

Directions: Change the sentences from active to passive. Include the *by*-phrase only if necessary.

1. Bob Smith built that house.
   → *That house was built by Bob Smith.*

2. Someone built this house in 1904.
   → *This house was built in 1904.* (*Someone* = unnecessary)

3. People grow rice in India.

4. Do people speak Spanish in Peru?

5. Alexander Graham Bell invented the telephone.

6. When did someone invent the first computer?

7. People sell hammers at a hardware store. People use them to pound nails.

8. Someone will list my name in the new telephone directory.

9. Charles Darwin wrote *The Origin of Species*.

10. Someone published *The Origin of Species* in 1859.

11. Has anyone ever hypnotized you?

12. Someone has changed the name of this street from Bay Avenue to Martin Luther King Way.

"*DEEP ASLEEP... DEEP ASLEEP.. YOU FEEL VERY SLEEPY.., DEEP...*"

Directions: <u>Underline</u> the passive verbs. Discuss use of the passive. If a *by*-phrase is included, discuss why.

1. The mail <u>is</u> usually <u>delivered</u> to Bob's apartment around eleven o'clock.
   → *The passive is used because it is unknown exactly who delivers the mail.*

2. A: That's a pretty picture.
   B: Yes. It <u>was drawn</u> by my eight-year-old son.
   → *The passive is used with a* by-*phrase. The focus of attention is on the picture. The* by-*phrase includes important information. The active could also be used: "Yes. My eight-year-old son drew it."*

3. Our classroom building was built in the 1950s.

4. Coffee is grown in Brazil.

5. A: These tomatoes are delicious!
   B: Yes. They taste so much better than the ones you can get in the grocery store. These tomatoes were grown by my uncle in his greenhouse.

6. Airplane travel is unpredictable. Yesterday Anna's flight was delayed for seven hours. That's a long time to spend in an airport waiting for your plane to leave.

7. We can't go to the school play tonight. All the tickets have already been sold.

8. "Thailand" means "land of the free." The country of Thailand has never been ruled by a foreign power.

9. One of the most significant inventions in the history of civilization was the wheel. It was invented around five thousand years ago. It allowed people to pull things in carts instead of carrying everything on their backs or in their arms.

10. The invention of the printing press changed the world because it allowed many people instead of few to have copies of books. It was invented by Johannes Gutenberg around 1440. Before that, books were copied by hand. Writing books by hand was a slow process.

☐ **EXERCISE 10. Active vs. passive. (Charts 10-1 → 10-4)**

Directions: Complete the sentences with the correct form of the verb (active or passive) in parentheses.

1. Yesterday our teacher *(arrive)* _____**arrived**_____ five minutes late.

2. Our morning paper *(read)* _____ by over 200,000 people every day.

3. Last night my favorite TV program *(interrupt)* _____ by a special news bulletin.

4. That's not my coat. It *(belong)* _____ to Louise.

5. Our mail *(deliver)* _____ before noon every day.

6. The "b" in "comb" *(pronounce, not)* _____ . It is silent.

7. A bad accident *(happen)* _____ on Highway 95 last night.

8. When I *(arrive)* _____ at the airport yesterday, I *(meet)* _____ by my cousin and a couple of her friends.

9. Yesterday I *(hear)* _____ about Margaret's divorce. I *(surprise)* _____ by the news. Janice *(shock)* _____ .

10. A new house *(build)* _____ next to ours next year.

11. Roberto *(write)* _____ this composition last week. That one *(write)* _____ by Abdullah.

12. Radium *(discover)* _____ by Marie and Pierre Curie in 1898.

13. At the soccer game yesterday, the winning goal *(kick)* _____ by Luigi. Over 100,000 people *(attend)* _____ the soccer game.

14. A: Do you understand the explanation in the book?

    B: No, I don't. I *(confuse)* _____ by it.

15. A: Where are you going to go to school next year?

    B: I *(accept)* _____ by Shoreline Community College.

16. A: I think football is too violent.

    B: I *(agree)* _____ with you. I *(prefer)* _____ baseball.

17. A: When *(your bike, steal)* _____ ?

B: Two days ago.

18. A: *(you, pay)* _____ your electric bill yet?

B: No, I haven't, but I'd better pay it today. If I don't, my electricity *(shut off)* _____ by the power company.

19. A: Did you hear about the accident?

B: No. What *(happen)* _____ ?

A: A bicyclist *(hit)* _____ by a taxi in front of the dorm.

B: *(the bicyclist, injure)* _____ ?

A: Yes. Someone *(call)* _____ an ambulance. The bicyclist *(take)* _____ to City Hospital and *(treat)* _____ in the emergency ward for cuts and bruises.

B: What *(happen)* _____ to the taxi driver?

A: He *(arrest)* _____ for reckless driving.

B: He's lucky that the bicyclist *(kill, not)* _____ .

20. The Eiffel Tower *(be)* _____ in Paris, France. It *(visit)* _____ by millions of people every year. It *(design)* _____ by Alexandre Eiffel (1832–1923). It *(erect)* _____ in 1889 for the Paris exposition. Since that time, it *(be)* _____ the most famous landmark in Paris. Today it *(recognize)* _____ _____ by people throughout the world.

☐ **EXERCISE 11. Active vs. passive. (Charts 10-1 → 10-4)**

Directions: Complete the sentences with the correct forms of the verbs in parentheses.

Almost everyone *(enjoy)* _____ **enjoys** _____ visiting a zoo. Today zoos are
 1

common. The first zoo *(establish)* _____ around 3500 years ago
 2

by an Egyptian queen for her personal enjoyment. Five hundred years later, a Chinese

emperor *(establish)* _____ a huge zoo to show his power and wealth.
 3

Later zoos *(establish)* _____ for the purpose of studying animals.
 4

Some of the early European zoos were dark holes or dirty cages. At that time, people

(disgust) _____ by the bad conditions and the mistreatment of
 5

the animals. Later, these early zoos *(replace)* _____ by scientific
 6

institutions where animals *(study)* _____ and *(keep)*
 7

_____ in good condition. These research centers *(become)* _____
 8 9

the first modern zoos.

As early as the 1940s, scientists *(understand)* _____ that
 10

many kinds of wild animals faced extinction. Since that time, zoos *(try)* _____
 11

_____ to save many endangered species, but relying on zoos to save

species such as the rhinoceros is not enough. In the 1980s, the number of rhinos in the

world *(reduce)* _____ from 10,000 to 400. Many rhinos *(kill)*
 12

_____ by poachers, but many also *(die)* _____ in
 13 14

captivity. Zoo breeding programs for rhinos have not been successful. The best method of

conservation *(be)* _____ to leave them in their natural habitat. By 1999,
 15

there *(be)* _____ more than 13,000 rhinos again living in the wild. These

rhinos *(save)* _____ from extinction by the strong conservation

16

17

methods of local communities, government agencies, and private landowners. Wildlife

biologists still fear that some subspecies of the rhino in Africa and Indonesia *(become)*

_____ extinct in the near future. Some scientists *(believe)*

18

_____ that half of all animal species in zoos will also be in danger of

19

extinction by the middle of this century.

Because zoos want to treat animals humanely and encourage breeding, today animals

(put) _____ in large, natural settings instead of small cages.

20

They *(watch)* _____ carefully for any signs of disease and *(feed)*

21

_____ a balanced diet. Most zoos *(have)* _____

22

23

specially trained veterinarians and a hospital for animals.

They also have specially trained keepers. Food *(prepare)* _____ in

24

the zoo kitchen. The food program *(design)* _____ to satisfy the

25

animals' particular needs. For example, some snakes *(feed)* _____ only

26

once a week, while some birds *(feed)* _____ several times a day. Today zoo

27

animals *(treat)* _____ well, and zoo breeding programs are important

28

in the attempt to save many species of wildlife.

10-5 THE PASSIVE FORMS OF THE PRESENT AND PAST PROGRESSIVE

ACTIVE	PASSIVE	
The secretary *is copying* some letters. Someone *is building* a new hospital.	(a) Some letters **are being copied** by the secretary. (b) A new hospital **is being built**.	Passive form of the present progressive: *am* *is* + **being** + *past participle* *are*
The secretary *was copying* some letters. Someone *was building* a new hospital.	(c) Some letters **were being copied** by the secretary. (d) A new hospital **was being built**.	Passive form of the past progressive: *was* *were* + **being** + *past participle*

☐ EXERCISE 12. Passive forms. (Chart 10-5)

Directions: Complete the sentences with the correct passive forms of the present and past progressive.

1. Mr. Rice is teaching our class today.

   → Our class _____is being taught_____ by Mr. Rice today.

2. Someone is building a new house on Elm Street.

   → A new house _____ on Elm Street.

3. The Smith Construction Company is building that house.

   → That house _____ by the Smith Construction Company.

4. We couldn't use our classroom yesterday because someone was painting it.

   → We couldn't use our classroom yesterday because it _____ .

5. Someone is organizing a student trip to the art museum.

   → A student trip to the art museum _____ .

6. Dogs usually wag their tails while people are petting them.

   → Dogs usually wag their tails while they _____ .

7. Many of the older people in the neighborhood were growing vegetables to help with the war effort.

   → Vegetables _____ by many of the older people in the neighborhood to help with the war effort.

8. According to one scientific estimate, we are losing 20,000 species of plants and animals each year due to the destruction of rainforests.

   → According to one scientific estimate, 20,000 species of plants and animals _____ each year due to the destruction of rainforests.

10-6 PASSIVE MODAL AUXILIARIES

ACTIVE MODAL AUXILIARIES	PASSIVE MODAL AUXILIARIES (MODAL + *BE* + PAST PARTICIPLE)		Modal auxiliaries are often used in the passive.
Bob *will mail* it.	It	*will be mailed* by Bob.	FORM: *modal* + *be* + *past participle*
Bob *can mail* it.	It	*can be mailed* by Bob.	(See Chapter 7 for information about
Bob *should mail* it.	It	*should be mailed* by Bob.	the meanings and uses of modal
Bob *ought to mail* it.	It	*ought to be mailed* by Bob.	auxiliaries.)
Bob *must mail* it.	It	*must be mailed* by Bob.	
Bob *has to mail* it.	It	*has to be mailed* by Bob.	
Bob *may mail* it.	It	*may be mailed* by Bob.	
Bob *might mail* it.	It	*might be mailed* by Bob.	
Bob *could mail* it.	It	*could be mailed* by Bob.	

☐ EXERCISE 13. Passive modals. (Chart 10-6)

Directions: Complete the sentences by changing the active modals to passive modals.

1. Someone must send this letter immediately.

   → This letter _____**must be sent**_____ immediately.

2. People should plant tomatoes in the spring.

   → Tomatoes _____ in the spring.

3. People cannot control the weather.

   → The weather _____ .

4. Someone had to fix our car before we left for Chicago.

   → Our car _____ before we left for Chicago.

5. People can reach me at 555-3815.

   → I _____ at 555-3815.

6. You can find flowers in almost every part of the world.

   → Flowers _____ in almost every part of the world.

7. Someone ought to wash these dirty dishes soon.

   → These dirty dishes _____ soon.

8. People may cook carrots or eat them raw.

   → Carrots _____ or _____ raw.

9. If the river floods, water could destroy the village.

   → The village _____ if the river floods.

10. You must keep medicine out of the reach of children.

    → Medicine _____ out of the reach of children.

11. You shouldn't pronounce the "b" in "lamb."

    → The "b" in "lamb" _____ .

12. People can wear some watches underwater.

    → Some watches _____
    underwater.

DO YOU HAVE THE TIME?

☐ EXERCISE 14. Active vs. passive. (Charts 10-1 → 10-6)

Directions: Complete the sentences with any appropriate tense, active or passive, of the verbs in parentheses.

In prehistoric times, huge herds of horses *(live)* ___**lived**___ throughout the
....1
Americas. But then, for some unknown reason, they *(disappear)* _____
....2
completely from North and South America. Even though the early horses *(die)*

_____ out in the Americas, they *(survive)* _____ in Asia.
...............3..4

Long ago, horses *(domesticate)*★ _____ by central Asian
....5
nomads. At first, horses *(use)* _____ in war and in hunting, and oxen
....6
(use) _____ for farming. Later, horses also *(become)* _____
..............7...8
farm animals.

Horses *(reintroduce)* _____ into the Americas by
....9
Spaniards early in the fifteenth century. Spanish explorers *(come)* _____ in
....10
ships to the New World with their horses on board. When the explorers *(return)*

_____ to Spain, they *(leave)* _____ some of their horses
...............11..12
behind. These *(develop)* _____ into wild herds. Native American
.....................................13
tribes in the western plains *(begin)* _____ to use horses around 1600. Wild
....14
horses *(capture)* _____ and *(tame)* _____ for
..........................15.....................................16
use in war and in hunting.

In the 1800s, there were several million wild horses in North America. By the 1970s,
that number had become less than 20,000. The wild horses *(hunt)* _____
....17
and *(kill)* _____ principally for use as pet food. Today in the United
..............18
States, wild horses *(protect)* _____ by law. They *(can kill, not)*
....19
_____ for sport or profit. What is your opinion?
..............20
(wild horses, should protect) _____ by law?
....21

_____

★People domesticate (tame) animals.

□ EXERCISE 15. Active vs. passive. (Charts 10-1 → 10-6)

Directions: All of the sentences in the following passage are active. Some of the sentences should be passive because it is unknown or unimportant to know exactly who performs certain actions. Change sentences to the passive as appropriate. Discuss your reasons for making changes and for not making changes.

(1) Cheese has been a principal food throughout much of the world for thousands of years.

The first cheese was probably made

(2) ~~Someone probably made the first cheese~~ in Asia around four thousand years ago. (3) Today people eat it in almost all the countries of the world. (4) People can eat it alone, or they may eat it with bread. (5) People can melt it and add it to noodles or vegetables. (6) People can use it as part of a main course or as a snack. (7) Throughout most of the world, cheese adds enjoyment and nutrition to many people's daily diets.

(8) Cheese is a milk product. (9) Cheesemakers make most cheese from cow's milk, but they can make it from the milk of goats, camels, yaks, and other animals, including zebras. (10) Some kinds of cheese, such as cheddar, are common in many parts of the world, but you can find other kinds only in small geographical areas.

(11) Cheesemakers produce cheese in factories. (12) They have to treat the milk in special ways. (13) They must heat it several times during the process. (14) At the end, they add salt, and they pack it into molds. (15) They age most cheese for weeks or months before they package and sell it. (16) They usually sell cheese to stores in large round pieces that they seal in wax.

(17) You can see these big rounds of cheese in food stores like delicatessens. (18) I like cheese and buy it often. (19) I don't know all the names of different kinds of cheese. (20) Often I can't pronounce the foreign name of the cheese I want. (21) When I go to the delicatessen near my apartment, I simply point to a kind of cheese that looks good to me. (22) I hold my

thumb and forefinger wide apart if I want a lot of cheese or close together if I want just a little.

(23) Frank and Anita, who work behind the cheese

counter at the deli, always seem to give me just the

right amount. (24) I'm glad cheese is nutritious

because it's one of my favorite kinds of food.

10-7 USING PAST PARTICIPLES AS ADJECTIVES (STATIVE PASSIVE)

<table>
<tr>
<td>

	BE	+	ADJECTIVE
(a) Paul	*is*		*young*.
(b) Paul	*is*		*tall*.
(c) Paul	*is*		*hungry*.
	BE	+	PAST PARTICIPLE
(d) Paul	*is*		*married*.
(e) Paul	*is*		*tired*.
(f) Paul	*is*		*frightened*.

</td>
<td>

Be can be followed by an adjective. The adjective describes or gives information about the subject of the sentence.

Be can be followed by a past participle (the passive form). The past participle is often like an adjective. The past participle describes or gives information about the subject of the sentence. Past participles are used as adjectives in many common, everyday expressions.

</td>
</tr>
<tr>
<td>

(g) Paul *is married **to*** Susan.
(h) Paul *was excited **about*** the game.
(i) Paul *will be prepared **for*** the exam.

</td>
<td>

Often the past participles in these expressions are followed by particular prepositions + an object.
For example:
    married is followed by ***to*** (+ an object)
    excited is followed by ***about*** (+ an object)
    prepared is followed by ***for*** (+ an object)

</td>
</tr>
</table>

SOME COMMON EXPRESSIONS WITH *BE* + PAST PARTICIPLE

1. *be acquainted (with)*	13. *be excited (about)*	25. *be opposed (to)*
2. *be bored (with, by)*	14. *be exhausted (from)*	26. *be pleased (with)*
3. *be broken*	15. *be finished (with)*	27. *be prepared (for)*
4. *be closed*	16. *be frightened (of, by)*	28. *be qualified (for)*
5. *be composed of*	17. *be gone (from)*	29. *be related (to)*
6. *be crowded (with)*	18. *be hurt*	30. *be satisfied (with)*
7. *be devoted (to)*	19. *be interested (in)*	31. *be scared (of, by)*
8. *be disappointed (in, with)*	20. *be involved (in, with)*	32. *be shut*
9. *be divorced (from)*	21. *be located in, south of, etc.*	33. *be spoiled*
10. *be done (with)*	22. *be lost*	34. *be terrified (of, by)*
11. *be drunk (on)*	23. *be made of*	35. *be tired (of, from)*★
12. *be engaged (to)*	24. *be married (to)*	36. *be worried (about)*

★I'm **tired *of*** the cold weather. = *I've had enough cold weather. I want the weather to get warm.*
  I'm **tired *from*** working hard all day. = *I'm exhausted because I worked hard all day.*

□ **EXERCISE 16. Stative passive. (Chart 10-7)**

Directions: Complete the sentences with the appropriate form of the verbs in *italics*. Include prepositions as necessary. Use the simple present.

1. *scare*   Most children ___are scared of___ loud noises.

2. *interest*   Jane _____ ecology.

3. *disappoint*   My parents _____ me because of my low grades.

4. *please*   My boss _____ my work.

5. *satisfy*   I _____ my progress in English.

6. *marry*   Tony _____ Sonia.

7. *relate*   Alice Jones _____ Anna Jones. They're first cousins.

8. *do*   This is the last item in this exercise. We _____ this exercise now.

□ **EXERCISE 17. Stative passive. (Chart 10-7)**

Directions: Complete the sentences with the expressions in the list. Use the simple present.

be acquainted	be exhausted	be related
be broken	be located	be satisfied
be composed	be lost	be scared
be crowded	be made	be spoiled
be disappointed	be qualified	✓be worried

1. Dennis isn't doing well in school this semester. He ___is worried___ about his grades.

2. My shirt _____ of cotton.

3. I live in a three-room apartment with six other people. Our apartment _____ _____ .

4. Vietnam _____ in Southeast Asia.

5. I'm going to go straight to bed tonight. It's been a hard day. I _____ _____ .

6. Excuse me, sir, but I _____ . Could you please tell me how to get to the bus station from here?

7. My tape recorder doesn't work. It _____ .

8. Holly and I are sisters. We _____ to each other.

9. We leave a light on in our son's bedroom at night because he _____
_____ of the dark.

10. Alice thinks her boss should pay her more money. She _____ not
_____ with her present salary.

11. The children _____ . I had promised to take them to
the beach today, but now we can't go because it's raining.

12. _____ you _____ with Mrs. Novinsky? Have you
ever met her?

13. According to the job description, an applicant must have a Master's degree and at least
five years of teaching experience. Unfortunately, I _____ not
_____ for that job.

14. This milk doesn't taste right. I think it _____ . I'm not going to
drink it.

15. Water _____ of hydrogen and oxygen.

□ EXERCISE 18. Stative passive. (Chart 10-7)
Directions: Complete the sentences with appropriate prepositions.

1. The day before a holiday, the food stores are usually crowded _____*with*_____
last-minute shoppers.

2. Are you qualified _____ that job?

3. Mr. Heath loves his family very much. He is devoted _____ them.

4. Our dog runs under the bed during storms. He's terrified _____ thunder.

5. My sister is married _____ a law student.

6. Are you prepared _____ the test?

7. I'll be finished _____ my work in another minute or two.

8. Jason is excited _____ going to Hollywood.

9. Ms. Brown is opposed _____ the new tax plan.

10. Jane isn't satisfied _____ her present apartment. She's looking for a
new one.

11. Janet doesn't take good care of herself. I'm worried _____ her health.

12. I'm tired _____ this rainy weather. I hope the sun shines tomorrow.

13. In terms of evolution, a hippopotamus is related _____ a horse.

14. The students are involved _____ many extracurricular activities.

15. Are you acquainted _____ this author? I think her books are excellent.

16. When will you be done _____ your work?

17. I'm starving! Right now I'm interested _____ only one thing: food.

18. The children want some new toys. They're bored _____ their old ones.

19. Sam is engaged _____ his childhood sweetheart.

20. Our daughter is scared _____ dogs.

21. You've done a good job. You should be very pleased _____ yourself.

☐ EXERCISE 19. Stative passive. (Chart 10-7)
Directions: Work in pairs.
Speaker A: Begin the item. Don't lower your intonation. Your book is open.
Speaker B: Finish the item with *a preposition* + ***someone*** or ***something***.
Speaker A: Decide whether B has used the correct preposition. (Refer to Chart 10-7, p. 292, if necessary.) Repeat the entire item, emphasizing the preposition.

Example:
SPEAKER A *(book open):* I'm worried . . . .
SPEAKER B *(book closed):* . . . about something.
SPEAKER A *(book open):* Right. I'm worried **about** something.

Switch roles.

1. I'm interested	10. I'm opposed . . . .
2. I'm married	11. I'm frightened . . . .
3. I'm scared	12. I'm excited . . . .
4. I'm related	13. I'm engaged . . . .
5. I'm disappointed	14. I'm exhausted . . . .
6. I'm qualified	15. I'm tired . . . .
7. I'm satisfied	16. I'm finished . . . .
8. I'm prepared	17. I'm done . . . .
9. I'm acquainted . . .	18. I'm involved . . . .

Repeat the exercise. Use only the past participles as cues, and make your own sentences.

Example: worried
SPEAKER A: worried
SPEAKER B: The students are worried about the next test.

□ EXERCISE 20. Stative passive. (Chart 10-7)
Directions: Complete the sentences with the words in *italics*. Use the passive form, simple present, or simple past. Include prepositions where necessary.

1. *close*   When we got to the post office, it ___was closed___ .

2. *make*   My earrings ___are made of___ gold.

3. *divorce*   Sally and Tom used to be married, but now they _____ .

4. *relate*   Your name is Tom Hood. _____ you _____
                 Mary Hood?

5. *spoil*   This fruit _____ . I think I'd better throw it out.

6. *exhaust*   Last night I _____ , so I went straight to bed.

7. *involve*   Last week I _____ a three-car accident.

8. *locate*   The University of Washington _____ Seattle.

9. *drink*   Ted _____ . He's making a fool of himself.

10. *interest*   I _____ learning more about that subject.

11. *devote*   Linda loves her job. She _____ her work.

12. *lose*   What's the matter, little boy? _____ you _____ ?

13. *terrify*   Once when we were swimming at the beach, we saw a shark. All of us

                 _____ .

14. *acquaint*   _____ you _____ Sue's roommate?

15. *qualify*   I didn't get the job. The interviewer said that I _____ not

                 _____ it.

16. *disappoint*   My son brought home a report card with all D's and F's. I can't

                 understand it. I _____ him.

17. *do*   At last, I _____ my homework. Now I can go to bed.

18. *crowd*   There are too many students in our class. The classroom _____

                 _____ .

19. *shut*   It's starting to rain. _____ all of the windows

_____ ?

20. *go*   Where's my wallet? It _____! Did you take it?

10-8 PARTICIPIAL ADJECTIVES: *-ED* vs. *-ING*

Indian art interests me.	The past participle *(-ed)*⋆ and the present participle *(-ing)* can be used as adjectives.
(a) I am *interested* in Indian art. INCORRECT: *I am interesting in Indian art.*	In (a): The past participle *(interested)* describes how a person feels.
(b) Indian art is *interesting*. INCORRECT: *Indian art is interested.*	In (b): The present participle *(interesting)* describes the **cause** of the feeling. The cause of the interest is Indian art.
The news surprised Kate.	In (c): *surprised* describes how Kate felt.
(c) Kate was *surprised*. (d) The news was *surprising*.	The past participle carries a passive meaning: *Kate was surprised* **by the news**. In (d): *the news* was the cause of the surprise.
(e) Did you hear the *surprising news?* (f) Roberto fixed the *broken window*.	Like other adjectives, participial adjectives may follow *be*, as in examples (a) through (d), or come in front of nouns, as in (e) and (f).

⋆ The past participle of regular verbs ends in *-ed*. Some verbs have irregular forms. See Chart 2-6, p. 32.

☐ **EXERCISE 21. Participial adjectives. (Chart 10-8)**

Directions: Complete the sentences with the *-ed* or *-ing* form of the verbs in *italics*.

1. Greg's classes *interest* him.

   a. Greg's classes are _____interesting_____ .

   b. Greg is an _____interested_____ student.

2. Emily is going to Australia. The idea of going on this trip *excites* her.

   a. Emily is _____ about going on this trip.

   b. She thinks it is going to be an _____ trip.

3. I like to study sea life. The subject of marine biology *fascinates* me.

   a. I'm _____ by marine biology.

   b. Marine biology is a _____ subject.

4. Mike heard some bad news. The bad news *depressed* him.

   a. Mike is very sad. In other words, he is _____ .

   b. The news made Mike feel sad. The news was _____ .

5. The exploration of space *interests* me.

    a. I'm _____ in the exploration of space.

    b. The exploration of space is _____ to me.

6. The nation's leader stole money. The scandal *shocked* the nation.

    a. It was a _____ scandal.

    b. The _____ nation soon replaced the leader.

7. I bought a new camera. I read the directions twice, but I didn't understand them.
They *confused* me.

    a. I was _____ when I tried to understand the directions.

    b. They were _____ directions.

8. I spilled my drink on the dinner table. This *embarrassed* me.

    a. I was very _____ when I spilled my drink.

    b. That was an _____ experience.

9. Jane's classes *bore* her.

    a. Jane's classes are _____ .

    b. Jane is a _____ student.

10. An article in the newspaper *surprised* Mrs. Perez.

    a. It was a very _____ article to her.

    b. Mrs. Perez was very _____ when she read it.

11. The loud noise *frightened* the children.

    a. It was a _____ sound.

    b. The _____ children ran into their house.

☐ **EXERCISE 22. Participial adjectives. (Chart 10-8)**
Directions: Complete the sentences with the appropriate *-ed* or *-ing* form of the words in *italics.*

Julie was walking along the edge of the fountain outside her office building. She was with her co-worker and friend Paul. Suddenly she lost her balance and accidentally fell in.

1. *embarrass*   Julie was really ___embarrassed___ .

2. *embarrass*   Falling into the fountain was really ___embarrassing___ .

3. *shock*   Her friend Paul was _____ .

4. *shock*   It was a _____ sight.

5. *surprise*   The people around the office building were very _____ when they saw Julie in the fountain.

6. *surprise*   It was a _____ sight.

7. *depress*   The next day Julie was _____ because she thought she had made a fool of herself.

8. *depress*   When she fell into the fountain, some people laughed at her. It was a _____ experience.

9. *interest*   Her friend Paul told her not to lose her sense of humor. He told her it was just another _____ experience in life.

10. *interest*   He said that people would be _____ in hearing about how she fell into a fountain.

□ EXERCISE 23. Participial adjectives. (Charts 10-7 and 10-8)

Directions: Complete the sentences with an **-ed** or **-ing** adjective and the **boldface** noun.

1. If you *spoil* **children**, they become _____ spoiled children.

2. If a **door** *revolves,* it is called a _____ revolving door.

3. If someone *steals* a **car**, it is a _____

4. If people *crowd* into a **room**, it is a _____

5. If **costs** *rise,* they are _____

6. If a **danger** *exists,* it is an _____

7. If you *dry* **fruit**, it becomes _____

8. If you *plan* an **event**, it is called a _____

9. If a **committee** *plans* something, it is called a _____

10. If **water** *is boiling,* we call it _____

11. If a **person** *is missing,* we call him or her a _____

12. If you *freeze* **vegetables**, they are called _____

13. If the **weather** *freezes* things, it is called _____

14. If you *break* your **pencil**, you have a _____

10-9 *GET* + ADJECTIVE; *GET* + PAST PARTICIPLE

GET + ADJECTIVE (a) I *am getting hungry.* Let's eat. (b) Eric *got nervous* before the job interview.	***Get*** can be followed by an adjective. ***Get*** gives the idea of change—the idea of becoming, beginning to be, growing to be. In (a): *I'm getting hungry.* = *I wasn't hungry before, but now I'm beginning to be hungry.*
GET + PAST PARTICIPLE (c) **I'm getting tired.** Let's stop working. (d) Steve and Rita *got married* last month.	Sometimes ***get*** is followed by a past participle. The past participle after ***get*** is like an adjective; it describes the subject of the sentence.

GET + ADJECTIVE

get angry	get dry	get quiet
get bald	get fat	get rich
get big	get full	get serious
get busy	get hot	get sick
get close	get hungry	get sleepy
get cold	get interested	get thirsty
get dark	get late	get well
get dirty	get nervous	get wet
get dizzy	get old	

GET + PAST PARTICIPLE

get acquainted	get drunk	get involved
get arrested	get engaged	get killed
get bored	get excited	get lost
get confused	get finished	get married
get crowded	get frightened	get scared
get divorced	get hurt	get sunburned
get done	get interested	get tired
get dressed	get invited	get worried

□ **EXERCISE 24. GET + adjective/past participle. (Chart 10-9)**
   Directions: Complete the sentences. Use each word in the list only one time.

angry	dirty	full	rich
bald	dizzy	hot	sick
busy	dressed	hurt	sleepy
✓cold	drunk	lost	tired

1. In winter, the weather gets _____cold_____ .

2. In summer, the weather gets _____ .

3. This food is delicious, but I can't eat any more. I'm getting _____ .

4. I think I'll go to bed. I'm getting _____ .

5. Let's stop working and take a break. I'm getting _____ .

6. Sam is wearing one brown sock and one blue sock today. He got _____
   in a hurry this morning and didn't pay attention to the color of his socks.

7. This work has to be done before we leave. We'd better get _____ and
   stop wasting time.

8. I didn't understand Jane's directions very well, so on the way to her house last night I
   got _____ . I couldn't find her house.

9. It's hard to work in a garage and stay clean. Paul's clothes always get _____
   from all the grease and oil.

10. Don't waste your money gambling. You won't ever get _____ that way.

11. Mr. Anderson is losing some of his hair. He's getting _____ .

12. Was it a bad accident? Did anyone get
    _____ ?

13. Calm down! Take it easy! You shouldn't
    get so _____ . It's not
    good for your blood pressure.

14. When I turned around and around in a
    circle, I got _____ .

15. I don't feel very good. I think I'm getting _____ . Maybe I should see a doctor.

16. My friends got _____ at the party Saturday night, so I drove them home in my car. They were in no condition to drive.

☐ EXERCISE 25. GET + adjective/past participle. (Chart 10-9)
Directions: Complete the sentences with appropriate forms of *get* and the words in the list.

cold	excite	lose	thirsty
crowd	hungry	marry	tired
dark	involve	sleep	well
dry	kill	✓sunburn	worry

1. When I stayed out in the sun too long yesterday, I ___got sunburned___ .

2. If you're sick, stay home and take care of yourself. You won't _____ if you don't take care of yourself.

3. Jane and Greg are engaged. They are going to _____ a year from now.

4. Sarah doesn't eat breakfast, so she always _____ by ten or ten-thirty.

5. In the winter, the sun sets early. It _____ outside by six or even earlier.

6. Put these socks back in the dryer. They didn't _____ the first time.

7. Let's stop working for a while. I'm _____ . I need to rest.

8. Sue has to vacate her apartment next week, and she hasn't found a new place to live. She's _____ .

9. Sitara always _____ after she eats salty food.

10. Toshiro was in a terrible car wreck and almost _____ . He's lucky to be alive.

11. The temperature is dropping. Brrr! I'm _____ . Can I borrow your sweater?

12. We were in a strange city without a map. It was easy for us to _____ . We had to ask a shopkeeper how to get back to our hotel.

13. Did you _____ when your team won the game? Did you clap and yell when they won?

14. Good restaurants _____ around dinner time. It's hard to find a seat because there are so many people.

15. When little Annie _____ , her father gave her a bottle and put her to bed.

16. I left when Ellen and Joe began to argue. I never _____ in other people's quarrels.

10-10 USING *BE USED/ACCUSTOMED TO* AND *GET USED/ACCUSTOMED TO*

(a) I **am used to** hot weather. (b) I **am accustomed to** hot weather.	(a) and (b) have the same meaning: "Living in a hot climate is usual and normal for me. I'm familiar with what it is like to live in a hot climate. Hot weather isn't strange or different to me."
(c) I *am used **to living*** in a hot climate. (d) I *am accustomed **to living*** in a hot climate.	Notice in (c) and (d): *to* (a preposition) is followed by the *-ing* form of a verb (a gerund).
(e) I just moved from Florida to Siberia. I have never lived in a cold climate before, but I **am getting used to (accustomed to)** the cold weather here.	In (e): *I'm getting used to/accustomed to* = something is beginning to seem usual and normal to me.

☐ EXERCISE 26. BE USED/ACCUSTOMED TO. (Chart 10-10)
    Directions: Complete the sentences with **be used to,** affirmative or negative.

1. Juan is from Mexico. He ___is used to___ hot weather. He ___isn't used to___ cold weather.

2. Alice was born and raised in Chicago. She _____ living in a big city.

3. My hometown is New York City, but this year I'm going to school in a town with a population of 10,000. I _____ living in a small town. I _____ living in a big city.

4. We do a lot of exercises in class. We _____ doing exercises.

Complete the sentences with **be accustomed to,** affirmative or negative.
NOTICE: **accustomed** is spelled with two "c"s and one "m."

5. Spiro recently moved to Canada from Greece. He ___is accustomed to___ eating Greek food. He ___isn't accustomed to___ eating Canadian food.

6. I always get up around 6:00 A.M. I _____ getting up early. I _____ sleeping late.

7. Our teacher always gives us a lot of homework. We _____

having a lot of homework every day.

8. Young schoolchildren rarely take multiple choice tests. They _____

_____ taking that kind of test.

☐ EXERCISE 27. BE USED/ACCUSTOMED TO. (Chart 10-10)
Directions: Talk about yourself. Use **be used/accustomed to**.

Example: cold weather
→ *I am* (OR *I am not*) *used / accustomed to cold weather.*

1. hot weather
2. cold weather
3. living in a warm climate
4. living in a cold climate
5. living in a big city
6. living in a small town
7. getting up early
8. sleeping late
9. eating a big breakfast
10. drinking coffee in the morning
11. *(a kind of)* food
12. being on my own*

☐ EXERCISE 28. BE USED/ACCUSTOMED TO. (Chart 10-10)
Directions: Work in pairs.
Speaker A: Pose the question. Your book is open.
Speaker B: Answer the question in a complete sentence. Your book is closed.

Example:
SPEAKER A *(book open):* What time are you accustomed to getting up?
SPEAKER B *(book closed):* I'm accustomed to getting up (at 7:30).

1. What time are you used to going to bed?

2. Are you accustomed to living in *(name of this city)*?

3. Are you used to speaking English every day?

4. Do you live with a roommate or do you live alone? Are you accustomed to that?

5. What are you accustomed to eating for breakfast?

Switch roles.
6. What kind of food are you accustomed to eating?

7. What time are you accustomed to getting up?

8. Are you accustomed to living in a big city or a small town?

9. Our weather right now is (hot/cold/humid/cold) and (wet/dry/etc.) Are you used to this kind of weather?

10. Are you used to speaking English every day, or does it seem strange to you?

———————

**To be on one's own is an idiom. It means to be away from one's family and responsible for oneself.

Directions: Discuss or write about one or more of the following topics.

1. James graduated from high school last month. Three days after graduation, he got married. The next week he started a job at a paint store. Within two weeks, his life changed a lot. What did he have to get used to?

2. Jane is going to leave her parents' house next week. She is going to move in with two of her cousins who work in the city. Jane will be away from her home for the first time in her life. What is she going to have to get accustomed to?

3. Think of a time you traveled in or lived in a foreign country. What weren't you used to? What did you get used to? What didn't you ever get used to?

4. Think of the first day of a job you have had. What weren't you used to? What did you get used to?

10-11 USED TO vs. BE USED TO

(a) I *used to* **live** in Chicago, but now I live in Tokyo. INCORRECT: I used to living in Chicago. INCORRECT: I am used to live in a big city.	In (a): ***Used to*** expresses the habitual past (see Chart 2-11, p. 52). It is followed by the **simple form of a verb**.
(b) I *am used to* **living** in a big city.	In (b): ***be used to*** is followed by the ***-ing* form of a verb** (a gerund).*

*NOTE: In both ***used to*** (habitual past) and ***be used to***, the "d" is not pronounced in *used.*

□ EXERCISE 30. USED TO vs. BE USED TO. (Chart 10-11)

Directions: Add an appropriate form of ***be*** if necessary. If no form of ***be*** is needed, write Ø in the blank.

1. I have lived in Malaysia for a long time. I _____*am*_____ used to warm weather.

2. I _____*Ø*_____ used to live in Finland, but now I live in France.

3. I _____ used to sitting at this desk. I sit here every day.

4. I _____ used to sit in the back of the classroom, but now I prefer to sit in the front row.

5. When I was a child, I _____ used to play games with my friends in a big field near my house after school every day.

6. It's hard for my children to stay inside on a cold, rainy day. They _____ used to playing outside in the big field near our house. They play there almost every day.

7. A teacher _____ used to answering questions. Students, especially good students, always have a lot of questions.

8. People _____ used to believe the world was flat.

☐ EXERCISE 31. USED TO vs. BE USED TO. (Chart 10-11)
Directions: Complete the sentences with **used to** or **be used to** and the correct form of the verb in parentheses.

1. Nick stays up later now than he did when he was in high school. He (go) _____used to go_____ to bed at ten, but now he rarely gets to bed before midnight.

2. I got used to going to bed late when I was in college, but now I have a job and I need my sleep. These days I (go) _____am used to going_____ to bed around ten-thirty.

3. I am a vegetarian. I (eat) _____ meat, but now I eat only meatless meals.

4. Ms. Wu has had a vegetable garden all her life. She (grow) _____ _____ her own vegetables.

5. Oscar has lived in Brazil for ten years. He (eat) _____ Brazilian food. It's his favorite.

6. Georgio moved to Germany to open his own restaurant. He (have) _____ _____ a small bakery in Italy.

7. I have taken the bus to work every day for the past five years. I (take) _____ _____ the bus.

8. Juanita travels by plane on company business. She (go) _____ by train, but now the distances she needs to travel are too great.

☐ EXERCISE 32. USED TO vs. BE USED TO. (Charts 2-9 and 10-11)
Directions: You are living in a new place (country, city, apartment, dorm, etc.) and going to a new school. What adjustments have you had to make? Write about them by completing the sentences with your own words.

1. I'm getting used to . . . .

2. I'm also getting accustomed to . . . .

3. I have gotten accustomed to . . . .

4. I haven't gotten used to . . . .

5. I can't get used to . . . .

6. Do you think I will ever get accustomed to . . . ?

7. I used to . . . , but now . . . .

10-12 USING *BE SUPPOSED TO*

(a) Mike *is supposed to call* me tomorrow. (IDEA: I expect Mike to call me tomorrow.) (b) We *are supposed to write* a composition. (IDEA: The teacher expects us to write a composition.)	*Be supposed to* is used to talk about an activity or event that is expected to occur. In (a): The idea of *is supposed to* is that Mike is expected (by me) to call me. I asked him to call me. He promised to call me. I expect him to call me.
(c) Alice *was supposed to be* home at ten, but she didn't get in until midnight. (IDEA: Someone expected Alice to be home at ten.)	In the past form, *be supposed to* often expresses the idea that an expected event did not occur, as in (c).

☐ EXERCISE 33. BE SUPPOSED TO. (Chart 10-12)
Directions: Create sentences with a similar meaning by using *be supposed to*.

1. The teacher expects us to be on time for class.
   → *We are supposed to be on time for class.*

2. People expect the weather to be cold tomorrow.

3. People expect the plane to arrive at 6:00.

4. My boss expects me to work late tonight.

5. I expected the mail to arrive an hour ago, but it didn't.

☐ EXERCISE 34. BE SUPPOSED TO. (Chart 10-12)
Directions: Correct the mistakes.

1. I'm supposed ⌄ call my parents tonight.
   _{to}

2. We're not suppose to tell anyone about the surprise.

3. You don't supposed to talk to Alan about the surprise.

4. My friend was supposing to call me last night, but he didn't.

5. Children supposed to respect their parents.

6. Didn't you supposed be at the meeting last night?

☐ EXERCISE 35. BE SUPPOSED TO. (Chart 10-12)

   Directions: Identify who is supposed to do something.

   1. TOM'S BOSS: Mail this package.
            TOM: Yes, sir.
      → *Tom is supposed to mail a package.*

   2. MARY: Call me at nine.
       ANN: Okay.

   3. MS. MARTINEZ: Please make your bed before you go to school.
           JOHNNY: Okay, Mom.

   4. MR. TAKADA: Put your dirty clothes in the laundry basket.
           SUSIE: Okay, Dad.

   5. MRS. WILSON: Bobby, pick up your toys and put them away.
           BOBBY: Okay, Mom.
      MRS. WILSON: Annie, please hang up your coat.
           ANNIE: Okay, Mom.

   6. DR. KETTLE: You should take one pill every eight hours.
         PATIENT: All right, Dr. Kettle. Anything else?
      DR. KETTLE: Drink plenty of fluids.

   7. PROF. THOMPSON: Read the directions carefully, and raise your hand if you have any
                      questions.
           STUDENTS: *(no response)*

☐ EXERCISE 36. BE SUPPOSED TO. (Chart 10-12)

   Directions: Create sentences with **be supposed to** by combining the subjects in Column A
   with the ideas in Column B. Use the simple present.

   Example: Visitors at a zoo are not supposed to feed the animals.

   Column A

   1. Visitors at a zoo
   2. Doctors
   3. Employees
   4. Air passengers
   5. Theatergoers
   6. Soldiers on sentry duty
   7. Children
   8. Heads of state
   9. A dog
   10. People who live in apartments

   Column B

   A. listen to their parents
   B. buckle their seatbelts before takeoff
   ✓C. not . . . feed the animals
   D. not . . . talk during a performance
   E. be on time for work
   F. obey its trainer
   G. pay their rent on time
   H. care for their patients
   I. not . . . fall asleep
   J. be diplomatic

Directions: Think of things the following people are or were supposed to do. Use **be supposed to**.

Example: a good friend of yours
> → *My friend Ji Ming is supposed to help me paint my apartment this weekend.*
> *Benito was supposed to go to dinner with me last Wednesday, but he forgot.*
> *Nadia is supposed to call me tonight.*

1. a good friend of yours
2. your roommate or spouse*
3. children
4. a student in your English class
5. your English teacher

6. the leader of your country
7. one or both of your parents
8. one of your siblings or cousins
9. yourself
10. (. . .)

☐ EXERCISE 38. Written. (Chapters 1 → 10)
Directions: In writing, describe how a particular holiday is celebrated in your country. What is done in the morning, in the afternoon, in the evening? What are some of the things that people typically do on this holiday?
NOTE: Many of your sentences will be active, but some of them should be passive.

☐ EXERCISE 39. Error analysis. (Chapter 10)
Directions: Correct the errors.

Example: I am agree with him.
> → *I agree with him.*

1. An accident was happened at the corner yesterday.

2. This pen is belong to me.

3. I am very surprise by the news.

4. I'm interesting in that subject.

5. He is marry with my cousin.

6. Thailand is locate in Southeast Asia.

7. Mary's dog was died last week.

8. Were you surprise when you saw him?

---

*If you have neither a roommate nor a spouse, invent one or simply skip to the next item.

9. When I went downtown, I get lost.

10. Last night I very tire.

11. The bus was arrived ten minutes late.

12. I am disagreed with that statement.

13. Our class is compose from immigrants.

14. I am not acustomed to cold weather.

15. We're not suppose to have pets in our apartment.

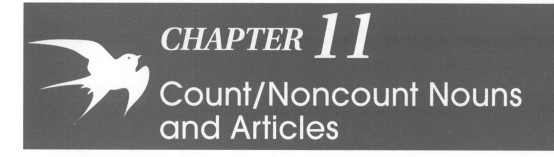

CHAPTER 11
Count/Noncount Nouns and Articles

□ EXERCISE 1. Preview: using A and AN. (Charts 11-1 and 11-2)
Directions: Add *a* or *an* as necessary.

1. I never wear ^*a* hat.

2. We had ^*an* easy test yesterday.

3. I rarely put salt on my food. OK *(no change)*

4. Jack has wallet in his back pocket.

5. We had good weather for our picnic yesterday.

6. There was earthquake in Turkey last week.

7. Ball is round object.

8. Linda likes to wear jewelry.

9. Anna is wearing ring on her fourth finger.

10. My father enjoys good health.

11. Simon Bolivar is hero to many people.

12. I called Jim by the wrong name. It was honest mistake.

13. I had unusual experience yesterday.

14. Ann had unique experience yesterday.

15. I often ask my parents for advice.

11-1 *A* vs. *AN*

(a) I have **a pencil**. (b) I live in **an apartment**. (c) I have **a small apartment**. (d) I live in **an old building**.	**A** and **an** are used in front of a singular noun (e.g., *pencil, apartment*). They mean "one." If a singular noun is modified by an adjective (e.g., *small, old*), **a** or **an** comes in front of the adjective, as in (c) and (d). **A** is used in front of words that begin with a consonant *(b, c, d, f, g, etc.)*: *a boy, a bad day, a cat, a cute baby.* **An** is used in front of words that begin with the vowels **a**, **e**, **i**, and **o**: *an apartment, an angry man, an elephant, an empty room, etc.*
(e) I have **an umbrella**. (f) I saw **an ugly picture**. (g) I attend **a university**. (h) I had **a unique experience**.	For words that begin with the letter **u**: (1) **An** is used if the **u** is a vowel sound, as in *an umbrella, an uncle, an unusual day.* (2) **A** is used if the **u** is a consonant sound, as in *a university, a unit, a usual event.*
(i) He will arrive in **an hour**. (j) New Year's Day is **a holiday**.	For words that begin with the letter **h**: (1) **An** is used if the **h** is silent: *an hour, an honor, an honest person.* (2) **A** is used if the **h** is pronounced: *a holiday, a hotel, a high point.*

□ EXERCISE 2. A vs. AN. (Chart 11-1)
Directions: Write **a** or **an** in the blanks.

1. _*a*_ mistake
2. ____ abbreviation
3. ____ dream
4. ____ interesting dream
5. ____ empty box
6. ____ box

7. ____ uniform
8. ____ union
9. ____ untrue story
10. ____ urgent message
11. ____ universal problem
12. ____ unhappy child

13. ____ hour or two
14. ____ hole in the ground
15. ____ hill
16. ____ handsome man
17. ____ honest man
18. ____ honor

□ EXERCISE 3. A vs. AN. (Chart 11-1)
Directions: Define the given words in complete sentences. Begin each sentence with **a** or **an**. Refer to a dictionary if necessary.

Example: indecisive person
→ *An indecisive person is a person who can't make up his mind.*

1. astronaut
2. microscope
3. enemy
4. ferry
5. absent-minded person

6. camel
7. umbrella
8. unicorn
9. onion
10. honeymoon trip

11. hourly wage
12. horn
13. unlit hallway
14. utensil
15. orchard

11-2 COUNT AND NONCOUNT NOUNS

	SINGULAR		PLURAL		A count noun:
COUNT NOUN	***a*** ***one***	chair chair	**Ø*** ***two*** ***some***	chairs chairs chairs	(1) can be counted with numbers: *one chair, two chairs, ten chairs, etc.* (2) can be preceded by ***a/an*** in the singular: *a chair.* (3) has a plural form ending in ***-s*** or ***-es***: *chairs.*******

NONCOUNT NOUN	**Ø**
	some
		furniture
		furniture
			Ø
			Ø
					A noncount noun:
					(1) cannot be counted with numbers.
					    INCORRECT: one furniture
					(2) is NOT immediately preceded by ***a/an***.
					    INCORRECT: a furniture
					(3) does NOT have a plural form (no final ***-s***).
					    INCORRECT: furnitures

*Ø = "nothing."

**See Chart 1-5, p. 13, and Chart 6-1, p. 157, for the spelling and pronunciation of *-s/-es*.

☐ EXERCISE 4. Count and noncount nouns. (Chart 11-2)

Directions: Correct the mistakes. Some sentences contain no errors. Use ***some*** with the noncount nouns.

1. I bought one chair for my apartment. OK *(no change)*

2. I bought ~~one~~ some furniture for my apartment.*

SOME FURNITURE

3. I bought four chairs for my apartment.

4. I bought four furnitures for my apartment.

5. I bought a chair for my apartment.

ONE CHAIR

6. I bought a furniture for my apartment.

7. I bought some chair for my apartment.

TWO CHAIRS

8. I bought some furnitures for my apartment.

SOME CHAIRS

---

*CORRECT: *I bought **some furniture** for my apartment.* OR *I bought **furniture** for my apartment.* See Chart 11–8, p. 326, for more information about the use of **Ø** and ***some***.

☐ **EXERCISE 5. Preview: count and noncount nouns. (Charts 11-2 and 11-3)**
　　Directions: Write *a*/*an* or *some* in the blanks. Identify count and noncount nouns.

1. I often have ____*some*____ **fruit** for dessert. 　　*fruit* 　→ count (noncount)
2. I had _____*a*_____ **banana** for dessert. 　　*banana* 　→ (count) noncount
3. I got _____ **letter** today. 　　*letter* 　→ count noncount
4. I got _____ **mail** today. 　　*mail* 　→ count noncount
5. Anna wears _____ **ring** on her left hand. 　*ring* 　→ count noncount
6. Maria is wearing _____ **jewelry** today. 　*jewelry* 　→ count noncount
7. I have _____ **homework** to finish. 　　*homework* 　→ count noncount
8. I have _____ **assignment** to finish. 　　*assignment* 　→ count noncount
9. I needed _____ **information**. 　　*information* 　→ count noncount
10. I asked _____ **question**. 　　*question* 　→ count noncount

11-3　NONCOUNT NOUNS

INDIVIDUAL PARTS = THE WHOLE	
(Count Nouns)	(Noncount Nouns)

(a) letters / postcards / bills / etc. → **mail**

(b) apples / bananas / oranges / etc. → **fruit**

(c) rings / bracelets / necklaces / etc. → **jewelry**

Noncount nouns usually refer to a whole group of things that is made up of many individual parts, a whole category made up of different varieties.

For example, *furniture* is a noncount noun; it describes a whole category of things: *chairs, tables, beds, etc.*

INDIVIDUAL PARTS = THE WHOLE

chairs / tables / beds / etc. → **furniture**

Mail, fruit, and *jewelry* are other examples of noncount nouns that refer to a whole category made up of individual parts.

SOME COMMON NONCOUNT NOUNS: WHOLE GROUPS MADE UP OF INDIVIDUAL PARTS

A. *clothing*	B. *homework*	E. *grammar*	G. *corn*
equipment	*housework*	*slang*	*dirt*
food	*work*	*vocabulary*	*flour*
fruit			*hair*
furniture	C. *advice*	F. *Arabic*	*pepper*
jewelry	*information*	*Chinese*	*rice*
mail		*English*	*salt*
money	D. *history*	*German*	*sand*
scenery	*literature*	*Indonesian*	*sugar*
stuff	*music*	*Spanish*	
traffic	*poetry*	*Etc.*	

□ EXERCISE 6. Count and noncount nouns. (Charts 11-2 and 11-3)
   Directions: Add final **-s/-es** if possible. Otherwise, write a slash (**/**) in the blank.

   1. I'm learning a lot of **grammar** __/__ .

   2. We're studying count and noncount **noun** _s_____ .

   3. City streets usually have a lot of **traffic** _____ .

   4. The streets are full of **automobile** _____ .

   5. We enjoyed the **scenery** _____ in the countryside.

   6. Nepal has high **mountain** _____ .

   7. I have some important **information** _____ for you.

   8. I have some important **fact** _____ for you.

   9. Olga knows a lot of English **word** _____ .

   10. Olga has learned a lot of new **vocabulary** _____ .

   11. The children learned a lot of new **song** _____ in nursery school.

   12. I enjoy listening to **music** _____ .

   13. Can you give me some **suggestion** _____ ?

   14. Can you give me some **advice** _____ ?

   15. I like to read good **literature** _____ .

   16. I like to read good **novel** _____ .

   17. I had **sand** _____ in my shoes from walking on the beach.

   18. Florida is famous for its white sand **beach** _____ .

11-4 MORE NONCOUNT NOUNS

(a) LIQUIDS		SOLIDS and SEMI-SOLIDS				GASES
coffee	soup	bread	meat	chalk	paper	air
milk	tea	butter	beef	glass	soap	pollution
oil	water	cheese	chicken	gold	toothpaste	smog
		ice	fish	iron	wood	smoke

(b) THINGS THAT OCCUR IN NATURE		
weather	darkness	thunder
rain	light	lightning
snow	sunshine	

(c) ABSTRACTIONS*					
beauty	fun	health	ignorance	patience	time
courage	generosity	help	knowledge	progress	violence
experience	happiness	honesty	luck		

*An abstraction is an idea. It has no physical form. A person cannot touch it.

☐ **EXERCISE 7. Count and noncount nouns. (Charts 11-2 → 11-4)**

Directions: Add final *-s*/*-es* if possible. Otherwise, write a slash (*/*) in the blank.

1. I made some **mistake** _s_____ on my algebra test.

2. In winter in Alaska, there (*is*), *are*) **snow** __/___ on the ground.

3. Alaska has a lot of cold **weather** _____ .

4. We have a lot of **storm** _____ in the winter.

5. There *(is, are)* some **chalk** _____ in this classroom.

6. Be sure to give the new couple my best **wish** _____ .

7. I want to wish them good **luck** _____ .

8. **Thunder** _____ and **lightning** _____ can be scary for children and animals.

9. **Gold** _____ *(is, are)* expensive. **Diamond** _____ *(is, are)* expensive too.

10. I admire Prof. Yoo for her extensive **knowledge** _____ of organic farming methods.

11. Prof. Yoo has a lot of good **idea** _____ and strong **opinion** _____ .

12. Teaching children to read requires **patience** _____ .

13. Doctors take care of **patient** _____ .

14. Mr. Fernandez's English is improving. He's making a lot of **progress** _____ .

15. Automobiles are the biggest source of **pollution** _____ in most cities.

16. Engineers build **bridge** _____ across **river** _____ and other **body** _____ of **water** _____ .

☐ **EXERCISE 8. Noncount abstractions. (Chart 11-4)**

Directions: Complete the sentences in Column A with words from Column B. The completed sentences will be common sayings in English.

Example: Ignorance is bliss.
("Ignorance is bliss" is a saying. It means: If you know about problems, you have to worry about them and solve them. If you don't know about problems, you can avoid them and be happy [*bliss* = *happiness*]. Do you agree with this saying?)

Column A	Column B
1. Ignorance is __D__	A. the best teacher.
2. Honesty is _____	B. the best medicine.
3. Time is _____	C. power.
4. Laughter is _____	✓D. bliss.
5. Beauty is _____	E. in the eye of the beholder.
6. Knowledge is _____	F. money.
7. Experience is _____	G. the best policy.

□ EXERCISE 9. Noncount abstractions. (Chart 11-4)
    Directions: In groups or by yourself, complete the lists with abstract nouns. (Abstract nouns are usually noncount. To find out if a noun is count or noncount, check your dictionary or discuss it with your teacher.)

    a. Name four good qualities you admire in a person.

    1. _____*patience*_____   3. _____

    2. _____   4. _____

    b. Name bad qualities people can have.

    1. _____*greed*_____   3. _____

    2. _____   4. _____

    c. What are some of the most important things in life?

    1. _____*good health*_____   3. _____

    2. _____   4. _____

    d. Certain bad conditions exist in the world. What are they?

    1. _____*hunger*_____   3. _____

    2. _____   4. _____

□ EXERCISE 10. Count and noncount nouns. (Charts 11-1 → 11-4)
    Directions: Choose one of the given topics. Make a written list of the things you see.

    Example: You're sitting in your office. List the things you see.

    Written:
    - two windows
    - three desk lamps
    - a lot of books—around 50 books about English grammar
    - office equipment—a Macintosh computer, a printer, a photocopy machine
    - typical office supplies—a stapler, paper clips, pens, pencils, a ruler
    - some photographs
    - etc.

    Topics:
    1. Sit in any room of your choosing. List the things you see (including things other people are wearing if you wish).
    2. Look out a window. List the things and people you see.
    3. Go to a place outdoors (a park, a zoo, a city street) and list what you see.
    4. Travel in your imagination to a room you lived in when you were a child. List everything you can remember about that room.

11-5 USING *SEVERAL, A LOT OF, MANY/MUCH,* AND *A FEW/A LITTLE*

	COUNT	NONCOUNT	
(a)	**several** chairs	Ø	**Several** is used only with *count* nouns.
(b)	**a lot of** chairs	**a lot of** furniture	**A lot of** is used with both *count* and *noncount* nouns.
(c)	**many** chairs	**much** furniture	**Many** is used with *count* nouns. **Much** is used with *noncount* nouns.
(d)	**a few** chairs	**a little** furniture	**A few** is used with *count* nouns. **A little** is used with *noncount* nouns.

☐ EXERCISE 11. SEVERAL, A LOT OF, and MANY/MUCH. (Charts 11-1 → 11-5)
  Directions: Correct the mistakes. Some sentences contain no errors. One sentence contains a spelling error.

1. Jack bought ~~several~~ *some* furniture.

2. He bought several chairs. OK (*no change*)

3. Ted bought a lot of chairs.

4. Sue bought a lot of furniture, too.

5. Alice bought too much furniture.

6. She bought too much chairs.

7. Dr. Lee bought a few furniture for his new office.

8. He bought a few chairs.

9. He has several new furnitures in his office.

10. He has several new chairs in his office.

11. There is alot of desk in this room.

12. There are a lot of furnitures in Dr. Lee's office.

□ EXERCISE 12. HOW MANY and HOW MUCH. (Charts 11-1 → 11-5)

Directions: Create questions with ***how many*** or ***how much***. Use the information in parentheses to form Speaker A's question.

1. A: How ___many children do the Millers have___?
   B: Three. (The Millers have three children.)

2. A: How ___much money does Jake make___?
   B: A lot. (Jake makes a lot of money.)

3. A: How _____ on a soccer team?
   B: Eleven. (There are eleven players on a soccer team.)

4. A: How _____ to do tonight?
   B: Just a little. (I have just a little homework to do tonight.)

5. A: How _____ in the baskets?
   B: A lot. (There are a lot of apples in the baskets.)

6. A: How _____ in the baskets?
   B: A lot. (There is a lot of fruit in the baskets.)

7. A: How _____ in Canada?
   B: Ten. (There are ten provinces in Canada.)

8. A: How _____ before you moved to Japan?
   B: Just a little. (I knew just a little Japanese before I moved to Japan.)

9. A: How _____ in the world?
   B: Approximately 22,000. (There are approximately 22,000 kinds of fish in the world.)

10. A: How _____?
    B: A lot. (You should buy a lot of cheese.) It looks really good.

11. A: How _____ every day?
    B: Two cups. (I drink two cups of coffee every day.)

12. A: How _____ in the chalk tray?
    B: Several pieces. (There are several pieces of chalk in the chalk tray.)

□ EXERCISE 13. MANY vs. MUCH. (Charts 11-1 → 11-5)
   Directions: Work in pairs.
   SPEAKER A: Using the cues, ask a question using **how much** or **how many**. You are looking for the answer to "**x**." Your book is open.
   SPEAKER B: Listen carefully for the correct use of **much** and **many**. Answer the question. If you don't know the answer, guess. Sometimes Speaker A is given the correct answer and can tell you how close you are to the correct answer. Your book is closed.

   Example: **water**: You drink **x** every day.
   SPEAKER A *(book open):*   How much water do you drink every day?
   SPEAKER B *(book closed):* I try to drink at least six glasses of water every day.

   Example: **page**: There are **x** in this chapter. *(Answer: 32)*
   SPEAKER A *(book open):*   How many pages are there in this chapter?
   SPEAKER B *(book closed):* I don't know. I'd guess there are about thirty.
   SPEAKER A *(book open):*   Very close! There are 32 pages in this chapter.

   1. **tea:**   You usually drink **x** every day.
   2. **word:**   There are **x** in the title of this book. *(Answer: 4)*
   3. **money:**   A pencil costs **x**.
   4. **bone:**   There are **x** in the human body. *(Answer: 206)*
   5. **tooth:**   The average person has **x**. *(Answer: 32)*
   6. **mail:**   You got **x** yesterday.

   Switch roles.
   7. **sugar:**   You put **x** in your tea.
   8. **language:**   You can speak **x**.
   9. **English:**   Had you studied **x** before you started attending this class?
   10. **people:**   There were **x** on earth 2,000 years ago. *(Answer: around 250 million)*
   11. **human being:** There are **x** in the world today. *(Answer: around six billion)*
   12. **butterfly:**   You can see **x** in one hour on a summer day in a flower garden.

□ EXERCISE 14. A FEW vs. A LITTLE. (Charts 11-1 → 11-5)
   Directions: Complete the sentences by using **a few** or **a little** and the given noun. Use the plural form of the noun when necessary.

   REMINDER: Use *a few* with a count noun: *a few songs.*
               Use *a little* with a noncount noun: *a little music.*

   1. *music*   I feel like listening to ____a little music____ tonight.
   2. *song*   We sang ____a few songs____ at the party.
   3. *help*   Do you need _____ with that?
   4. *pepper*   My grandfather doesn't use extra salt, but he always puts _____
                 _____ on his hard-boiled egg
   5. *thing*   I need to pick up _____ at the market on my way home from work tonight.

6. *apple*   I bought _____ at the market.*

7. *fruit*   I bought _____ at the market.

8. *advice*   I need _____ .

9. *money*   If I accept that job, I'll make _____ more _____ .

10. *coin*   Annie put _____ in her pocket.

11. *friend*   _____ came by last night to visit us.

12. *rain*   It looks like we might get _____ today.
             I think I'll take my umbrella with me.

13. *French*   I can speak _____ , but I don't know
              any Italian at all.

14. *hour*   Ron's plane will arrive in _____ more _____ .

15. *toothpaste*   Tommy, put just _____ on your
                  toothbrush, not half the tube!

16. *chicken*   I'm still hungry. I think I'll have _____ more
               _____ .

17. *chicken*   When I was a child, we raised _____ in
               our backyard.

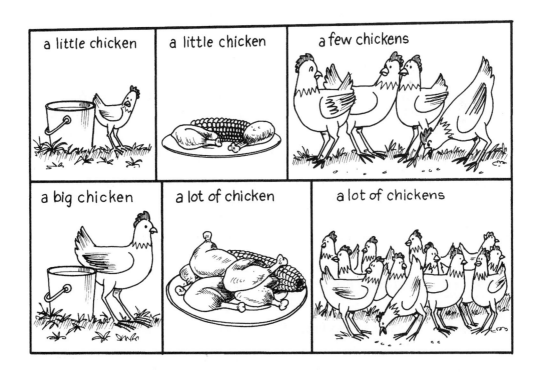

a little chicken   a little chicken   a few chickens

a big chicken   a lot of chicken   a lot of chickens

_____

I bought a few apples. = I bought a small number of apples.
 I bought a little apple. = I bought one apple, and it was small, not large.

11-6 NOUNS THAT CAN BE COUNT OR NONCOUNT

Quite a few nouns can be used as either count or noncount nouns. Examples of both count and noncount usages for some common nouns follow.

NOUN	USED AS A **NONCOUNT** NOUN	USED AS A **COUNT** NOUN
glass	(a) Windows are made of *glass*.	(b) I drank *a glass* of water. (c) Janet wears *glasses* when she reads.
hair	(d) Rita has brown *hair*.	(e) There's *a hair* on my jacket.
iron	(f) *Iron* is a metal.	(g) I pressed my shirt with *an iron*.
light	(h) I opened the curtain to let in *some light*.	(i) Please turn off *the lights* (lamps).
paper	(j) I need *some paper* to write a letter.	(k) I wrote *a paper* for Professor Lee. (l) I bought *a paper* (a newspaper).
time	(m) How *much time* do you need to finish your work?	(n) How *many times* have you been in Mexico?
work	(o) I have *some work* to do tonight.	(p) That painting is *a work* of art.
coffee	(q) I had *some coffee* after dinner.	(r) *Two coffees*, please.
chicken/ fish	(s) I ate *some chicken/some fish*.	(t) She drew a picture of *a chicken/a fish*.
experience	(u) I haven't had *much experience* with computers. (I don't have much knowledge or skill in using computers.)	(v) I had *many* interesting *experiences* on my trip. (Many interesting events happened to me on my trip.)

☐ EXERCISE 15. Nouns that can be count or noncount. (Chart 11-6)

Directions: Complete the sentences with the given words. Choose words in parentheses as necessary.

1. *chicken*   Joe, would you like (a, some) __some chicken__ for dinner tonight?

2. *chicken*   My grandmother raises ____chickens____ in her yard.

3. *time*   It took a lot of _____ to write my composition.

4. *time*   I really like that movie. I saw it three _____.

5. *paper*   Students in Prof. Young's literature class have to write a lot of

   _____.

6. *paper*   Students who take thorough lecture notes use a lot of _____.

7. *paper*   *The New York Times* is *(a, some)* famous _____ .

8. *work*   Rodin's statue of "The Thinker" is one of my favorite _____ of art.

9. *work*   I have a lot of _____ to do tomorrow at my office.

10. *light*   If _____ accidentally *(get, gets)* in a darkroom, *(it, they)* can ruin photographic negatives.

11. *light*   There *(is, are)* a lot of fluorescent _____ on the ceilings of the school building.

12. *hair*   Erin has straight _____ , and Sara has curly _____ .

13. *hair*   Brian has a white cat. When I stood up from Brian's sofa, my black slacks were covered with short white _____ .

14. *glass*   I wear _____ because I'm nearsighted.

15. *glass*   In some countries, people use _____ for their tea; in other countries, they use cups.

16. *glass*   Framed paintings are usually covered with _____ to protect them.

17. *iron*   _____ *(is, are)* necessary to animal and plant life.

18. *iron*   _____ *(is, are)* used to make clothes look neat.

19. *experience*   Grandfather had a lot of interesting _____ in his long career as a diplomat.

20. *experience*   You should apply for the job at the electronics company only if you have a lot of _____ in that field.

11-7 USING UNITS OF MEASURE WITH NONCOUNT NOUNS

(a) I had some tea. (b) I had **two cups of** tea. (c) I ate some toast. (d) I ate **one piece of** toast.	To mention a specific quantity of a noncount noun, speakers use units of measure such as *two cups of* or *one piece of*. A unit of measure usually describes **the container** (*a cup of, a bowl of*), **the amount** (*a pound of, a quart of*),* or **the shape** (*a bar of soap, a sheet of paper*).

*Weight measure: *one pound* = 0.45 kilograms/kilos.
  Liquid measure: *one quart* = 0.95 litres/liters; four quarts = one gallon = 3.8 litres/liters.

☐ **EXERCISE 16. Units of measure with noncount nouns. (Chart 11-7)**
   Directions: What units of measure are usually used with the following nouns? More than one unit of measure can be used with some of the nouns.

   PART I. You are going to the store. What are you going to buy? Choose from these units of measure.

bag	bottle	box	can* (tin)	jar

   1. a _____can/jar_____ of olives

   2. a _____box_____ of crackers

   3. a _____ of mineral water

   4. a _____ of jam or jelly

   5. a _____ of tuna fish

   6. a _____ of soup

   7. a _____ of sugar

   8. a _____ of wine

   9. a _____ of corn

   10. a _____ of peas

   11. a _____ of flour

   12. a _____ of soda pop

   13. a _____ of paint

   14. a _____ of breakfast cereal

   RICE
   TOASTIES
   ALL THE
   VITAMINS
   YOU WILL
   EVER NEED

   _____
   *a can in American English = a tin in British English.

PART II. You are hungry and thirsty. What are you going to have? Choose from these units of measure.

bowl	cup	glass	piece	slice

15. a ___cup/glass___ of green tea

16. a ___bowl___ of cereal

17. a _____ of candy

18. a _____ of bread

19. a _____ of apple pie

20. a _____ of orange juice

21. a _____ of soup

22. a _____ of cantaloupe

23. a _____ of beer

24. a _____ of noodles

25. a _____ of mineral water

26. a _____ of popcorn

27. a _____ of cheese

28. a _____ of rice

29. a _____ of strawberries and ice cream

☐ **EXERCISE 17. Writing activity: count and noncount nouns. (Charts 11-1 → 11-7)**
Directions: In several paragraphs, describe the perfect meal. Use your imagination. If you use the name of a dish that your reader is probably unfamiliar with, describe it in parentheses. For example:

I'm going to imagine for you the perfect meal. I am on a terrace high on a hillside in Nepal. When I look out, I see snow-capped mountains in the distance. The valley below is hazy and beautiful. I'm with my friends Olga and Roberto. The table has a while tablecloth and a vase of blue flowers. I'm going to eat all of my favorite kinds of food.

First the waiter is going to bring escargots. (Escargots are snails cooked in butter and seasoned with garlic and other herbs.) Etc.

11-8 GUIDELINES FOR ARTICLE USAGE

	USING *A* OR Ø (NO ARTICLE)		USING *A* OR *SOME*
SINGULAR COUNT NOUNS	(a) *A dog* makes a good pet. (b) *A banana* is yellow. (c) *A pencil* contains lead.	A speaker uses *a* with a singular count noun when s/he is making a generalization. In (a): The speaker is talking about any dog, all dogs, dogs in general.	(j) I saw *a dog* in my yard. (k) Mary ate *a banana*. (l) I need *a pencil*.
PLURAL COUNT NOUNS	(d) Ø *Dogs* make good pets. (e) Ø *Bananas* are yellow. (f) Ø *Pencils* contain lead.	A speaker uses no article (Ø) with a plural count noun when s/he is making a generalization.* In (d): The speaker is talking about any dog, all dogs, dogs in general. Note: (a) and (d) have the same meaning.	(m) I saw *some dogs* in my yard. (n) Mary bought *some bananas*. (o) Bob has *some pencils* in his pocket.
NONCOUNT NOUNS	(g) Ø *Fruit* is good for you. (h) Ø *Coffee* contains caffeine. (i) I like Ø *music*.	A speaker uses no article (Ø) with a noncount noun when s/he is making a generalization. In (g): The speaker is talking about any fruit, all fruit, fruit in general.	(p) I bought *some fruit*. (q) Bob drank *some coffee*. (r) Would you like to listen to *some music*?

*Sometimes a speaker uses an expression of quantity (e.g., *almost all, most, some)* when s/he makes a generalization:
Almost all dogs make good pets. Most dogs are friendly. Some dogs have short hair.

	USING *THE*	

A speaker uses *a* with a singular count noun when s/he is talking about one thing (or person) that is not specific.
 	
In (j): The speaker is saying, "I saw one dog (not two dogs, some dogs, many dogs). It wasn't a specific dog (e.g., your dog, the neighbor's dog, that dog). It was only one dog out of the whole group of animals called dogs."
	(s) Did you feed **the dog**?
	(t) I had a banana and an apple. I gave **the banana** to Mary.
	(u) **The pencil** on that desk is Jim's.
	(v) **The sun** is shining.
	(w) Please close **the door**.
	(x) Mary is in **the kitchen**.
		The is used in front of
		  (1) singular count nouns: *the dog*.
		  (2) plural count nouns: *the dogs*.
		  (3) noncount nouns: *the fruit*.
		A speaker uses *the* (not *a*, *Ø*, or *some*) when the speaker and the listener are thinking about the same specific person(s) or thing(s).

A speaker often uses *some*★ with a plural count noun when s/he is talking about things (or people) that are not specific. In (m): The speaker is saying, "I saw more than one dog. They weren't specific dogs (e.g., your dogs, the neighbor's dogs, those dogs). The exact number of dogs isn't important (two dogs, five dogs); I'm simply saying that I saw an indefinite number of dogs."	(y) Did you feed **the dogs**? (z) I had some bananas and apples. I gave **the bananas** to Mary. (aa) **The pencils** on that desk are Jim's. (bb) Please turn off **the lights**.	In (s): The speaker and the listener are thinking about the same specific dog. The listener knows which dog the speaker is talking about: the dog that they own, the dog that they feed every day. There is only one dog that the speaker could possibly be talking about. In (t): A speaker uses *the* when s/he mentions a noun the second time. First mention: *I had **a banana** . . . .* Second mention: *I gave **the banana** . . . .* In the second mention, the listener now knows which banana the speaker is talking about: the banana the speaker had (not the banana John had, not the banana in that bowl).
A speaker often uses *some*★ with a noncount noun when s/he is talking about something that is not specific. In (p): The speaker is saying, "I bought an indefinite amount of fruit. The exact amount (e.g., two pounds of fruit, four bananas, and two apples) isn't important. And I'm not talking about specific fruit (e.g., that fruit, the fruit in that bowl.)"	(cc) **The fruit** in this bowl is ripe. (dd) I drank some coffee and some milk. **The coffee** was hot. (ee) I can't hear you. **The music** is too loud. (ff) **The air** is cold today.	

★In addition to *some*, a speaker might use *several*, *a few*, *a lot of*, *etc.*, with a plural count noun, or *a little*, *a lot of*, *etc.*, with a noncount noun. (See Chart 11-5, p. 318.)

Directions: Discuss Speaker A's use of articles in the following dialogues. Why does Speaker A use *a, some, the,* or Ø? Discuss what both Speaker A and Speaker B are thinking about.

DIALOGUE 1:

A: *A dog* makes a good pet. B: I agree.

DIALOGUE 2:

A: I saw *a dog* in my yard.

DIALOGUE 4:

A: *Dogs* make good pets. B: I agree.

DIALOGUE 5:

A: I saw *some dogs* in my yard.

DIALOGUE 7:

A: *Fruit* is good for you. B: I agree.

DIALOGUE 8:

A: I ate *some fruit*.

B: Oh?

DIALOGUE 3:

A: Did you feed *the dog?*   B: Yes.

B: Oh?

DIALOGUE 6:

A: Did you feed *the dogs?*   B: Yes.

B: Oh?

DIALOGUE 9:

A: *The fruit* in this bowl is ripe.   B: Good.

□ **EXERCISE 19. THE vs. A/AN. (Chart 11-8)**

Directions: Here are some conversations. Try to decide whether the speakers would probably use *the* or *a/an*. Are the speakers thinking about the same objects or persons?

1. A: Did you have a good time at __the__ party last night?

   B: Yes.

   A: So did I. I'm glad that you decided to go with me.

2. A: What did you do last night?

   B: I went to __a__ party.

   A: Oh? Where was it?

3. A: Do you have _____ car?

   B: No. But I have _____ bicycle.

4. A: Do you need _____ car today, honey?

   B: Yes. I have a lot of errands to do. Why don't I drive you to work today?

   A: Okay. But be sure to fill _____ car up with gas sometime today.

5. A: I bought _____ table yesterday.

   B: Oh? I didn't know you went shopping for furniture.

6. A: Have you seen my keys?

   B: Yes. They're on _____ table next to _____ front door.

7. A: Is Mr. Jones _____ graduate student?

   B: No. He's _____ professor.

8. A: Where's _____ professor?

   B: She's absent today.

9. A: Would you like to go to _____ zoo this afternoon?

   B: Sure. Why not?

10. A: Does San Diego have _____ zoo?

    B: Yes. It's world famous.

11. A: Let's listen to _____ radio.

    B: Okay. I'll turn it on.

12. A: Does your car have _____ radio?

    B: Yes, and _____ CD player.

13. A: Did you lock _____ door?

    B: Yes.

    A: Did you check _____ stove?

    B: Yes.

    A: Did you close all _____ windows downstairs?

    B: Yes.

    A: Did you set _____ alarm?

    B: Yes.

    A: Then let's turn out _____ lights.

    B: Goodnight, dear.

    A: Goodnight, dear.

14. A: Where's Dennis?

    B: He's in _____ kitchen.

15. A: Do you like your new apartment?

    B: Yes. It has _____ big kitchen.

□ **EXERCISE 20. Using A or Ø for generalizations. (Chart 11-8)**
    Directions: Write **a** or **Ø** in the blank before each singular noun. Then write the plural form of the noun if possible.

Singular Subjects	**Plural Subjects**
1. __*A*__ bird has feathers.	__Birds have feathers.__
2. __Ø__ C ¢orn is nutritious.	__Ø (none possible)__
3. _____ milk is white.	_____
4. _____ flower is beautiful.	_____
5. _____ water is a clear liquid.	_____
6. _____ horse is strong.	_____
7. _____ jewelry is expensive.	_____
8. _____ soap produces bubbles.	_____
9. _____ shirt has sleeves.	_____
10. _____ honey comes from bees.	_____

□ **EXERCISE 21. Using THE for specific statements. (Chart 11-8)**
    Directions: Complete the sentences with the given nouns. Use ***the*** for specific statements.
    Do not use ***the*** for general statements.

1. *flowers*   a. _____The flowers_____ in that vase are beautiful.

    b. _____Flowers_____ are beautiful.

2. *mountains* a. _____ are beautiful.

    b. _____ in Colorado are beautiful.

3. *water*   a. _____ consists of hydrogen and oxygen.

    b. I don't want to go swimming today. _____ is

    too cold.

4. *information* a. _____ in today's newspaper is

    alarming.

    b. The Internet is a widely used source of _____ .

5. *health*   a. _____ is more important than money.

    b. Doctors are concerned with _____ of their

    patients.

6. *men*   a. _____ generally have stronger muscles

   women   than _____ .

    b. At the party last night, _____ sat on one side

    of the room, and _____ sat on the other.

7. *problems*   a. Everyone has _____ .

    b. Irene told me about _____ she had with her

    car yesterday.

8. *happiness* a. I can't express _____ I felt when I

    heard the good news.

    b. Everyone seeks _____ .

9. *vegetables* a. _____ are good for you.

    b. _____ we had for dinner last

    night were overcooked.

10. *gold*   a. _____ is a precious metal.

    b. _____ in Mary's ring is 24 karats.

□ **EXERCISE 22. Using THE for specific statements. (Chart 11-8)**
Directions: Add **the** if necessary. Otherwise, use **Ø** to show that no article is necessary.

1. Please pass me _____the_____ butter.

2. _____Ø_____ Ɓutter is a dairy product.

3. _____ air is free.

4. _____ air is humid today.

5. A: _____ windows are closed. Please open them.

   B: Okay.

6. _____ windows are made of _____ glass.

7. As every parent knows, _____ children require a lot of time and attention.

8. A: Frank, where are _____ children?

   B: Next door at the Jacksons'.

9. _____ paper is made from _____ trees or other plants.

10. _____ paper in my notebook is lined.

11. _____ nurses are trained to care for sick and injured people.

12. When I was in Memorial Hospital, _____ nurses were wonderful.

13. I'm studying _____ English. I'm studying _____ grammar.

14. _____ grammar in this chapter isn't easy.

15. All of our food comes from _____ plants. Some food, such as _____ fruit and _____ vegetables, comes directly from _____ plants. Other food, such as _____ meat, comes indirectly from _____ plants.

16. I'm not very good at keeping houseplants alive. _____ plants in my apartment have to be tough. They survive in spite of me.

□ **EXERCISE 23. Using THE for second mention. (Chart 11-8)**
Directions: Write **a/an, some,** or **the** in the blanks.

1. I had ____a____ banana and ____an____ apple. I gave ____the____ banana to Mary. I ate ____the____ apple.

2. I had ____some____ bananas and ____some____ apples. I gave ____the____ bananas to Mary. I ate ____the____ apples.

3. I have _____ desk and _____ bed in my room. _____ desk is hard. _____ bed is hard, too, even though it's supposed to be soft.

4. I forgot to bring my things with me to class yesterday, so I borrowed _____ pen and _____ paper from Joe. I returned _____ pen, but I used _____ paper for my homework.

5. A: What did you do last weekend?

   B: I went on _____ picnic Saturday and saw _____ movie Sunday.

   A: Did you have fun?

   B: _____ picnic was fun, but _____ movie was boring.

6. Yesterday I saw _____ dog and _____ cat. _____ dog was chasing _____ cat. _____ cat was chasing _____ mouse. _____ mouse ran into _____ hole, but _____ hole was very small. _____ cat couldn't get into _____ hole, so it ran up _____ tree. _____ dog tried to climb _____ tree too, but it couldn't.

7. I bought _____ bag of flour and _____ sugar to make _____ cookies. _____ sugar was okay, but I had to return _____ flour. When I opened _____ flour, I found _____ little bugs in it. I took it back to the people at the store and showed them _____ little bugs. They gave me _____ new bag of flour. _____ new bag didn't have any bugs in it.

8. Once upon a time, _____ princess fell in love with _____ prince. _____ princess wanted to marry _____ prince, who lived in _____ distant land. She summoned _____ messenger to take _____ things to _____ prince to show him her love. _____ messenger took _____ jewels and _____ robe made of yellow and red silk to _____ prince. _____ princess anxiously awaited _____ messenger's return. She hoped that _____ prince would send her _____ tokens of his love. But when _____ messenger returned, he brought back _____ jewels and _____ beautiful silk robe that _____ princess had sent. Why? Why? she wondered. Then _____ messenger told her: _____ prince already had _____ wife.

☐ EXERCISE 24. Summary: A/AN vs. Ø vs. THE. (Charts 11-1 → 11-8)
    Directions: Write **a/an, Ø,** or ***the*** in the blanks.

1. I have __*a*__ window in my bedroom. I keep it open at night because I like __Ø__ fresh air. __The__ window is above my bed.

2. Kathy bought _____ radio. She likes to listen to _____ music when she studies.

3. A: Would you please turn _____ radio down? _____ music is too loud.
   B: No problem.

4. _____ good book is _____ friend for _____ life.

5. Last week I read _____ book about _____ life of Gandhi.

6. A: Let's go swimming in _____ lake today.
   B: That sounds like _____ good idea.

7. _____ lake is a body of _____ water that is smaller than _____ sea but larger than _____ pond. _____ ocean is larger than _____ sea.

8. During our vacation in Brazil, we walked along _____ beach in front of our hotel and looked at _____ ocean.

9. _____ water is essential to human life, but don't drink _____ water in the Flat River. It'll kill you! _____ pollution in that river is terrible.

10. People can drink _____ fresh water. They can't drink _____ seawater because it contains _____ salt.

11. Ted, pass _____ salt, please. And _____ pepper. Thanks.

12. _____ different countries have _____ different geography. Italy is located on _____ peninsula. Japan is _____ island nation.

13. A: How did you get here? Did you walk?
   B: No, I took _____ taxi.

14. There are some wonderful small markets in my neighborhood. You can always get _____ fresh fish at Mr. Rico's fish market.

15. _____ good food keeps us healthy and adds _____ pleasure to our lives.

16. A: Well, are you ready to leave?

B: Anytime you are.

A: Let me take just one last sip of coffee. I've really enjoyed this meal.

B: I agree. _____ food was excellent—especially _____ fish. And _____ service was exceptionally good. Let's leave _____ waitress _____ good tip.

A: Yes, let's do that. I usually tip around fifteen percent, sometimes eighteen percent. Does that sound about right to you?

17. A: We're ready to go, kids. Get in _____ car.

B: Just a minute! We forgot something.

A: Marge, can you get _____ kids in _____ car, please?

B: Just a minute, Harry. They're coming.

18. In ancient times, people did not use _____ coins for money. Instead they used _____ shells, _____ beads, or _____ salt. The first coins were made around 2600 years ago. Today, most money is made from _____ paper. In the future, maybe we'll use only _____ plastic cards and there will be no paper money.

19. A: Can I have some money, Dad?

B: What for?

A: I want to go to the movies with my friends and hang around the mall.

B: What you need is a job! _____ money doesn't grow on _____ trees, you know.

20. A doctor cures _____ sick people. _____ farmer grows _____ crops. _____ architect designs _____ buildings. _____ artist creates _____ new ways of looking at _____ world and _____ life.

21. _____ earthquakes are _____ rare events in central Africa.

22. My city experienced _____ earthquake recently. I was riding my bicycle when _____ earthquake occurred. _____ ground beneath me trembled so hard that it shook me off my bike.

23. A: I saw _____ good program on TV last night.

B: Oh? What was it?

A: It was _____ documentary about wildlife in Indonesia. It was really interesting. Did you see it too?

B: No, I watched _____ old movie. It wasn't very good. I wish I'd known about _____ documentary. I would have watched it.

24. _____ modern people, just like their ancestors, are curious about _____ universe. Where did _____ moon come from? Does _____ life exist on other planets? What is _____ star? How large is _____ universe? How long will _____ sun continue to burn?

☐ **EXERCISE 25. Preview: using THE or Ø with names. (Chart 11-9)**
Directions: Complete with ***the*** or **Ø**.

I would like to know more about . . .

1. __the__ Amazon River.
2. __Ø__ Korea.
3. _____ Mexico City.
4. _____ Indian Ocean.
5. _____ Ural Mountains.
6. _____ Australia.
7. _____ Mississippi River.
8. _____ Red Sea.
9. _____ Lake Michigan.
10. _____ Mount Fuji.

11-9 USING *THE* OR Ø WITH NAMES

(a) We met **Ø** *Mr. Wang.* I know **Ø** *Doctor Smith.* **Ø** *President Rice* has been in the news.	***The*** is NOT used with titled names. INCORRECT: *We met the Mr. Wang.*
(b) He lives in **Ø** *Europe.* **Ø** *Asia* is the largest continent. Have you ever been in **Ø** *Africa?*	***The*** is NOT used with the names of continents. INCORRECT: *He lives in the Europe.*
(c) He lives in **Ø** *France.* **Ø** *Brazil* is a large country. Have you ever been in **Ø** *Thailand?*	***The*** is NOT used with the names of most countries. INCORRECT: *He lives in the France.*
(d) He lives in **the** *United States.* **The** *Netherlands* is in Europe. Have you ever been in **the** *Philippines?*	***The*** is used in the names of only a few countries, as in the examples. Others: *the Czech Republic, the United Arab Emirates, the Dominican Republic.*
(e) He lives in **Ø** *Paris.* **Ø** *New York* is the largest city in the United States Have you ever been in **Ø** *Istanbul?*	***The*** is NOT used with the names of cities. INCORRECT: *He lives in the Paris.*
(f) **The** *Nile River* is long. They crossed **the** *Pacific Ocean.* **The** *Yellow Sea* is in Asia.	***The*** is used with the names of rivers, oceans, and seas.
(g) Chicago is on **Ø** *Lake Michigan.* **Ø** *Lake Titicaca* lies on the border between Peru and Bolivia.	***The*** is NOT used with the names of lakes.
(h) We hiked in **the** *Alps.* **The** *Andes* are in South America.	***The*** is used with the names of mountain ranges.
(i) He climbed **Ø** *Mount Everest.* **Ø** *Mount Fuji* is in Japan.	***The*** is NOT used with the names of individual mountains.

☐ EXERCISE 26. Using THE or Ø with names. (Chart 11-9)
   Directions: Complete with ***the*** or **Ø**.

1. ___Ø___ Rome is in ___Ø___ Italy.

2. ___The___ Rhine River flows through ___Ø___ Germany.

3. _____ Moscow is the capital of _____ Russia.

4. _____ Yangtze is a famous river.

5. _____ Atlantic Ocean is smaller than _____ Pacific.

6. _____ Rocky Mountains are located in _____ Canada and _____
   United States.

7. _____ Doctor Anderson is a good physician.

8. _____ Lake Victoria is located in _____ Africa.

11-10 CAPITALIZATION

CAPITALIZE		
1. The first word of a sentence	(a) **W**e saw a movie last night. **I**t was very good.	*Capitalize* = use a big letter, not a small letter.
2. The names of people	(b) I met **G**eorge **A**dams yesterday.	
3. Titles used with the names of people	(c) I saw **D**octor (**D**r.) Smith. Do you know **P**rofessor (**P**rof.) Alston?	COMPARE I saw a **d**octor. I saw **D**octor Wilson.
4. Months, days, holidays	(d) I was born in **A**pril. Bob arrived last **M**onday. It snowed on **T**hanksgiving **D**ay.	NOTE: Seasons are not capitalized: *spring, summer, fall/autumn, winter*
5. The names of places: city state/province country continent	(e) He lives in **C**hicago. She was born in **C**alifornia. They are from **M**exico. Tibet is in **A**sia.	COMPARE She lives in a **c**ity. She lives in **N**ew **Y**ork City.
ocean lake river desert mountain	They crossed the **A**tlantic **O**cean. Chicago is on **L**ake **M**ichigan. The **N**ile **R**iver flows north. The **S**ahara **D**esert is in Africa. We visited the **R**ocky **M**ountains.	COMPARE They crossed a **r**iver. They crossed the **Y**ellow **R**iver.
school business	I go to the **U**niversity of **F**lorida. I work for the **G**eneral **E**lectric **C**ompany.	COMPARE I go to a **u**niversity. I go to the **U**niversity of **T**exas.
street building park, zoo	He lives on **G**rand **A**venue. We have class in **R**itter **H**all. I went jogging in **F**orest **P**ark.	COMPARE We went to a **p**ark. We went to **C**entral **P**ark.
6. The names of courses	(f) I'm taking **C**hemistry 101 this term.	COMPARE I'm reading a book about **p**sychology. I'm taking **P**sychology 101 this term.
7. The titles of books, articles, movies	(g) *Gone with the **W**ind* *The **O**ld **M**an and the **S**ea*	Capitalize the first word of a title. Capitalize all other words except articles *(the, a/an)*, coordinating conjunctions *(and, but, or)*, and short prepositions *(with, in, at, etc.)*.
8. The names of languages and nationalities	(h) She speaks **S**panish. We discussed **J**apanese customs.	Words that refer to the names of nations, nationalities, and languages are always capitalized.
9. The names of religions	(i) **B**uddism, **C**hristianity, **H**induism, **I**slam, and **J**udaism are major religions in the world. Talal is a **M**oslem.	Words that refer to the names of religions are always capitalized.
10. The pronoun "I"	(j) Yesterday **I** fell off my bicycle.	The pronoun "I" is always capitalized.

Directions: Add capital letters where necessary.

1. We're going to have a test next Ṫuesday.

2. Do you know richard smith? he is a professor at this university.

3. I know that professor smith teaches at the university of arizona.

4. The nile river flows into the mediterranean sea.

5. John is a catholic. ali is a moslem.

6. Anna speaks french. she studied in france for two years.

7. I'm taking a history course this semester.

8. I'm taking modern european history 101 this semester.

9. We went to vancouver, british columbia, for our vacation last summer.

10. Venezuela is a spanish-speaking country.

11. Canada is in north america.*

12. Canada is north of the united states.

13. The sun rises in the east.

14. The mississippi river flows south.

15. The amazon is a river in south america.

16. We went to a zoo. We went to brookfield zoo in chicago.

17. The title of this book is fundamentals of english grammar.

18. I enjoy studying english grammar.

19. On valentine's day (february 14), sweethearts give each other presents.

20. I read a book entitled *the cat and the mouse in my aunt's house.*

---

*When **north, south, east,** and **west** refer to the direction on a compass, they are not capitalized:
    *Japan is **east** of China.*
When they are part of a geographical name, they are capitalized: *Japan is in the Far **East**.*

Directions: Capitalize as necessary.

(1) Jane goodall is a famous scientist. She became famous for her studies of chimpanzees in tanzania.

(2) Even though she was born in the heart of london, england, as a child she was always fascinated by animals of all sorts. Her favorite books were *the jungle book,* by rudyard kipling, and books about tarzan, a fictional character who was raised by apes.

(3) Her dream from childhood was to go to africa. After high school, she worked as a secretary and a waitress to earn enough money to go there. During that time, she took evening courses in journalism and english literature. One of her favorite poets was t. s. eliot. She saved every penny. She put her wages under the carpet in her mother's living room until she had enough money for passage to africa.

(4) In the spring of 1957, she sailed through the red sea and southward down the african coast to mombasa in kenya. Her uncle had arranged a job for her in nairobi with a british company. When she was there, she met louis leakey, a famous anthropologist. Under his guidance she began her lifelong study of chimpanzees on the eastern shore of lake tanganyika.

(5) Jane goodall lived alone in a tent near the lake. Through months and years of patience, she won the trust of the chimps and was able to observe them at close hand. Her observations changed forever how we view chimpanzees—and all other animals we share the world with as well.

(6) As a young woman, jane couldn't afford to go to a university. She never received an undergraduate degree, but later in her life she received a Ph.D. from cambridge university and became a professor at stanford university. She has written several books. One of them is *my friends, the wild chimpanzees.* She works tirelessly on behalf of endangered species and in support of the humane treatment of animals in captivity.

□ EXERCISE 29. Error analysis. (Chapter 11)
    Directions: Correct the mistakes.

    1. Lions are wild animal.

    2. There are a lot of informations in that book.

    3. The oil is a natural resource.

    4. I was late because there were too many traffics.

    5. I drank two waters.

    6. Our teacher gives us too many homeworks.

    7. Nadia knows a lot of vocabularies.

    8. I had a egg for breakfast.

    9. There is many kind of trees in the world.

   10. I'm studying the english.

   11. My cousin living in United State.

   12. Only twelve student were in class yesterday.

   13. I need some advices.

   14. We all have a few problem in the life.

   15. There were no job, and people didn't have much moneys.

   16. I don't know anything about farm animals except for chicken.

   17. When I am a children, my family had a big farm with the Horses.

   18. I live with two friend. One is from the chile, and the other is from the Saudi Arabia.

   19. I think the english is difficult language.

   20. When people use a lot of slangs, I can't understand them.

CHAPTER 12
Adjective Clauses

CONTENTS

12-1 ADJECTIVE CLAUSES: INTRODUCTION

ADJECTIVES	ADJECTIVE CLAUSES
An **adjective** modifies a noun. "Modify" means to change a little. An adjective describes or gives information about the noun. (See Chart 6-8, p. 166.)	An **adjective clause★** modifies a noun. It describes or gives information about a noun.
An adjective usually comes in front of a noun.	An adjective clause follows a noun.
(a) I met a *adjective* + *noun* **kind** man. (b) I met a *adjective* + *noun* **famous** man.	(c) I met a *noun* man + *adjective clause* **who is kind to everybody**. (d) I met a *noun* man + *adjective clause* **who is a famous poet**. (e) I met a *noun* man + *adjective clause* **who lives in Chicago**.

★GRAMMAR TERMINOLOGY	
(1) ***I met a man*** = an independent clause; it is a complete sentence. (2) ***He lives in Chicago*** = an independent clause; it is a complete sentence. (3) ***who lives in Chicago*** = a dependent clause; it is NOT a complete sentence. (4) ***I met a man who lives in Chicago*** = an independent clause + a dependent clause; a complete sentence.	A **clause** is a structure that has a subject and a verb. There are two kinds of clauses: **independent** and **dependent**. • An **independent clause** is a main clause and can stand alone as a sentence. • A **dependent clause** cannot stand alone as a sentence; it must be connected to an independent clause.

12-2 USING *WHO* AND *WHOM* IN ADJECTIVE CLAUSES

(a) The man is friendly.
 	
    S   V
    He lives next to me.
    ↓
    who
    ↓
    S   V
    who lives next to me
	In (a): ***He*** is a subject pronoun. ***He*** refers to "the man."
	To make an adjective clause, change ***he*** to ***who***. ***Who*** is a subject pronoun. ***Who*** refers to "the man."

(b) The man ***who lives next to me*** is friendly.	In (b): An adjective clause immediately follows the noun it modifies. *INCORRECT: The man is friendly who lives next to me.*

(c) The man was friendly.
 	
    S   V   O
    I met ***him***.
    ↓
       whom
    ↓
    O   S   V
    whom I met
	In (c): ***him*** is an object pronoun. ***Him*** refers to "the man."
	To make an adjective clause, change ***him*** to ***whom***.
	Whom is an object pronoun.
	Whom refers to "the man."
	Whom comes at the beginning of an adjective clause.

(d) The man ***whom I met*** was friendly.	In (d): An adjective clause immediately follows the noun it modifies. *INCORRECT: The man was friendly whom I met.*

☐ EXERCISE 1. Adjective clauses with WHO and WHOM. (Charts 12-1 and 12-2)
    Directions: Combine the two sentences into one sentence. Make "b" an adjective clause.
    Use ***who*** or ***whom***.

    1. a. Do you know the people?   b. They live in the white house.
        → *Do you know the people who live in the white house?*

    2. a. The woman gave me some information.   b. I called her.
        → *The woman whom I called gave me some information.*

    3. a. The police officer was friendly.   b. She gave me directions.
        The police officer who gave me directions was friendly

    4. a. The waiter was friendly.   b. He served us dinner.
        The waiter who served us dinner was friendly

    5. a. The people were very nice.   b. I met them at the party last night.
        The people whom I met at the party last night were very nice.

    6. a. The people have three cars.   b. They live next to me.
        The people who live next to me have three cars.

    7. a. The man talked a lot.   b. I met him on the plane.
        The man whom I met on the plane talked a lot.

    8. a. The man talked a lot.   b. He sat next to me.
        The man who sat next to me talked a lot.

    9. a. Three women walked into my office.   b. I didn't know them.
        Three women whom I didn't know walked into my office.

   10. a. I talked to the women.   b. They walked into my office.
        I talked to the women who walked into my office.

☐ EXERCISE 2. Adjective clauses with WHO and WHOM. (Charts 12-1 and 12-2)

Directions: Complete the sentences with **who** or **whom**. Put parentheses around the entire adjective clause. Identify the subject and verb of the adjective clause.

1. The children (_____who_____ live down the street in the yellow house) are always polite.

2. The children (_____whom_____ we watched in the park) were feeding ducks in a pond.

3. The people _____whom_____ we visited gave us tea and a light snack.

4. I know some people _____who_____ live on a boat.

5. I talked to the woman _____who_____ was sitting next to me.

6. I saw the people _____who_____ were playing football at the park.

7. My mother is a person _____whom_____ I admire tremendously.

8. Marie and Luis Escobar still keep in touch with many of the students _____whom_____ they met in their English class five years ago.

9. People _____who_____ listen to very loud music may suffer gradual hearing loss.

10. At the supermarket yesterday, one of the store employees caught a man _____who_____ had put a beefsteak in his coat pocket and attempted to walk out without paying.

11. The couple _____whom_____ I invited to dinner at my home were two hours late. I thought that was very rude. They didn't call. They didn't have an excuse. They didn't apologize. I'll never invite them again.

☐ EXERCISE 3. Adjective clauses with WHO. (Charts 12-1 and 12-2)
   Directions: Insert ***who*** where it is necessary.

1. The man ∧ *who* answered the phone was polite.

2. I liked the people *who* sat next to us at the soccer game.

3. People *who* paint houses for a living are called house painters.

4. I'm uncomfortable around married couples *who* argue all the time.

5. While I was waiting at the bus stop, I stood next to an elderly gentleman *who* started a conversation with me about my educational plans.

☐ EXERCISE 4. Adjective clauses with WHO. (Charts 12-1 and 12-2)
   Directions: Complete the sentences in Column A with the adjective clauses in Column B. Consult your dictionary if necessary.

   Example: A Bostonian is someone . . . .
   → *A Bostonian is someone who lives in Boston.*

Column A	Column B
1. A Bostonian is someone	A. who has trouble sleeping.
2. A pilot is a person	B. who seeks to overthrow the government.
3. A procrastinator is someone	C. who flies an airplane.
4. A botanist is a scientist	D. who studies weather phenomena.
5. An insomniac is somebody	✓E. who lives in Boston.
6. A revolutionary is someone	F. who hates people.
7. A misanthrope is a person	G. who always puts off doing things.
8. A meteorologist is a person	H. who knows a lot about a little and a little about a lot.
9. A jack-of-all-trades is someone	I. who has many skills.
10. An expert can be defined as a person	J. who studies plants.

☐ EXERCISE 5. Adjective clauses with WHO. (Charts 12-1 and 12-2)
   Directions: Complete the sentences with your own words. Consult your dictionary if necessary.

1. A baker is a person who . . . . *makes bread, cakes, pies, etc.*

2. A mechanic is someone who . . . .

3. A bartender is a person who . . . .

4. A philatelist is someone who . . . .

5. A spendthrift is somebody who . . . .

6. An astronomer is a scientist who . . . .

7. A carpenter is a person who . . . .

8. A miser is someone who . . . .

12-3 USING *WHO, WHO(M)*, AND *THAT* IN ADJECTIVE CLAUSES

(a) The man is friendly. **He** (S) lives next to me. (V) ↓ **who** **that**	In addition to **who**, **that** can be used as the subject of an adjective clause. (b) and (c) have the same meaning.
(b) The man **who** *lives next to me* is friendly. (S V) (c) The man **that** *lives next to me* is friendly.	A subject pronoun cannot be omitted: INCORRECT: *The man lives next to me is friendly.* CORRECT: *The man who/that lives next to me is friendly.*
(d) The man was friendly. I met (S V) **him.** (O) ↓ **whom** **that**	In addition to **who(m)**,* **that** can be used as the object in an adjective clause. (e) and (f) have the same meaning.
(e) The man **who(m)** (O) *I met* (S V) was friendly. (f) The man **that** *I met* was friendly. (g) The man **Ø** *I met* was friendly.	An object pronoun can be omitted from an adjective clause. (e), (f), and (g) have the same meaning. In (g): The symbol "**Ø**" means "nothing goes here."

*The parentheses around the "m" in **who(m)** indicate that (especially in everyday conversation) **who** is often used as an object pronoun instead of the more formal **whom**.

☐ EXERCISE 6. Adjective clauses with WHO, WHO(M), and THAT. (Chart 12-3)
Directions: Complete the sentences using **who, who(m)**, and **that**. Write **Ø** if the pronoun can be omitted.

1. The woman ___who(m) / that / Ø___ I met last night was interesting.

2. The man ___who / that___ answered the phone was polite.

3. The people ___who / that___ (Nadia) is visiting live on Elm Street.

4. The students ___who / that___ came to class late missed the quiz.

5. The man ___who / that___ married my mother is now my stepfather.

6. The man ___who / that / Ø___ my mother married is now my stepfather.

7. Do you know the boy ___who / that___ is talking to Anita?

8. I've become good friends with several of the people ___whom / that / Ø___ I met in my English class last year.

9. The woman ___whom / that / Ø___ I saw in the park was feeding the pigeons.

10. The woman ___who / that___ was feeding the pigeons had a sackful of bread crumbs.

Should not use whom in front of name just use in pronoun.

12-4 USING *WHICH* AND *THAT* IN ADJECTIVE CLAUSES

(a) The river is polluted. ⎡ **S** ↓ **which** **that** ⎤ **It** → **V** flows through the town.	*Who* and *whom* refer to people. *Which* refers to things. *That* can refer to either people or things.
	In (a): To make an adjective clause, change *it* to *which* or *that*. *It*, *which*, and *that* all refer to a thing (the river). (b) and (c) have the same meaning.
(b) The river **S which** **V** flows through the town is polluted. (c) The river **that** *flows through the town* is polluted.	When *which* and *that* are used as the subject of an adjective clause, they CANNOT be omitted. *INCORRECT: The river flows through town is polluted.*
(d) The books were expensive. I bought **S V** ⎡ **O** ***them.*** ↓ ***which*** ***that*** ⎤	*Which* or *that* can be used as an object in an adjective clause, as in (e) and (f).
	An object pronoun can be omitted from an adjective clause, as in (g). (e), (f), and (g) have the same meaning.
(e) The books **O which** **S V** *I bought* were expensive. (f) The books **that** *I bought* were expensive. (g) The books **Ø** *I bought* were expensive.	

☐ **EXERCISE 7. Adjective clauses with WHO, WHO(M), WHICH, and THAT.**
   (Charts 12-3 and 12-4)

Directions: Combine the two sentences into one sentence. Make "b" an adjective clause. Give all the possible forms.

1. a. The pill made me sleepy.   b. I took it.
    → *The pill which I took made me sleepy.*
    → *The pill that I took made me sleepy.*
    → *The pill Ø I took made me sleepy.*

2. a. The soup was too salty.   b. I had it for lunch.

3. a. I have a class.   b. It begins at 8:00 A.M.

4. a. I know a man.   b. He doesn't have to work for a living.

5. a. The information helped me a lot.   b. I found it on the Internet.

6. a. The people waved at us.   b. We saw them on the bridge.

7. a. My daughter asked me a question.   b. I couldn't answer it.

8. a. The woman predicted my future.
   b. She read my palm.

9. a. Where can I catch the bus?
   b. It goes downtown.

10. a. All of the people can come.
    b. I asked them to my party.

□ **EXERCISE 8. Adjective clauses with WHO and THAT. (Charts 12-3 and 12-4)**

Directions: Complete the definitions that begin in Column A with the information given in Column B. Use adjective clauses with **who** or **that** in the definitions.★ Consult your dictionary if necessary.

Example: A hammer is a tool . . . .
   → *A hammer is a tool that is used to pound nails.*

Column A

1. A hammer is a tool . . . .
2. A barometer is an instrument . . . .
3. Plastic is a synthetic material . . . .
4. An architect is someone . . . .
5. A puzzle is a problem . . . .
6. A vegetarian is a person . . . .
7. Steam is a gas . . . .
8. A turtle is an animal . . . .
9. A hermit is a person . . . .
10. A pyramid is a structure . . . .

Column B

A. She or he leaves society and lives completely alone.

✓B. It is used to pound nails.

C. It forms when water boils.

D. It is square at the bottom and has four sides that come together in a point at the top.

E. He (or she) designs buildings.

F. It measures air pressure.

G. It can be shaped and hardened to form many useful things.

H. It is difficult to solve.

I. He or she doesn't eat meat.

J. It has a hard shell and can live in water or on land.

★NOTE: In usual usage, one pattern is often favored over another.
   (1) As subject pronouns:
   • **who** is more commonly used than **that** (*A doctor is someone who takes care of sick people*);
   • **that** is more commonly used than **which** (*A pencil is an instrument that is used for writing*).
   (2) Object pronouns are usually omitted.

□ **EXERCISE 9. Adjective clauses. (Charts 12-1 → 12-3)**

Directions: In groups or pairs, provide definitions for the words listed below. Consult your dictionaries if necessary.

Example: A telephone directory is a book . . . .
→ *A telephone directory is a book that lists telephone numbers.*

1. A dictionary is a book . . . .

2. A nurse is someone . . . .

3. Birds are creatures . . . .

4. A key is a piece of metal . . . .

5. A prisoner is a person . . . .

6. A giraffe is an animal . . . .

7. Photographers are people . . . .

8. A hero is a person . . . .

9. An adjective is a word . . . .

10. A friend is a person . . . .

□ **EXERCISE 10. Object pronouns in adjective clauses. (Charts 12-3 and 12-4)**

Directions: Cross out the incorrect pronouns in the adjective clauses.

1. The books I bought ~~them~~ at the bookstore were expensive.

2. I like the shirt you wore ~~it~~ to class yesterday.

3. Amanda Jones is a person I would like you to meet ~~her~~.

4. The apartment we wanted to rent ~~it~~ had two bedrooms.

5. My wife and I are really enjoying the TV set that we bought ~~it~~ for ourselves last week.

6. The woman you met ~~her~~ at Aunt Martha's house is a pharmacist.

7. Anna has a cat that ~~it~~ likes to catch birds.

8. The birds that Anna's cat catches ~~them~~ are very frightened.

9. Yesterday, Anna rescued a bird that the cat had brought ~~it~~ into the house. When she set it free, it flew away quickly.

□ EXERCISE 11. Adjective clauses with WHO, WHO(M), WHICH, THAT, and Ø.
   (Charts 12-3 and 12-4)
   Directions: Write the pronouns that can be used to connect the adjective clauses to the main clause: **who, who(m), which,** or **that.** Also write **Ø** if the pronoun can be omitted.

Example: The manager 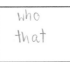 fired Tom is a difficult person to work for.

1. The box 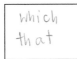 I mailed to my sister was heavy.

2. The people sat in the stadium cheered for the home team.

3. The calendar 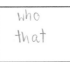 hangs in Paul's office has pictures of wildlife.

4. The teenagers counted the money they earned at the car wash.

5. The people my brother called didn't answer their phone.

6. The tree branch was lying in the street was a hazard to motorists.

□ EXERCISE 12. Identifying adjective clauses. (Charts 12-3 and 12-4)
   Directions: <u>Underline</u> the adjective clause. Circle the noun it modifies.

1. I lost the (scarf) <u>I borrowed from my roommate.</u>

2. The (food) <u>we ate at the sidewalk cafe</u> was delicious.

3. A storekeeper is a (person) <u>who owns or operates a store.</u>

4. The (bus) <u>I take to school every morning</u> is usually very crowded.

5. (Pizza) <u>that is sold by the piece</u> is a popular lunch in many cities and towns throughout
   the world.

6. Two hundred years ago, people on ships and in coastal towns greatly feared the (pirates) who sailed the South China Sea and the Gulf of Thailand.

correct 7. The earth receives less than one-billionth of the enormous amount of heat the sun produces. The rest of the sun's energy disappears into outer space.

8. Piranhas are (dangerous fish) that can tear the flesh off an animal as large as a horse in a few minutes.

9. The heart of education is in a culture's literature. (People) who read gain not only knowledge but also pleasure. A (person) who does not read is no better off than a person who cannot read.

10. Cedar waxwings are gray-brown birds that live in most parts of North America. If you see a (crested bird) that is a little larger than a sparrow and has a band of yellow across the end of its tail, it may be a cedar waxwing.

☐ EXERCISE 13. Review: adjective clauses. (Charts 12-1 → 12-4)
Directions: Answer the questions in complete sentences. Use any appropriate pattern of adjective clause. Use *the* with the noun that is modified by the adjective clause.

1. • One phone wasn't ringing.
   • The other phone was ringing.
   QUESTION: Which phone did Sam answer?
   → *Sam answered* **the** *phone that was ringing.*
   QUESTION: Which phone didn't he answer?
   → *He didn't answer* **the** *phone that wasn't ringing.*

2. • We ate some food from our garden.
   • We ate some food at a restaurant.
   QUESTION: Which food was expensive?
   → ***The*** *food we ate . . . .*
   QUESTION: Which food wasn't expensive?

3. • One student raised her hand in class.
   • Another student sat quietly in his seat.
   QUESTIONS: One of them asked the teacher a question. Which one?
   Which one didn't ask the teacher a question?

4. • One girl won the foot race.
   • The other girl lost the foot race.

   QUESTIONS: Which girl is happy? Which girl isn't happy?

5. • One man was sleeping.
   • Another man was listening to the radio.

   QUESTIONS: One of the men heard the news bulletin about the earthquake in China. Which one did? Which one didn't?

6. • One person bought a *(make of car)*.
   • Another person bought a *(make of car)*.

   QUESTION: Which person probably spent more money than the other?

7. • Amanda bought some canned vegetables at a supermarket.
   • Tom picked some fresh vegetables from his grandfather's garden.

   QUESTION: Which vegetables probably tasted fresher than the others?

8. • One young musician practiced hours and hours every day.
   • The other young musician had a regular job and practiced only in the evenings and on the weekends.

   QUESTIONS: Which musician showed a great deal of improvement during the course of a year? Which one didn't show as much improvement?

9. • One city provides clean water and a modern sewer system for its citizens.
   • Another city uses its rivers and streams as both a source of water and a sewer.

   QUESTIONS: Which city has a high death rate from infectious diseases such as typhoid and cholera? Which one doesn't?

12-5 SINGULAR AND PLURAL VERBS IN ADJECTIVE CLAUSES

(a) I know the **man** *who **is** sitting over there.*	In (a): The verb in the adjective clause *(is)* is singular because ***who*** refers to a singular noun, *man.*
(b) I know the **people** *who **are** sitting over there.*	In (b): The verb in the adjective clause *(are)* is plural because ***who*** refers to a plural noun, *people.*

□ EXERCISE 14. Subject–verb agreement in adjective clauses. (Chart 12-5)
   Directions: Circle the correct word in parentheses. <u>Underline</u> the noun that determines whether the verb should be singular or plural.

1. A saw is a <u>tool</u> that *((is,) are)* used to cut wood.

2. Hammers are <u>tools</u> that *(is, (are))* used to pound nails.

3. I recently met a <u>woman</u> who *(live, (lives))* in Montreal.

4. Most of the <u>people</u> who *((live,) lives)* in Montreal speak French as their first language.

5. I have a <u>cousin</u> who *((works,) work)* as a coal miner.

6. Some coal <u>miners</u> who *(works, (work))* underground suffer from lung disease.

7. A professional <u>athlete</u> who *(play, (plays))* tennis is called a tennis pro.

8. <u>Professional athletes</u> who *((play,) plays)* tennis for a living can make a lot of money.

9. Biographies are <u>books</u> which *(tells, (tell))* the stories of people's lives.

10. A <u>book</u> that *((tells,) tell)* the story of a person's life is called a biography.

11. I talked to the <u>men</u> who *(was, (were))* sitting near me.

12. The <u>woman</u> that *((was,) were)* sitting in front of me at the movie was wearing a big hat.

12-6 USING PREPOSITIONS IN ADJECTIVE CLAUSES

			PREP	**Obj.**		*Whom*, *which*, and *that* can be used as the object of a preposition in an adjective clause.
(a) The man was helpful.		I talked	*to*	*him*.		REMINDER: An object pronoun can be omitted from an adjective clause, as in (d) and (i).

		Obj.	**PREP**	
(b) The man		*whom*	*I talked to*	was helpful.
(c) The man		*that*	*I talked to*	was helpful.
(d) The man		Ø	*I talked to*	was helpful.
	PREP	**Obj.**		
(e) The man	*to*	*whom*	*I talked*	was helpful.

In very formal English, a preposition comes at the beginning of an adjective clause, as in (e) and (j). The preposition is followed by either *whom* or *which* (not *that* or *who*), and the pronoun CANNOT be omitted.

(b), (c), (d), and (e) have the same meaning.

			PREP	**Obj.**
(f) The chair is hard.		I am sitting	*in*	*it*.

	Obj.		**PREP**	
(g) The chair	*which*	*I am sitting*	*in*	is hard.
(h) The chair	*that*	*I am sitting*	*in*	is hard.
(i) The chair	Ø	*I am sitting*	*in*	is hard.
	PREP	**Obj.**		
(j) The chair	*in*	*which*	*I am sitting*	is hard.

(g), (h), (i), and (j) have the same meaning.

☐ **EXERCISE 15. Prepositions in adjective clauses. (Chart 12-6)**

Directions: Combine the two sentences in each pair. Use "b" as an adjective clause. Give all the possible forms of the adjective clauses, and <u>underline</u> them.

1. a. The movie was interesting.　　b. We went **to** it.
   - → *The movie <u>which we went **to**</u> was interesting.*
   - → *The movie <u>that we went **to**</u> was interesting.*
   - → *The movie <u>Ø we went **to**</u> was interesting.*
   - → *The movie <u>**to** which we went</u> was interesting.*

2. a. The man is over there.　　b. I told you **about** him.

3. a. The woman pays me a fair salary.　　b. I work **for** her.

4. a. Alicia likes the family.　　b. She is living **with** them.

5. a. The picture is beautiful.　　b. Tom is looking **at** it.

6. a. I enjoyed the music.　　b. We listened **to** it after dinner.

Directions: Add an appropriate preposition to each sentence.* Draw parentheses around the adjective clause.

1. I spoke _____to_____ a person. The person (I spoke _____to_____) was friendly.

2. We went _____to_____ a movie. The movie (we went _____to_____) was very good.

3. We stayed _____in_____ a motel. The motel (we stayed _____in_____) was clean and comfortable.

4. We listened _____to_____ a new CD. I enjoyed the new CD (we listened _____to_____).

5. Sally was waiting _____for_____ a person. The person (Sally was waiting _____for_____) never came.

6. I talked _____to_____ a man. The man _____to_____ whom I talked was helpful.

7. I never found the book that (I was looking _____for_____).

8. The bank I borrowed money _____from_____ charges high interest on its loans.

9. The news article we talked _____about_____ in class concerned a peace conference.

10. One of the subjects I've been interested _____in_____ for a long time is global economics.

11. The interviewer wanted to know the name of the college I had graduated _____from_____.

12. Oscar likes the Canadian family _____with_____ whom he is living.

13. The man I was staring _____at_____ started to stare back at me.

14. Organic chemistry is a subject that I'm not familiar _____with_____.

15. My sister and I have the same ideas about almost everything. She is the one person _____to_____ whom I almost always agree.

16. The person _____to_____ whom you speak at the airline counter will ask to see your passport and ticket.

17. What's the name of the person you introduced me _____to_____ at the restaurant last night? I've already forgotten.

18. My father is someone I've always been able to depend _____on_____ when I need advice or help.

19. Look. The sailor you waved _____to_____ is walking toward us. Now what are you going to say?

20. Your building supervisor is the person _____to_____ whom you should complain if you have any problems with your apartment.

_____

*See Appendix 2, p. 463, for a list of preposition combinations.

□ EXERCISE 17. Review: adjective clauses. (Charts 12-1 → 12-6)
Directions: Work in pairs.
Speaker A: Read the cue aloud to your partner.
Speaker B: Combine the sentences, using the second sentence as an adjective clause.
Practice omitting the object pronoun (*whom, which, that*). Look at your book
only if necessary.
Speaker A: If Speaker B's information is correct, respond with "yes" and repeat the
information.

Example:
SPEAKER A: The taxi was expensive. **I** took it to the airport.
SPEAKER B: The taxi **you** took to the airport was expensive.
SPEAKER A: Yes. The taxi **I** took to the airport was expensive.

1. The plane leaves at 7:08 P.M. I'm taking it to Denver.
2. The university is in New York. I want to go to it.
3. I met the people. You told me about them.
4. The bananas were too ripe. My husband/wife bought them.
5. The shirt/blouse is made of cotton. The teacher is wearing it.
6. The market has fresh vegetables. I usually go to it.

Switch roles.
7. I couldn't understand the woman. I talked to her on the phone.
8. The scrambled eggs were cold. I had them for breakfast at the cafeteria.
9. I had a good time on the trip. I took it to Hawaii.
10. The doctor prescribed some medicine for my sore throat. I went to him yesterday.
11. The cream was spoiled. I put it in my coffee.
12. The fast-forward button on the tape recorder doesn't work. I bought it last month.
13. I'm going to call about the want ad. I saw it in last night's paper.

□ EXERCISE 18. Review: adjective clauses. (Charts 12-1 → 12-6)
Directions: <u>Underline</u> the adjective clauses in the following passages. Circle the nouns that
the adjective clauses modify.

1. Frogs are small, tailless (animals) <u>that live near water</u>.

2. Flowers that bloom year after year are called perennials. Flowers that bloom only one
season are called annuals.

3. Flamingos are large pink birds that have long legs and curved bills.

4. A fossil is the remains of an animal or plant that lived in the past.

5. A: Who's that boy?

   B: Which boy? Are you talking about the boy who's wearing the striped shirt or the boy who has on the T-shirt?

   A: I'm not talking about either one of them. I'm talking about the boy who just waved at us. Look. Over there. Do you see the kid that has the red baseball cap?

   B: Sure. I know him. That's Al Jordan's kid. His name is Josh or Jake or Jason. Nice kid. Did you wave back?

6. Hiroki is from Japan. When he was sixteen, he spent four months in South America. He stayed with a family who lived near Quito, Ecuador. Their way of life was very different from his. At first, many of the things they did and said seemed strange to Hiroki: their eating customs, political views, ways of expressing emotion, work habits, sense of humor, and more. He felt homesick for people who were like him in their customs and habits.

   As time went on, Hiroki began to appreciate the way of life that his host family followed. Many of the things he did with his host family began to feel natural to him. He developed a strong bond of friendship with them. At the beginning of his stay in Ecuador, he had noticed only the things that were different between his host family and himself. At the end, he appreciated the many things they had in common as human beings despite their differences in cultural background.

7. Many of the problems that exist today have existed since the beginning of recorded history. One of these problems is violent conflict between people who come from different geographical areas or cultural backgrounds. One group may distrust and fear another group of people who are different from themselves in language, customs, politics, religion, and/or appearance. These irrational fears are the source of much of the violence that has occurred throughout the history of the world.

12-7 USING *WHOSE* IN ADJECTIVE CLAUSES

(a) The man called the police. **His car** → **whose car** was stolen.	***Whose*** shows possession. In (a): *His car* can be changed to *whose car* to make an adjective clause. In (b): *whose car was stolen* = an adjective clause.
(b) The man ***whose car*** *was stolen* called the police.	
(c) I know a girl. **Her brother** → **whose brother** is a movie star.	In (c): *Her brother* can be changed to *whose brother* to make an adjective clause.
(d) I know a girl ***whose brother*** *is a movie star.*	
(e) The people were friendly. We bought **their house.** → **whose house**	In (e): *Their house* can be changed to *whose house* to make an adjective clause.
(f) The people ***whose house*** *we bought* were friendly.	

*****Whose*** and ***who's*** have the same pronunciation but NOT the same meaning.
Who's = ***who is***: ***Who's*** *(Who is) your teacher?*

□ EXERCISE 19. WHOSE in adjective clauses. (Chart 12-7)
   Directions: Combine the two sentences into one sentence. Make "b" an adjective clause. Use ***whose***.

   SITUATION: You and your friend are at a party. You are telling your friend about the people at the party.

   1. a. There is the man.   b. His car was stolen.
      → *There is the man whose car was stolen.*

   2. a. There is the woman.   b. Her cat died.

   3. a. Over there is the man.   b. His daughter is in my English class.

   4. a. Over there is the woman.   b. You met her husband yesterday.

   5. a. There is the professor.   b. I'm taking her course.

   6. a. That is the man.   b. His daughter is an astronaut.

7. a. That is the girl.   b. I borrowed her camera.

8. a. There is the boy.   b. His mother is a famous musician.

9. a. They are the people.   b. We visited their house last month.

10. a. That is the couple.   b. Their apartment was burglarized.

☐ EXERCISE 20. WHOSE in adjective clauses. (Chart 12-7)
Directions: Work in pairs.
Speaker A: Read the cue aloud.
Speaker B: Combine the sentences. Use **whose**. Look at your book only if necessary.
Speaker A: If Speaker B's information is correct, say "yes" and repeat the sentence.

Example:
SPEAKER A: The people were very kind. **I** stayed at their house.
SPEAKER B: The people whose house **you** stayed at were very kind.
SPEAKER A: Yes, the people whose house **I** stayed at were very kind.

1. The man called the police. His car was stolen.
2. The woman was sad. Her cat died.
3. The man is friendly. His daughter is in my English class.
4. The professor gives hard tests. I'm taking her course.
5. The man is very proud. His daughter is an astronaut.
6. The girl is a good friend of mine. I borrowed her camera.
7. The people were very nice. I visited their house.

Switch roles.
8. I have a friend. Her brother is a police officer.
9. I have a neighbor. His dog barks all day long.
10. I like the people. We went to their house.
11. I thanked the woman. I borrowed her dictionary.
12. The woman shouted "Stop! Thief!" Her purse was stolen.
13. The man is famous. His picture is in the newspaper.
14. I know a girl. Her family never eats dinner together.

☐ EXERCISE 21. Review: adjective clauses. (Chapter 12)
Directions: Which of the following can be used in the blanks: **who, who(m), which, that, whose,** and/or **Ø**?

1. The people _____ who / that _____ moved into town are Italian.

2. The lamp _____ which / that / ø _____ I bought downtown is beautiful but quite expensive.

3. Everyone ___ who | that _____ came to the audition got a part in the play.

4. Ms. Laura Rice is the teacher _____*whose*_____ class I enjoy most.

5. Flowers _____*which , that*_____ grow in tropical climates usually have vibrant colors.

6. The man _____*whom , that , ∅*_____ I found in the doorway had collapsed from exhaustion.

7. I like the people with _____*whom*_____ I work.

8. I have a friend _____*whose*_____ father is a famous artist.

9. The camera _____*which , that*_____ I bought has a zoom lens.

10. Students _____*who , that*_____ have part-time jobs have to budget their time very carefully.

11. The person to _____*whom*_____ you should send your application is the Director of Admissions.

12. Flying squirrels _____*that*_____ live in tropical rainforests stay in the trees their entire lives without ever touching the ground.

13. The people _____*whose*_____ window I broke got really angry.

14. Monkeys will eat eggs, grass, fruit, birds, snakes, insects, nuts, flowers, leaves, and frogs. Monkeys will eat almost anything _____ they can find.

15. A: A magazine _____ I read at the doctor's office had an article _____ you ought to read. It's about the importance of exercise in dealing with stress.

B: Why do you think I should read an article _____ deals with exercise and stress?

A: If you stop and think for a minute, you can answer that question yourself. You're under a lot of stress, and you don't get any exercise.

B: The stress _____ I have at work doesn't bother me. It's just a normal part of my job. And I don't have time to exercise.

A: Well, you should make time. Anyone _____ job is as stressful as yours should make physical exercise part of their daily routine.

☐ EXERCISE 22. Written: adjective clauses. (Chapter 12)
Directions: Imagine that you are in a room full of people. You know everyone who is there. I (your reader) know no one. Tell me who these people are. Write your description of these people. Practice using adjective clauses.

Begin your composition with: *I'm glad you came to the party. Let me tell you about the people who are here. The woman who . . . .*

☐ EXERCISE 23. Review: adjective clauses. (Chapter 12)
Directions: Work in pairs, in groups, or as a class.
Speaker A: Write the main sentence on the board or on a piece of paper for Speaker B to refer to. Give the cue.
Speaker B: Use Speaker A's information to add an adjective clause to the main sentence.

PART I. MAIN SENTENCE: **The man was nice.**

Example:
SPEAKER A: **I** met him yesterday.
SPEAKER B: The man (whom/that/Ø) **you** met yesterday was nice.

1. He helped me yesterday.
2. I spoke to him on the phone.
3. I called him.
4. He answered the phone.
5. I introduced you to him.
6. I had dinner with him last week.
7. He opened the door for me.
8. I told you about him.

9. (. . .) went to a movie with him last night.
10. He gave me directions to the post office.
11. (. . .) roomed with him.
12. He visited our class yesterday.
13. We visited his house.
14. He helped us at the hardware store.
15. I borrowed his pen.
16. I met him at the party last night.

PART II. MAIN SENTENCE: **Do you know the woman?**

Example:

SPEAKER A: She is standing over there.

SPEAKER B: Do you know the woman who/that is standing over there?

1. (. . .) is talking to her.
2. Her car was stolen.
3. (. . .) is going to marry her.
4. (. . .) is talking about her.
5. She is waving at us.

6. Her apartment was burglarized.
7. She works in that office.
8. She is sitting over there.
9. My brother is engaged to her.
10. Her son was arrested by the police.

PART III. MAIN SENTENCE *(written on the board):* **The movie was good.**

Example:

SPEAKER A: **I** saw it yesterday.

SPEAKER B: The movie which/that **you** saw yesterday was good.

1. I went to it.
2. I watched it on TV last night.
3. (. . .) told me about it.

4. It was playing at *(name of a local theater)*.
5. (. . .) saw it.
6. It starred *(name of an actor/actress)*.

☐ **EXERCISE 24. Review: adjective clauses. (Chapter 12)**

Directions: Use the given information in the list to complete the sentences using adjective clauses. Omit the object pronoun from the adjective clause if possible.

> *Their specialty is heart surgery.*
> ✓*James chose the color of paint for his bedroom walls.*
> *Its mouth was big enough to swallow a whole cow in one gulp.*
> *You drink it.*
> *It erupted in Indonesia recently.*
> *His son was in an accident.*
> *They lived in the jungles of Southeast Asia.*
> *They have been used countless times before in countless ways.*
> *I slept on it in a hotel last night.*

1. The color of paint _____James chose for his bedroom walls_____ was an unusual blue.

2. The man _____ called an ambulance.

3. My back hurts today. The mattress _____ was too soft.

4. A volcano _____ killed six people and damaged large areas of rice, coconut, and clove crops.

5. Doctors and nurses _____

   are some of the best-trained medical personnel in the world.

6. Early human beings hunted animals for food, including chickens. Originally, chickens

   were wild birds _____. At

   some point in time, humans learned how to domesticate them and raise them for food.

7. In prehistoric times, there was a dinosaur _____

   _____.

8. Every glass of water _____ has molecules

   _____.

☐ EXERCISE 25. Review: adjective clauses. (Chapter 12)
   Directions: <u>Underline</u> the adjective clauses in the following passage. Circle the noun that
   each adjective clause modifies. Work in pairs or groups.
       There are ten adjective clauses in the passage (including the one in the first
   sentence). Can your team find all of them?

   (1) Parents are (people) <u>who provide love, care, and education for children</u>. Parents

   may be defined as the principal people who raise a child. These people may or may not

   have physically produced the child. Many children are brought up by relatives or other

   caring adults when their biological parents, through death, disability, or uncontrollable

   circumstances, are not present to care for them. The role of any parents,

   biological or not, is to take care of their children's emotional, physical,

   and social needs.

   (2) Children need love and affection to grow strong emotionally. It

   is important for all children to have at least one adult with whom they

   can form a loving, trusting relationship. A strong bond with adults is

   essential from birth through adolescence. For example, babies who are

   not picked up frequently and held lovingly may have slow physical and mental growth even

   though they receive adequate food and exercise. Youngsters who are raised in an

   institution without bonding with an older person who functions as a parent often have

   difficulty forming trusting relationships when they are adults.

(3) In addition to love, children need physical care. Babies are completely dependent upon adults for food, shelter, and safety. Children who are denied such basics in their early lives may suffer chronic health problems and feelings of insecurity throughout their lifetimes. One of the greatest responsibilities that parents have is to provide for the physical well-being of their children.

(4) Children's education is also the responsibility of the parents. Girls and boys must learn to speak, dress themselves, eat properly, and get along with others. They must learn not to touch fire, to look carefully before they cross the street, and not to use violence to solve problems. The lessons that parents teach their children are numerous. As children get older and enter school, teachers join parents in providing the education that young people need in order to become independent, productive members of society.

☐ EXERCISE 26. Adjective clauses. (Chapter 12)
Directions: <u>Underline</u> the adjective clause and complete each sentence with your own words.

1. One of the things <u>I like best</u>   is* hot and spicy food. _____

2. One of the places I want to visit someday _____

3. One of the people I admire most in the world _____

4. Some of the cities I would like to visit   are* _____

5. Some of the places I hope to visit someday _____

6. One of the cities I would like to visit while I'm in this country _____

7. One of the programs my roommate likes to watch on TV _____

8. One of the subjects I would like to know more about _____

9. Some of the things I like most in life _____

10. One of the best books I've ever read _____

11. One of the hardest classes I've ever taken _____

12. One of the most fascinating people I've ever met _____

_____

One of the + *plural noun* (+ *adjective clause*) + **singular** *verb*.
 Some of the + *plural noun* (+ *adjective clause*) + **plural** *verb*.

☐ EXERCISE 27. Written: adjective clauses. (Chapter 12)
Directions: Complete the sentences with your own words.

1. My friend told me about a man who . . . .
2. I have a friend whose . . . .
3. I returned the book that . . . .
4. The person who . . . .
5. The people I . . . .
6. The movie we . . . .
7. The people whose . . . .
8. Do you know the woman that . . . ?
9. The book I . . . .
10. The person to whom . . . .
11. One of the places I . . . .
12. Some of the things I . . . .

☐ EXERCISE 28. Error analysis: adjective clauses. (Chapter 12)
Directions: Correct the mistakes.

1. The book that I bought ɪ̷t at the bookstore was very expensive.

2. The woman was nice that I met yesterday.

3. The people which live next to me are friendly.

4. I met a woman who her husband is a famous lawyer.

5. Do you know the people who lives in that house?

6. The professor teaches Chemistry 101 is very good.

7. I wrote a thank-you note to the people who I visited their house on Thanksgiving Day.

8. The people who I met them at the party last night were interesting.

9. I enjoyed the music that we listened to it.

10. The man was very angry who's bicycle was stolen.

11. A clock is an instrument measures time.

12. The apple tree is producing fruit that we planted it last year.

13. Before I came here, I don't have the opportunity to speak to people who their native

    tongue is English.

14. One of the thing I need to get a new alarm clock.

15. The people who was waiting in line for tickets to the game they were happy and

excited because their team had made it to the championship series.

☐ EXERCISE 29. Adjective clauses. (Chapter 12)
Directions: Discuss one or more of the following topics in groups or as a class. Practice using adjective clauses in your sentences as much as possible (but not every sentence needs to have an adjective clause).

Example:
SPEAKER A: What are the qualities of a friend?
SPEAKER B: A friend is someone you can depend on in times of trouble.
SPEAKER C: A friend is a person who accepts you as you are.
SPEAKER D: Friends don't talk about you behind your back.
SPEAKER E: I agree. A friend is someone you can trust with secrets.
SPEAKER F: Etc.

1. What is your idea of the ideal roommate?
   (Suggested beginning: *An ideal roommate is someone who . . . .*)

2. What kind of people make good leaders?
   (Good leaders are people who . . . .)

3. What are the qualities of a good neighbor?
   (A good neighbor is a person who . . . .)

4. What kind of people make good parents?
   (People who . . . .)

5. What is your idea of the ideal classroom?
   (Students need a classroom that . . . .)

6. What are the qualities of a good boss and a bad boss?
   (A good boss is someone who . . . , but a bad boss . . . .)

☐ EXERCISE 30. Adjective clauses. (Chapter 12)
Directions: Write a few sentences on one (or more) of the topics in Exercise 29 and/or the following topics. Practice using adjective clauses in some of your sentences.

Additional topics:
1. The qualities of the ideal wife/husband.
2. The qualities of the ideal apartment.
3. The qualities of a good student.
4. The qualities of a good teacher.
5. The qualities of a good novel.

CHAPTER *13*
Gerunds and Infinitives

13-1 VERB + GERUND

	verb gerund	A gerund is the *-ing* form of a verb. It is used as a noun. In (a): *walking* is a gerund. It is used as the object of the verb *enjoy*.
(a) I	*enjoy* *walking* in the park.	

COMMON VERBS FOLLOWED BY GERUNDS			The verbs in the list are followed by gerunds. The list also contains phrasal verbs (e.g., *put off*) that are followed by gerunds.
enjoy	(b)	I *enjoy working* in my garden.	
finish	(c)	Ann *finished studying* at midnight.	The verbs in the list are NOT followed by *to* + *the simple form of a verb* (an infinitive).
stop	(d)	It *stopped raining* a few minutes ago.	INCORRECT: *I enjoy to walk in the park.*
quit	(e)	David *quit smoking*.	INCORRECT: *Bob finished to study.*
mind	(f)	Would you *mind opening* the window?	INCORRECT: *I'm thinking to go to*
postpone	(g)	I *postponed doing* my homework.	*Hawaii.*
put off	(h)	I *put off doing* my homework.	See Chart 2-5, p. 29, for the spelling of *-ing* verb forms.
keep (on)	(i)	*Keep (on) working.* Don't stop.	
consider	(j)	I'm *considering going* to Hawaii.	
think about	(k)	I'm *thinking about going* to Hawaii.	
discuss	(l)	They *discussed getting* a new car.	
talk about	(m)	They *talked about getting* a new car.	

(n) I *considered not going* to class.	Negative form: *not* + *gerund*

☐ EXERCISE 1. Verb + gerund. (Chart 13-1)

Directions: Complete the sentences by using gerunds. Add a preposition after the gerund if necessary.

1. It was cold and rainy yesterday, so we postponed ___going to / visiting___ the zoo.

2. The Porters' house is too small. They're considering ___buying/ moving___ ___into /renting___ a bigger house.

3. We discussed _____ Colorado for our vacation.

4. When Martha finished _____ the floor, she dusted the furniture.

5. Sometimes students put off _____ their homework.

6. We had a blizzard yesterday, but it finally stopped _____ around 10:00 P.M.

7. I quit _____ comic books when I was twelve years old.

8. I'm thinking about _____ a biology course next semester.

9. Beth doesn't like her job. She's talking about _____ a different job.

10. I enjoy _____ sports.

11. I'm considering _____ New York City.

12. A: Are you listening to me?
    B: Yes. Keep _____ . I'm listening.

13. A: Do you want to take a break?
    B: No. I'm not tired yet. Let's keep on _____ for another hour or so.

14. A: Would you mind _____ the window?
    B: Not at all. I'd be glad to.

15. A: I'm thinking about not _____ the meeting tomorrow.
    B: Really? Why? I hope you decide to go. We need your input.

□ **EXERCISE 2. Verb + gerund. (Chart 13-1)**

Directions: Complete the sentences in the dialogues. Use the expressions in the list or your own words. Be sure to use a gerund in each sentence.

buy a new car	✓rain
do my homework	read a good book
do things	repeat that
get a Toyota	smoke
go to the zoo on Saturday	tap your fingernails on the table
help him	try

1. A: Would you like to go for a walk?

   B: Has it stopped _____ *raining** _____ ?

   A: Yes.

   B: Let's go.

2. A: I've been having a lot of trouble with my old Volkswagen the last couple of months. It's slowly falling apart. I'm thinking about _____ .

   B: Do you think you'll get another Volkswagen?

   A: No. I'm considering _____ .

3. A: What do you usually do in your free time in the evening?

   B: I enjoy _____ .

4. A: Good news! I feel great. I don't cough any more, and I don't run out of breath when I walk up a hill.

   B: Oh?

   A: I quit _____ .

   B: That's wonderful!

5. A: I've been working on this math problem for the last half hour, and I still don't understand it.

   B: Well, don't give up. Keep _____ . If at first you don't succeed, try, try again.

---

*The object following **stop** is a gerund, NOT an infinitive. *INCORRECT: It stopped to rain.* But in special circumstances, **stop** can be followed by an infinitive of purpose: *in order to* (see Chart 13-9, p. 391). *While I was walking down the hall, I dropped my pen. **I stopped to pick** it up. = I stopped walking in order to pick it up.*

6. A: Are you a procrastinator?

   B: A what?

   A: A procrastinator. That's someone who always postpones _____

      _____ .

   B: Oh. Well, sometimes I put off _____ .

7. A: What are you doing?

   B: I'm helping Teddy with his homework.

   A: When you finish _____ , could you help me in the

      kitchen?

   B: Sure.

8. A: Could you please stop doing that?

   B: Doing what?

   A: Stop _____ . It's driving me crazy!

9. A: Do you have any plans for this weekend?

   B: Henry and I talked about _____ .

10. A: I didn't understand what you said. Would you mind _____

      _____ ?

    B: Of course not. I said, "Three free trees."

☐ **EXERCISE 3. Verb + gerund. (Chart 13-1)**
   Directions: Complete the sentences in Column A by using a verb from Column B and your own words. Use the verbs in Column B only once.

   Example: I often postpone + write
   → *I often postpone writing thank you notes, and then I have to apologize for sending them late.*

Column A	Column B	
1. I often postpone	buy	listen
2. I enjoy	close	love
3. I'm considering	do	make
4. Would you mind	eat	open
5. I finished	exercise	play
6. I'll never stop	finish	take
7. Do you ever think about	give	teach
8. You should keep	go	try
9. Sometimes I put off	help	visit
	learn	watch
	leave	✓write

13-2   GO + -ING

(a) **Did** you **go shopping** yesterday? (b) I **went swimming** last week. (c) Bob **hasn't gone fishing** in years.	**Go** is followed by a gerund in certain idiomatic expressions about activities. Notice: There is no **to** between **go** and the gerund. INCORRECT: *Did you go to shopping?*

COMMON EXPRESSIONS WITH *GO* + *-ING*

go boating	go dancing	go jogging	go (window) shopping	go (water) skiing
go bowling	go fishing	go running	go sightseeing	go skydiving
go camping	go hiking	go sailing	go (ice) skating	go swimming

☐ **EXERCISE 4. GO + -ING. (Chart 13-2)**

   Directions: Answer the questions. Use the expressions with **go** + **-ing** listed in Chart 13-2.

   1. Ann often goes to the beach. She spends hours in the water. What does she like to do?
      → *She likes to go swimming.*
   2. Nancy and Frank like to spend the whole day on a lake with poles in their hands. What do they like to do?
   3. Last summer Adam went to a national park. He slept in a tent and cooked his food over a fire. What did Adam do last summer?
   4. Tim likes to go to stores and buy things. What does he like to do?
   5. Laura takes good care of her health. She runs a couple of miles every day. What does Laura do every day? (*NOTE: There are two possible responses.*)
   6. On weekends in the winter, Fred and Jean sometimes drive to a resort in the mountains. They like to race down the side of a mountain in the snow. What do they like to do?

7. Joe likes to take long walks in the woods. What does Joe like to do?

8. Sara prefers indoor sports. She goes to a place where she rolls a thirteen-pound ball at some wooden pins. What does Sara often do?

9. Liz and Greg know all the latest dances. What do they probably do a lot?

10. The Taylors are going to go to a little lake near their house tomorrow. The lake is completely frozen now that it's winter. The ice is smooth. What are the Taylors **going** to do tomorrow?

11. Alex and Barbara live near the ocean. When there's a strong wind, they like to spend the whole day in their sailboat. What do they like to do?

12. Tourists often get on buses that take them to see interesting places in an area. What do tourists do on buses?

13. Colette and Ben like to jump out of airplanes. They don't open their parachutes until the last minute. What do they like to do?

14. What do you like to do for exercise and fun?

13-3 VERB + INFINITIVE

(a) Tom **offered to lend** me some money. (b) I've **decided to buy** a new car.	Some verbs are followed by an infinitive: AN INFINITIVE = **to** + *the simple form of a verb.*
(c) I've **decided not to keep** my old car.	Negative form: **not** + *infinitive.*

COMMON VERBS FOLLOWED BY INFINITIVES

want	*hope*	*decide*	*seem*	*learn (how)*
need	*expect*	*promise*	*appear*	*try*
would like	*plan*	*offer*	*pretend*	
would love	*intend*	*agree*		*(can't) afford*
	mean	*refuse*	*forget*	*(can't) wait*

☐ **EXERCISE 5. Verb + infinitive. (Chart 13-3)**

Directions: Complete the sentences by using infinitives. Add a preposition after the infinitive if necessary.

1. I'm planning ___*to go to / to visit / to fly to*___ Chicago next week.

2. I've decided _____ a new apartment.

3. Jack promised not _____ late for the wedding.

4. I forgot _____ some rice when I went to the grocery store.

5. I would like _____ the Grand Canyon.

6. My husband and I would love _____ Arizona.

7. I need _____ my homework tonight.

8. What time do you expect _____ Chicago?

9. I want _____ a ball game on TV after dinner tonight.

10. You seem _____ in a good mood today.

11. Susie appeared _____ asleep, but she wasn't. She was only pretending.

12. Susie pretended _____ asleep. She pretended not _____
when I spoke to her.

13. The Millers can't afford _____ a house.

14. George is only seven, but he intends _____ a doctor when he grows up.

15. My friend offered _____ me a little money.

16. Tommy doesn't like peas. He refuses _____ them.

17. My wife and I wanted to do different things this weekend. Finally, I agreed
_____ a movie with her Saturday, and she agreed _____
the football game with me on Sunday.

18. I hope _____ all of my courses this term. So far my grades have
been pretty good.

19. I try _____ class on time every day.

20. I can't wait _____ my family again! It's been a long time!

21. I'm sorry. I didn't mean _____ you.

22. I learned (how) _____ when I was around six or
seven.

13-4 VERB + GERUND OR INFINITIVE

(a) It *began* **raining**. (b) It *began* **to rain**.	Some verbs are followed by either a gerund or an infinitive. Usually there is no difference in meaning. (a) and (b) have the same meaning.

COMMON VERBS FOLLOWED BY EITHER A GERUND OR AN INFINITIVE		
begin	*like★*	*hate*
start	*love★*	*can't stand*
continue		

★COMPARE: ***Like*** and ***love*** can be followed by either a gerund or an infinitive:
  I like going/to go to movies. I love playing/to play chess.
  Would like and ***would love*** are followed by infinitives:
  I would like ***to go*** *to a movie tonight. I'd love* ***to play*** *a game of chess right now.*

□ EXERCISE 6. Verb + gerund or infinitive. (Charts 13-3 and 13-4)
    Directions: Use the given words to create sentences with gerunds and infinitives.

    1. start + snow around midnight
        → *It started snowing around midnight. It started to snow around midnight.*
    2. continue + work even though everyone else stopped
    3. like + get a lot of e-mails from my friends
    4. love + go to baseball games
    5. hate + talk to pushy salespeople
    6. can't stand + wait in lines for a long time

□ EXERCISE 7. Verb + gerund or infinitive. (Charts 13-3 and 13-4)
    Directions: Discuss what you like and don't like to do. Use the given ideas to make sentences that begin with words from this list.

I like	*I don't like*	*I don't mind*
I love	*I hate*	
I enjoy	*I can't stand*	

    1. cook
        → *I like to cook / I like cooking / I hate to cook / I hate cooking / I don't mind cooking / I don't enjoy cooking, etc.*
    2. live in this city
    3. wash dishes
    4. fly
    5. wait in airports
    6. read novels in my spare time
    7. eat a delicious meal slowly
    8. speak in front of a large group
    9. play cards for money
    10. drive on city streets during rush hour
    11. go to parties where I don't know a single person
    12. listen to the sounds of the city while I'm trying to get to sleep
    13. visit with friends I haven't seen in a long time
    14. get in between two friends who are having an argument
    15. travel to strange and exotic places

□ EXERCISE 8. Gerunds vs. infinitives. (Charts 13-1 → 13-4)
    Directions: Complete the sentences with the infinitive or gerund form of the words in parentheses.

    1. I need *(study)* _____to study_____ tonight.

    2. I enjoy *(cook)* _____cooking_____ fancy meals.

3. Ellen started *(talk)* __to talk / talking__ about her problem.

4. Bud and Sally have decided *(get)* _____ married.

5. We finished *(eat)* _____ around seven.

6. I like *(meet)* _____ new people.

7. My roommate offered *(help)* _____ me with my English.

8. I'd just begun *(watch)* _____ a movie on TV when the phone rang.

9. Please stop *(crack)* _____ your knuckles!

10. Did you remember *(feed)* _____ the cat this morning?

11. I won't be late. I promise *(be)* _____ on time.

12. I'm considering *(move)* _____ to a new apartment.

13. Some children hate *(go)* _____ to school.

14. I forgot *(lock)* _____ the door when I left my apartment this morning.

15. I don't mind *(live)* _____ with four roommates.

16. Shhh. My roommate is trying *(take)* _____ a nap.

17. My boss refused *(give)* _____ me a raise, so I quit.

18. The company will continue *(hire)* _____ new employees as long as new production orders keep *(come)* _____ in.

19. That's not what I meant! I meant *(say)* _____ just the opposite.

20. I want *(go)* _____ *(shop)* _____ this afternoon.

21. Alex seems *(want)* _____ *(go)* _____ *(sail)* _____ this weekend.

22. My wife can't stand *(sleep)* _____ in a room with all of the windows closed.

23. Sam's tomato crop always failed. Finally he quit *(try)* _____ *(grow)* _____ tomatoes in his garden.

24. I enjoy *(be)* _____ a teacher.

□ **EXERCISE 9. Gerunds vs. infinitives. (Charts 13-1 → 13-4)**

Directions: Work in pairs.

Student A: Read the cues. Your book is open.

Student B: Complete the sentences with either **to go** or **going** + *the name of a place.*
Your book is closed.

Example:

STUDENT A *(book open):* I expect . . . .

STUDENT B *(book closed):* to go (to Mack's Bar and Grill for dinner tonight).

STUDENT A *(book open):* I like . . . .

STUDENT B *(book closed):* to go (to Hawaii). OR going (to Hawaii).

	Switch roles.
1. I expect	13. I enjoy . . . .
2. I like	14. I don't need . . . .
3. I would like	15. I'm going to try . . . .
4. I enjoy	16. I hate . . . .
5. I'd love	17. I love . . . .
6. I promised	18. My friend and I discussed . . . .
7. I can't stand	19. I've decided . . . .
8. I intend	20. Sometimes I put off . . . .
9. I am thinking about	21. Yesterday I forgot . . . .
10. Are you considering	22. I can't wait . . . .
11. I've always wanted	23. My friend and I agreed . . . .
12. I can't afford	24. Would you mind . . . .

□ **EXERCISE 10. Gerunds vs. infinitives. (Charts 13-1 → 13-4)**

Directions: Complete the sentences with a form of the words in parentheses.

1. I want *(stay)* _____to stay_____ home tonight.

2. I want *(relax)* _____ tonight.

3. I want *(stay)* _____ home and *(relax)** _____
tonight.

4. I want *(stay)* _____ home, *(relax)* _____ , and
(go) _____ to bed early tonight.

5. I enjoy *(get)* _____ up early in the morning.

6. I enjoy *(watch)* _____ the sunrise.

7. I enjoy *(get)* _____ up early in the morning and *(watch)*
_____ the sunrise.

_____

*When infinitives are connected by **and**, it is not necessary to repeat **to**.

*Example: I need **to stay** home **and** (to) **study** tonight.*

8. I enjoy *(get)* _____ up early in the morning, *(watch)* _____ the sunrise, and *(listen)* _____ to the birds.

9. Mr. and Mrs. Brown are thinking about *(sell)* _____ their old house and *(buy)* _____ a new one.

10. Kathy plans *(move)* _____ to New York City, *(find)* _____ a job, and *(start)* _____ a new life.

11. Have you finished *(paint)* _____ your apartment yet?

12. Steve needs *(go)* _____ to the shopping mall tomorrow and *(buy)* _____ winter clothes.

13. Do you enjoy *(go)* _____ to an expensive restaurant and *(have)* _____ a gourmet dinner?

14. Most nonsmokers can't stand *(be)* _____ in a smoke-filled room.

15. Let's postpone *(go)* _____ abroad until the political situation improves.

16. The children promised *(stop)* _____ *(make)* _____ so much noise.

17. Kevin is thinking about *(quit)* _____ his job and *(go)* _____ back to school.

18. Linda plans *(leave)* _____ for Chicago on Tuesday and *(return)* _____ on Friday.

19. I often put off *(wash)* _____ the dinner dishes until the next morning.

20. Don't forget *(unplug)* _____ the coffee pot, *(turn off)* _____ all the lights, and *(lock)* _____ the door before you leave for work this morning.

21. Sometimes when I'm listening to someone who is speaking English very fast, I nod my head and pretend *(understand)* _____ .

22. After Isabel got a speeding ticket and had to pay a big fine, she decided *(stop)* _____ *(drive)* _____ over the speed limit on interstate highways.

23. I've been trying *(reach)* _____ Carol on the phone for the last three days, but she is never at home. I intend *(keep)* _____ *(try)* _____ until I finally get her.

☐ EXERCISE 11. Gerunds vs. infinitives. (Charts 13-1 → 13-4)

Directions: Create sentences from the given words. Use *I.* Use any tense. Work in pairs, in groups, or as a class.

Example: *want* and *go*
→ *I want to go (to New York City next week).*

1. *plan* and *go*
2. *consider* and *go*
3. *offer* and *lend*
4. *like* and *visit*
5. *enjoy* and *read*
6. *intend* and *get*
7. *decide* and *get*
8. *seem* and *be*
9. *put off* and *write*
10. *forget* and *go*
11. *can't afford* and *buy*
12. *try* and *learn*
13. *need* and *learn*
14. *would love* and *take*
15. *would like* and *go* and *swim*

16. *promise* and *come*
17. *finish* and *study*
18. *would mind* and *help*
19. *hope* and *go*
20. *think about* and *go*
21. *quit* and *try*
22. *expect* and *stay*
23. *stop* and *eat*
24. *refuse* and *lend*
25. *agree* and *lend*
26. *postpone* and *go*
27. *begin* and *study*
28. *continue* and *walk*
29. *talk about* and *go*
30. *keep* and *try* and *improve*

☐ EXERCISE 12. Gerunds vs. infinitives. (Charts 13-1 → 13-4)

Directions: Complete the sentences with the correct form, gerund or infinitive, of the words in parentheses.

A: Have you made any vacation plans?

B: I was hoping *(go)* ____to go____ to an island off the Atlantic coast, but my
   1

wife wanted *(drive)* _____ down the Pacific coast. We've decided
                        2

(compromise) _____ by going to neither coast. We've
                        3

agreed *(find)* _____ a place where both of us want
                        4

(go) _____ .
          5

A: So where are you going?

B: Well, we've been considering *(go)* _____ *(fish)* _____ in
                                            6   7

Canada. We've also discussed *(take)* _____ a train across central and
                                            8

western Canada. We've also been talking about *(rent)* _____ a sailboat
                                                            9

and *(go)* _____ *(sail)* _____ in the Gulf of Mexico.
          10   11

A: Have you ever thought about *(stay)* _____ home and *(relax)*

_____ ?
13

B: That's not a vacation to me. If I stay home during my vacation, I always end up doing

all the chores around the house that I've put off *(do)* _____ for the past
14

year. When I go on a holiday, I like *(visit)* _____ new places and *(do)*
15

_____ new things. I enjoy *(see)* _____ parts of the
16   17

world I've never seen before.

A: What place would you like *(visit)* _____ the most?
18

B: I'd love *(go)* _____ *(camp)* _____ in New Zealand. My
19   20

wife loves *(camp)* _____ in new places too, but I'm afraid she might
21

refuse *(go)* _____ to New Zealand. She doesn't like long plane flights.
22

A: Why don't you just pick a spot on a map? Then call and make a hotel reservation.

B: Neither of us can stand *(spend)* _____ two whole weeks at a
23

luxury hotel. I don't mean *(say)* _____ anything bad about big hotels,
24

but both of us seem *(like)* _____ more adventurous vacations.
25

A: Well, keep *(think)* _____ about it. I'm sure you'll figure out a
26

really great place for your vacation.

B: We'll have to stop *(think)* _____ about it sometime soon and
27

make a decision.

A: I can't wait *(find)* _____ out where you decide *(go)* _____ .
28   29

I'll expect *(hear)* _____ from you when you make a decision. Don't
30

forget *(call)* _____ me.
31

B: Hmmm. Maybe we should go *(ski)* _____ in Switzerland. Or perhaps
32

we could go *(waterski)* _____ on the Nile. Then there's the
33

possibility of going *(hike)* _____ in the Andes. Of course, we'd
34

probably enjoy *(swim)* _____ off the Great Barrier Reef of
35

Australia. And we shouldn't postpone *(explore)* _____ the

Brazilian rainforest much longer. Someday I'd really like *(climb)* _____

to the top of an active volcano and *(look)* _____ inside the crater. Or

maybe we could . . . .

13-5 PREPOSITION + GERUND

(a) Kate *insisted **on coming*** with us.	A preposition is followed by a gerund, not an infinitive.
(b) We're *excited **about going*** to Tahiti.	In (a): The preposition *(on)* is followed by a gerund
(c) I *apologized **for being*** late.	*(coming)*.

COMMON EXPRESSIONS WITH PREPOSITIONS FOLLOWED BY GERUNDS

be afraid **of** (doing something)	forgive (someone) ***for***	plan **on**
apologize **for**	be good **at**	be responsible **for**
believe **in**	insist **on**	stop (someone) ***from***
dream **about**	be interested **in**	thank (someone) ***for***
be excited **about**	look forward **to**	be tired **of**
feel **like**	be nervous **about**	worry **about**/be worried **about**

☐ **EXERCISE 13. Preposition + gerund. (Chart 13-5 and Appendix 2)**
  Directions: Complete the sentences with a preposition and the given words.

  1. I'm looking forward + go to the zoo → *I'm looking forward to going to the zoo.*
  2. Thank you + open the door
  3. I'm worried + be late for the concert
  4. Are you interested + go to the museum with us
  5. I apologized + be late
  6. Are you afraid + fly in small planes
  7. Are you nervous + take your driver's test

8. We're excited   + go to a soccer game
9. Jack insisted   + pay the restaurant bill
10. Annie dreams   + be a horse trainer someday
11. I don't feel   + eat right now
12. Please forgive me   + not call you sooner
13. I'm tired   + live with five roommates
14. I believe   + be honest at all times
15. Let's plan   + meet at the restaurant at six
16. Who's responsible   + clean the classroom
17. The police stopped us   + enter the building
18. Jake's not very good   + cut his own hair

☐ EXERCISE 14. Preposition + gerund. (Chart 13-5 and Appendix 2)

Directions: Work in pairs.

Speaker A: Complete the sentence with a preposition and "doing something."

Speaker B: Ask a question about A's statement. Begin with "What . . ." and end with "doing."

Speaker A: Answer the question in a complete sentence using your own words.

Example: I'm looking forward . . . .

SPEAKER A: I'm looking forward to doing something.

SPEAKER B: What are you looking forward to doing?

SPEAKER A: I'm looking forward to going to a movie tonight.

Switch roles.

1. I'm interested . . . .
2. I'm worried . . . .
3. I thanked my friend . . . .
4. I apologized . . . .
5. I'm afraid . . . .

6. I'm nervous . . . .
7. I'm excited . . . .
8. I feel . . . .
9. I'm planning . . . .
10. I'm tired . . . .

☐ EXERCISE 15. Preposition + gerund. (Chart 13-5 and Appendix 2)

Directions: Using the verbs in parentheses, complete the sentences with prepositions and gerunds.

1. I believe _____in_____ *(tell)* _____telling_____ the truth no matter what.

2. I wish the weather would get better. I'm tired _____of_____ *(be)* _____being_____ inside all the time.

3. I don't go swimming because I'm afraid _____ *(drown)* _____ .

4. Greg is nervous _____ *(meet)* _____ his girlfriend's parents for the first time.

5. I don't know how to thank you _____ (help) _____ me.

6. Are you interested _____ (go) _____ to a bullfight?

7. I just can't get excited _____ (visit) _____ Disneyland for the third time in two years.

8. Why do you constantly worry _____ (please) _____ your parents?

9. Every summer, I look forward _____ (take) _____ a vacation with my family.

10. Do you feel _____ (tell) _____ me why you're so sad?

11. I apologize _____ (lie) _____ , but I was trying to protect you from the truth. Sometimes the truth hurts.

12. Why do you always insist _____ (pay) _____ for everything when we go out for dinner?

13. I want you to know that I'm sorry. I don't know if you can ever forgive me _____ (cause) _____ you so much trouble.

14. I'm not very good _____ (remember) _____ names.

15. I'm not happy in my work. I often dream _____ (quit) _____ my job.

16. How do you stop someone _____ (do) _____ something you know is wrong?

17. I'm too tired to cook, but I hadn't planned _____ (eat) _____ out tonight.

18. Who's responsible _____ (spill) _____ these coffee beans all over the floor?

19. Anna made a lot of big mistakes at work. That's why she was afraid _____ (lose)* _____ her job.

---

*Note that lose is spelled with one "o." The word loose, with two "o"s, is an adjective meaning "not tight." (E.g., My shirt is big and loose.) Pronunciation difference: lose = /luwz/; loose = /luws/.

□ **EXERCISE 16. Preposition + gerund. (Chart 13-5 and Appendix 2)**

Directions: Make up a quiz. Use the given word or phrase + ONE of the suggested verbs in parentheses. Hand your quiz to a classmate to complete. When s/he finishes it, correct the answers.

Example: apologize to (. . .) + (interrupt, be, call)

Quiz item:

You should apologize to Tarik _____ (interrupt)_____ him. OR

I apologized to my friend _____ (be)_____ late. OR

Rosa apologized to me _____ (call)_____ after midnight.

1. thank + (open / help / invite)

2. feel + (go / have / take)

3. worry + (lose / not have / be)

4. insist + (answer / drive / fly)

5. believe + (help / tell / trust)

6. be nervous + (speak / go / get)

7. look forward + (do / stop / skydive)

8. apologize to (. . .) + (sell / give / leave)

9. forgive (. . .) + (lie / take / quit)

10. be excited + (go / hear / move)

13-6 USING *BY* AND *WITH* TO EXPRESS HOW SOMETHING IS DONE

(a) Pat turned off the tape recorder ***by pushing*** the stop button.	***By*** + *a gerund* is used to express how something is done.
(b) Mary goes to work ***by bus***. (c) Andrea stirred her coffee ***with a spoon***.	***By*** or ***with*** followed by a noun is also used to express how something is done.

BY IS USED FOR MEANS OF TRANSPORTATION AND COMMUNICATION

by (air)plane★	*by subway*★★	*by mail*	*by air*
by boat	*by taxi*	*by (tele)phone*	*by land*
by bus	*by train*	*by fax*	*by sea*
by car	*by foot* (OR *on foot*)	*by e-mail*	

OTHERS

by chance	*by mistake*	*by check* (but *in cash*)
by choice	*by hand*★★★	*by credit card*

WITH IS USED FOR INSTRUMENTS OR PARTS OF THE BODY
I cut down the tree *with an ax* (by using an ax).
I swept the floor *with a broom*.
She pointed to a spot on the map *with her finger*.

★*airplane* = American English; *aeroplane* = British English.

★★*by subway* = American English; *by underground, by tube* = British English.

★★★The expression ***by hand*** is usually used to mean that something was made by a person, not by a machine: *This rug was made **by hand**.* (A person, not a machine, made this rug.)

COMPARE: *I touched his shoulder **with my hand**.*

☐ **EXERCISE 17. BY + a gerund. (Chart 13-6)**

Directions: Complete the following by using **by** + a gerund. Use the words in the list or your own words.

eat	smile	wag	wave
drink	stay	wash	✓write
guess	take	watch	

1. Students practice written English ___by writing___ compositions.

2. We clean our clothes _____ them in soap and water.

3. Khalid improved his English _____ a lot of TV.

4. We show other people we are happy _____ .

5. We satisfy our hunger _____ something.

6. We quench our thirst _____ something.

7. I figured out what "quench" means _____ .

8. Alex caught my attention _____ his arms in the air.

9. My dog shows me she is happy _____ her tail.

10. Carmen recovered from her cold _____ in bed and _____ care of herself.

Complete the following with your own words. Use **by** *and gerunds.*

11. You can destroy bacteria in meat _____ it.

12. You can cook an egg _____ it, _____ it, or _____ it.

13. We can improve our English _____ .

14. Each of us, in our own small way, can help conserve the world's natural resources _____ .

15. You can favorably impress a job interviewer _____ .

16. People can improve their health _____ .

17. Parents can help their young children learn to read _____ .

18. We can make the world a better place for future generations _____ .

☐ EXERCISE 18. Using WITH. (Chart 13-6)
Directions: Complete the sentences using **with** and appropriate words from the list.

✓a broom	a pair of scissors	a spoon
a hammer	a saw	a thermometer
a needle and thread	a shovel	

1. I swept the floor _____with a broom_____ .

2. I sewed a button on my shirt _____ .

3. I cut the wood _____ .

4. I took my temperature _____ .

5. I stirred my coffee _____ .

6. I dug a hole in the ground _____ .

7. I nailed two pieces of wood together

   _____ .

8. I cut the paper _____ .

☐ EXERCISE 19. Using BY or WITH. (Chart 13-6)
Directions: Complete the sentences with **by** or **with**.

1. I opened the door _____with_____ a key.

2. I went to Cherryville _____by_____ bus.

3. I dried the dishes _____ a dishtowel.

4. I went from Portland to San Francisco _____ train.

5. Ted drew a straight line _____ a ruler.

6. Is there any way you could touch the ceiling _____ your foot?

7. Some advertisers try to reach target audiences _____ mail.

8. Rebecca tightened the screw in the corner of her eyeglasses _____ her fingernail.

9. I called Bill "Paul" _____ mistake.

10. The fastest way to send a copy of a piece of paper halfway around the world is _____ fax.

11. The chef sliced the partially frozen meat into thin strips _____ a razor-sharp knife.

12. Some people pay their bills _____ computer.

13. Sally protected her eyes from the sun _____ her hand.

14. My grandmother makes tablecloths _____ hand.

13-7 USING GERUNDS AS SUBJECTS; USING *IT* + INFINITIVE

(a) **Riding** horses is fun. (b) **It** is fun **to ride** horses. (c) **Coming** to class on time is important. (d) **It** is important **to come** to class on time.	(a) and (b) have the same meaning. In (a): A gerund *(riding)* is the subject of the sentence.* Notice: The verb *(is)* is singular because a gerund is singular. In (b): The word **it** is used as the subject of the sentence. The word **it** has the same meaning as the infinitive phrase at the end of the sentence: **it** means *to ride horses.*

*It is also correct (but less common) to use an infinitive as the subject of a sentence: *To ride horses is fun.*

☐ EXERCISE 20. Gerunds as subjects. (Chart 13-7)
> *Directions:* Create sentences with the same meaning by using a gerund as the subject.

1. It is important to get daily exercise. → *Getting daily exercise is important.*
2. It isn't hard to make friends.
3. It is easy to cook rice.
4. It is relaxing to take a long walk.
5. Is it difficult to learn a second language?
6. It is wrong to cheat during a test.
7. Is it expensive to live in an apartment?
8. It isn't easy to live in a foreign country.
9. It takes time to make new friends.

☐ EXERCISE 21. IT + infinitive. (Chart 13-7)
> *Directions:* Create sentences with the same meaning by using **it** + an infinitive.

1. Having good friends is important. → *It's important to have good friends.*
2. Playing tennis is fun.
3. Being polite to other people is important.
4. Learning about other cultures is interesting.
5. Walking alone at night in that part of the city is dangerous.
6. Is riding a motorcycle easy?
7. Having a cold isn't much fun.
8. Learning a second language takes a long time.
9. Cooking a soft-boiled egg takes three minutes.

☐ EXERCISE 22. Gerunds as subjects; IT + infinitive. (Chart 13-7)
> *Directions:* Work in pairs.
> Speaker A: Ask the given question. Your book is open.
> Speaker B: Answer the question. Begin with "*It's* . . ." and use an **infinitive**. Your book is closed.
> Speaker A: Respond by saying "*I agree*" followed by a **gerund** subject. (Or, if you wish, say "*I don't agree. I think that* . . ." followed by a gerund subject.)

Example:

SPEAKER A *(book open):*   Which is easier: to make money or to spend money?
SPEAKER B *(book closed):*   It's easier to spend money than (it is) to make money.
SPEAKER A *(book open):*   I agree. Spending money is easier than making money.   OR
                                    I don't agree. I think that making money is easier than spending money.

1. Which is more fun: to study at the library or to go to a movie?
2. Which is more difficult: to write English or to read English?
3. Which is easier: to write English or to speak English?
4. Which is more expensive: to go to a movie or to go to a concert?
5. Which is more interesting: to talk to people or to watch people?

Switch roles.
6. Which is more comfortable: to wear shoes or to go barefoot?
7. Which is more satisfying: to give gifts or to receive them?
8. Which is more dangerous: to ride in a car or to ride in an airplane?
9. Which is more important: to come to class on time or to get an extra hour of sleep in the morning?
10. Which is better: to light one candle or to curse the darkness?

13-8   IT + INFINITIVE: USING *FOR (SOMEONE)*

(a) *You* should study hard. (b) It is important *for you* to study hard. (c) *Mary* should study hard. (d) It is important *for Mary* to study hard. (e) *We* don't have to go to the meeting. (f) It isn't necessary *for us* to go to the meeting. (g) *A dog* can't talk. (h) It is impossible *for a dog* to talk.	(a) and (b) have a similar meaning. Notice the pattern in (b): *it is* + *adjective* + *for (someone)* + *infinitive phrase*

☐ EXERCISE 23. Using FOR (SOMEONE). (Chart 13-8)
   Directions: Use the given information to complete each sentence. Use *for (someone)* and an infinitive phrase in each completion.

1. *Students should do their homework.*

   It's important ____for students to do their homework____.

2. *Teachers should speak clearly.*

   It's important _____.

3. *We don't have to hurry.*

   There's plenty of time. It isn't necessary _____.

4. *A fish can't live out of water for more than a few minutes.*

   It's impossible _____ .

5. *Students have to budget their time carefully.*

   It's necessary _____ .

6. *A child usually can't sit still for a long time.*

   It's difficult _____ .

7. *My family always eats turkey on Thanksgiving Day.*

   It's traditional _____ .

8. *People can take trips to the moon.*

   Will it be possible _____

   within the next fifty years?

9. *I usually can't understand Mr. Alvarez.*

   It's hard _____ . He talks too fast.

10. *The guests usually wait until the hostess begins to eat.*

    At a formal dinner party, it's customary _____ .

    After she takes the first bite, the guests also start to eat.

11. *The bride usually feeds the groom the first piece of*

    wedding cake.

    It's traditional _____

    _____ .

12. *I can understand our teacher.*

    It's easy _____ .

☐ **EXERCISE 24. Gerunds as subjects; IT + infinitive. (Charts 13-7 and 13-8)**

Directions: Create sentences by combining ideas from Column A and Column B. Use gerund subjects or *it* + an infinitive.

Example: Riding a bicycle is easy / dangerous / fun / relaxing.   OR
It's easy / dangerous / fun / relaxing to ride a bicycle.

Column A	Column B
1. ride a bicycle	A. against the law
2. read newspapers	B. boring
3. study grammar	C. dangerous
4. play tennis	D. easy
5. steal cars	E. educational
6. listen to a two-hour speech	F. embarrassing
7. predict the exact time of an earthquake	G. exciting
8. forget someone's name	H. frightening
9. walk alone through a dark forest at night	I. fun
10. go fishing with your friends	J. hard
11. know the meaning of every word in a dictionary	K. important
12. be honest with yourself at all times	L. impossible
13. change a flat tire	M. relaxing
14. visit museums	N. a waste of time
15. log on to the Internet	

☐ **EXERCISE 25. IT + FOR (SOMEONE) + infinitive. (Charts 13-7 and 13-8)**

Directions: Create sentences using *it* + *for (someone)* + an infinitive by combining ideas from Columns A, B, and C. Add your own words if you wish.

Example: difficult
→ *It's difficult for me to be on time for class.*
It's difficult for some people to learn how to swim.
It's difficult for children to understand adults' behavior.

Column A	Column B	Column C
1. difficult	anyone	spend time with friends
2. easy	children	predict the exact time of an earthquake
3. fun	me	change a flat tire
4. important	most people	be on time for class
5. impossible	some people	understand adults' behavior
6. enjoyable	students	obey their parents
7. interesting		observe animals in their wild habitat
8. possible		visit new places
		learn how to swim
		live on the planet Mars

☐ **EXERCISE 26. IT + FOR (SOMEONE) + infinitive. (Charts 13-7 and 13-8)**

Directions: Complete the sentences with your own words.

1. It's easy for . . . to . . . .

2. It's traditional for . . . to . . . .

3. It's impossible for . . . to . . . .

4. It takes *(a length of time)* for . . . to . . . .

5. It's sensible for . . . to . . . .

6. Is it necessary for . . . to . . . ?

7. It's important for . . . to . . . .

8. It's difficult for . . . to . . . .

☐ **EXERCISE 27. IT + TAKE + infinitive. (Charts 5-13 and 13-8)**

Directions: Use your own words to complete the sentences.

Example: It takes . . . hours to . . . .
→ **It takes** *five* **hours to** *fly from Los Angeles to Honolulu.*

Example: It takes a lot of work for . . . to . . . .
→ **It takes a lot of work for** *most small businesses* **to** *succeed.*

1. It takes time for . . . to . . . .

2. It takes a lot of money to . . . .

3. It takes . . . minutes to . . . .

4. How long does it take to . . . ?

5. It will take . . . years for . . . to . . . .

6. It takes patience / courage / skill to . . . .

7. It takes hard work for . . . to . . . .

8. It takes stamina and determination to . . . .

13-9 EXPRESSING PURPOSE WITH *IN ORDER TO* AND *FOR*

—*Why did you go to the post office?* (a) I went to the post office *because I wanted to mail a letter.* (b) I went to the post office ***in order to mail*** *a letter.* (c) I went to the post office ***to mail*** *a letter.*	***In order to*** expresses purpose. It answers the question "Why?" In (c): ***in order*** is frequently omitted. (a), (b), and (c) have the same meaning.
(d) I went to the post office ***for*** *some stamps.* (e) I went to the post office ***to buy*** *some stamps.* INCORRECT: *I went to the post office for to buy some stamps.* INCORRECT: *I went to the post office for buying some stamps.*	***For*** is also used to express purpose, but it is a preposition and is followed by a noun phrase, as in (d).

☐ EXERCISE 28. Using IN ORDER TO. (Chart 13-9)
Directions: Add *in order* to the sentences whenever possible.

1. I went to the bank to cash a check.
   → *I went to the bank in order to cash a check.*

2. I'd like to see that movie.
   → *(No change. The infinitive does not express purpose.)*

3. Sam went to the hospital to visit a friend.

4. I need to go to the bank today.

5. I need to go to the bank today to deposit my paycheck.

6. On my way home from school, I stopped at the drugstore to buy some shampoo.

7. Carmen looked in her dictionary to find the correct spelling of a word.

8. Masako went to the cafeteria to eat lunch.

9. Jack and Linda have decided to get married.

10. Pedro watches TV to improve his English.

11. I didn't forget to pay my rent.

12. Kim wrote to the university to ask for a catalog.

13. Sally touched my shoulder to get my attention.

14. Donna expects to graduate next spring.

15. Jerry needs to go to the bookstore to buy a spiral notebook.

☐ EXERCISE 29. Using (IN ORDER) TO. (Chart 13-9)
Directions: Complete the sentences in Column A by using the ideas in Column B.
Connect the ideas with *(in order) to*.

Example: I called the hotel desk . . .
   → *I called the hotel desk (in order) to ask for an extra pillow.*

Column A

1. I called the hotel desk . . .

2. I turned on the radio . . .

3. I looked on the Internet . . .

4. People wear boots . . .

5. Andy went to Egypt . . .

6. Ms. Lane stood on tiptoes . . .

7. The dentist moved the light closer to my face . . .

8. I clapped my hands and yelled . . .

9. Maria took a walk in the park . . .

10. I offered my cousin some money . . .

Column B

A. keep their feet warm and dry

B. reach the top shelf

C. listen to a ball game

D. find the population of Malaysia

✓E. ask for an extra pillow

F. chase a stray dog away

G. help her pay the rent

H. get some fresh air and exercise

I. see the ancient pyramids

J. look into my mouth

□ EXERCISE 30. Expressing purpose with TO and FOR. (Chart 13-9)
    Directions: Complete the sentences by using *to* or *for*.

1. I went to Chicago _____for_____ a visit.

2. I went to Chicago _____to_____ visit my aunt and uncle.

3. I take long walks _____ relax.

4. I take long walks _____ relaxation.

5. I'm going to school _____ a good education.

6. I'm going to school _____ get a good education.

7. I'm not going to school just _____ have fun.

8. I'm not going to school just _____ fun.

9. I turned on the radio _____ listen to the news.

10. I listened to the radio _____ news about the earthquake in Peru.

11. I sent a card to Carol _____ wish her a happy birthday.

12. Two police officers came to my apartment _____ ask me about my cousin.

13. Mr. Wong works in his garden _____ the pure pleasure of it.

14. I looked in the encyclopedia _____ information about Ecuador.

15. My three brothers, two sisters, and parents all came to town _____
    attend my graduation.

□ EXERCISE 31. Expressing purpose with TO and FOR. (Chart 13-9)
    Directions: Answer *why*-questions in your own words. Show purpose by using an infinitive phrase or a *for*-phrase. Work in pairs or as a class.

Example:
SPEAKER A: Yesterday you turned on the TV. Why?
SPEAKER B: Yesterday I turned on the TV (to listen to the news / for the latest news about the earthquake / etc.).

1. You went to the supermarket. Why?
2. You need to go to the bookstore. Why?
3. You went to the post office. Why?
4. You went to the health clinic. Why?
5. You reached into your pocket/purse. Why?

(Switch roles if working in pairs.)
6. You came to this school. Why?
7. You borrowed some money from (. . .). Why?
8. You stopped at the service station. Why?
9. You play (soccer, tennis, etc.). Why?
10. You had to go out last night. Why?

13-10 USING INFINITIVES WITH *TOO* AND *ENOUGH*

TOO + ADJECTIVE + (FOR SOMEONE) + INFINITIVE (a) A piano is **too** *heavy* **to** *lift.* (b) That box is **too** *heavy* **for** *me* **to** *lift.* (c) That box is **too** *heavy* **for** *Bob* **to** *lift.*	Infinitives often follow expressions with **too**. **Too** comes in front of an adjective. In the speaker's mind, the use of **too** implies a negative result. COMPARE *The box is too heavy. I can't lift it.* *The box is very heavy, but I can lift it.*
ENOUGH + NOUN + INFINITIVE (d) I don't have **enough** *money* **to** *buy* that car. (e) Did you have **enough** *time* **to** *finish* the test?	Infinitives often follow expressions with **enough**. **Enough** comes in front of a noun.★ **Enough** follows an adjective.
ADJECTIVE + ENOUGH + INFINITIVE (f) Jimmy isn't *old* **enough** **to** *go* to school. (g) Are you *hungry* **enough** **to** *eat* three sandwiches?	

★**Enough** can also follow a noun: *I don't have* **money enough** *to buy that car.* In everyday English, however, **enough** usually comes in front of a noun.

☐ **EXERCISE 32. TOO and ENOUGH + infinitive. (Chart 13-10)**
Directions: Combine the sentences.

> **PART I.** Use **too**.
>
> 1. We can't go swimming today. It's very cold.
>   → *It's too cold (for us) to go swimming today.*
> 2. I couldn't finish my homework last night. I was very sleepy.
> 3. This jacket is very small. I can't wear it.
> 4. Mike couldn't go to his aunt's housewarming party. He was very busy.
> 5. I live far from school. I can't walk there.
> 6. Some movies are very violent. Children shouldn't watch them.
>
> **PART II.** Use **enough**.
>
> 7. I can't reach the top shelf. I'm not that tall.
>   → *I'm not tall enough to reach the top shelf.*
> 8. I can't lift a horse. I'm not that strong.
> 9. It's not warm today. We can't go outside in shorts and sandals.
> 10. I didn't stay home and miss work. I wasn't really sick, but I didn't feel good all day.

☐ **EXERCISE 33. TOO and ENOUGH + infinitive. (Chart 13-10)**
Directions: Complete the sentences by choosing from the words in *italics*. Use **too** or **enough** + an infinitive.

> 1. *strong/lift*   I'm not ____strong enough to lift____ a refrigerator.
>
> 2. *weak/lift*   Most people are ____too weak to lift____ a refrigerator without help.
>
> 3. *busy/answer*   I was _____ the phone. I let it
>
>   keep ringing until the caller gave up.
>
> 4. *early/get*   We got to the concert _____ good seats.

5. *full/hold*   My suitcase is _____

_____ any more clothes.

6. *large/hold*   My suitcase isn't _____

_____ all the

clothes I want to take on my trip.

7. *big/get*   Rex is _____ into

Bobo's doghouse.

8. *big/hold*   Julie's purse is _____ her dog

Pepper.

□ EXERCISE 34. TOO and ENOUGH + infinitive. (Chart 13-10)
   Directions: Complete the sentences with *too* and *enough*. Use Ø if nothing is needed.

1. Alan is _____too_____ smart _____Ø_____ to make that kind of mistake.

2. Alan is _____Ø_____ smart __enough__ to understand how to solve that

problem.

3. My pocket is _____ big _____ to hold my wallet. I always carry

my wallet there.

4. A horse is _____ big _____ for a person to lift.

5. I'm uncomfortable. This room is _____ hot _____. Why don't

you open the window?

6. That watch is _____ expensive _____. I can't afford it.

7. Are you _____ tall _____ to reach that book for me? The green

one on the top shelf. Thanks.

8. Ask John to move that box. He's _____ strong _____ to lift it.

9. I am _____ busy _____ to help you right now.

☐ EXERCISE 35. TOO and ENOUGH + infinitive. (Chart 13-10)
   Directions: Complete the following sentences. Use infinitives in the completions.

1. I'm too short . . . .
2. I'm not tall enough . . . .
3. I'm not strong enough . . . .
4. Last night I was too tired . . . .
5. Yesterday I was too busy . . . .
6. A Mercedes-Benz is too expensive . . . .
7. I don't have enough money . . . .
8. Yesterday I didn't have enough time . . . .
9. A teenager is old enough . . . . but too young . . . .
10. I know enough English . . . . but not enough . . . .

☐ EXERCISE 36. Review: gerunds vs. infinitives. (Chapter 13)
   Directions: Complete the sentences with the words in parentheses: gerund or infinitive.

1. It's difficult for me *(remember)* _____to remember_____ phone numbers.

2. My cat is good at *(catch)* _____catching_____ mice.

3. I bought a newspaper *(look)* _____ at the ads for apartments for rent.

4. Tourists like *(go)* _____ *(swim)* _____ in the warm
   ocean in Hawaii.

5. I called my friend *(invite)* _____ her for dinner.

6. Hillary talked about *(go)* _____ to graduate school.

7. Sarosh found out what was happening by *(listen)* _____ carefully
   to everything that was said.

8. Children, stop *(draw)* _____ pictures on the tablecloth!

9. Professor Amani has a strong accent. It is difficult for his students *(understand)*
   _____ him. He needs *(improve)* _____
   his pronunciation if he wants *(be)* _____ a good lecturer. *(lecture)*
   _____ requires good communication skills.

10. A: Hi! I'm home!

    B: Welcome back. Did you have a good trip?

    A: Yes, thanks. How's everything? How are my goldfish? I hope you didn't forget
       (feed) _____ them.

    B: Oh, my gosh!

11. Dan's goldfish died when he was away on a trip because his roommate forgot *(feed)* _____ them. Dan is considering *(get)* _____ a new roommate.

12. My friend Akihiko has goldfish in a pond in his garden. He enjoys *(feed)* _____ them one by one with chopsticks.

13. Michelle Yin Yin Ko works sixteen hours a day *(earn)* _____ enough money *(take)* _____ care of her elderly parents and her three children.

14. It takes care, patience, and a little luck *(take)* _____ a really good photograph of wildlife.

15. No matter how wonderful a trip is, it's always good *(get)* _____ back home and *(sleep)* _____ in one's own bed.

16. A: Quit *(stare)* _____ at the phone. Greg isn't going to call.

    B: I keep *(think)* _____ the phone will ring any second.

    A: I don't mean *(be)* _____ unsympathetic, but I think you'd better forget about Greg. It's over.

17. It's important to your health for you *(work)* _____ at a job you like. If you hate *(go)* _____ to your job, you should seriously think about *(look)* _____ for a different kind of job. The stress of *(do)* _____ work you hate day in and day out can damage your health.

18. *(ask)* _____ others about themselves and their lives is one of the secrets of *(get)* _____ along with other people. If you want *(make)* _____ and *(keep)* _____ friends, it is important *(be)* _____ sincerely interested in other people's lives.

19. I keep *(forget)* _____ *(call)* _____ my friend Louise. I'd better write myself a note.

20. I like *(travel)* _____ to out-of-the-way places. I don't like *(go)* _____ to usual tourist places when I'm on holiday.

21. Large bee colonies have 80,000 workers. These worker bees must visit fifty million flowers *(make)* _____ one kilogram (2.2 pounds) of honey. It's no wonder that "busy as a bee" is a common expression.

22. Exercise is good for you. Why don't you walk up the stairs instead of *(take)*

    _____ the elevator?

23. Stop *(crack)* _____ those nuts with your teeth! Here. Use a

    nutcracker. Do you want *(be)* _____ toothless by the time you're thirty?

24. Different cultures have different gestures. When North Americans meet someone, they

    usually offer a strong handshake and look the other person straight in the eye. In

    some countries, however, it is impolite *(shake)* _____ hands

    firmly, and *(look)* _____ a person in the eye is equally rude.

25. How close do you stand to another person when you are speaking? North Americans

    prefer *(stand)* _____ just a little less than an arm's length from

    someone. Many people in the Middle East and Latin America like *(move)*

    _____ in closer than that during a conversation.

26. *(smile)* _____ at another person is a universal, cross-cultural

    gesture. Everyone throughout the world understands the meaning of a smile.

☐ EXERCISE 37. Error analysis. (Chapter 13)
   Directions: Correct the errors.

    1. Do you enjoy ~~to go~~ going to the zoo?

    2. I went to the store for getting some toothpaste.

    3. Did you go to shopping yesterday?

    4. I usually go to the cafeteria for to get a cup of coffee in the morning.

    5. Bob needed to went downtown yesterday.

    6. I cut the rope by a knife.

    7. I thanked him for drive me to the airport.

    8. Is difficult to learn a second language.

    9. It is important getting an education.

    10. Timmy isn't enough old too get married.

11. Do you want go to swimming tomorrow?

12. I went to the bank for cashing a check.

13. I was to sleepy to finish my homework last night.

14. Is easy this exercise to do.

15. Last night too tired no do my homework.

16. I've never gone to sailing, but I would like to.

17. Reading it is one of my hobby.

18. The man began to built a wall around his garden.

19. I like to travel because you learn too much about other countries and cultures.

20. Instead of settle down in one place, I'd like to travel around the world.

21. My grandmother likes to fishing.

22. Mary would like to has a big family.

☐ **EXERCISE 38. Speaking. (Chapter 13)**

Directions: Form small groups. Make a list of several topics that can be used for a one-minute impromptu speech. The topics should be gerund phrases. Exchange topics with another group. After your group has its topics, each member in turn should give a one-minute speech to the rest of the group. One group member should keep time. After all the speeches have been given, choose one speech from your group to be presented to the rest of the class. Examples of topics: *eating at fast-food restaurants, traveling to a foreign country, taking care of your health*.

☐ **EXERCISE 39. Writing. (Chapter 13)**

Directions: What do you do for fun and recreation in your spare time? Write about one or two spare-time activities that you enjoy. What do you do? Where? When? Why? Mention some interesting experiences. Try to get your readers interested in doing the same things in their free time. Do you enjoy exploring caves? Is playing tennis one of your passions? Have you ever gone skydiving? Maybe collecting ceramic horses is one of your hobbies. Have you ever gone waterskiing? Do you enjoy simple pleasures such as walking in a park? Do you go jogging for recreation? Maybe watching sports on television is your way of relaxing. It is important for all of us to have spare-time activities that we enjoy. What are yours?

□ **EXERCISE 40. Review: verb forms. (Chapters 1 → 13)**

Directions: Complete the sentences by writing the correct form of the verb in parentheses.

What is your most *(embarrass)* _____**embarrassing**_____ experience? Let me tell you
                                              1

what happened to my Uncle Ernesto when he *(go)* _____ to Norway for a
                                                                        2

business meeting last year.

First, I must tell you about my uncle. He *(be)* _____ a businessman from
                                                                3

Buenos Aires, Argentina. He *(manufacture)* _____ a new kind of
                                                                        4

computer compass for ships. Computer compasses *(make)* _____ by
                                                                        5

many companies in the world, so my uncle *(have)* _____ a lot of
                                                                        6

competition for his product. In order to sell his product, he *(need)* _____
                                                                                              7

(meet) _____ with companies that might want to buy it. He *(travel)*
                        8

_____ frequently to other countries.
          9

Last year, he *(go)* _____ to Norway *(meet)* _____ with a
                              10   11

shipping company. It was his first trip to Scandinavia. My Uncle Ernesto *(speak)*

_____ Spanish, of course, and also *(know)* _____ a little
          12   13

English, but he *(know, not)* _____ any Norwegian. While he
                                              14

(stay) _____ in Norway, he *(have)* _____ a problem.
                    15   16

Uncle Ernesto *(stay)* _____ at a small hotel in Oslo. One
                                    17

morning, while he *(get)* _____ ready to take a shower, he *(hear)*
                                    18

_____ a knock at the door. He *(walk)* _____ to the
          19   20

door, *(open)* _____ it, and *(find)* _____ no one. He *(take)*
                        21   22

_____ a step out of his room and *(look)* _____ down the
          23   24

hall. He *(see)* _____ no one. So he *(turn)* _____ *(go)*
                        25   26

_____ back into his room, but the door *(close)* _____! It
          27   28

(lock) _____ , and he *(have, not)* _____
                    29   30

his key. This was a very big problem for my unfortunate uncle because he *(dress, not)*

_____ properly. In fact, he *(wear)* _____

31
32

nothing but a towel. Poor Uncle Ernesto! "What *(I, do)* _____?"

33

he asked himself.

    Instead of *(stand)* _____ in the hallway with only a towel, he

34

(decide) _____ *(get)* _____ help. So he *(start)*

35   36

_____ *(walk)* _____ down the hall toward the

37   38

elevator. He thought about *(knock)* _____ on someone else's door

39

(ask) _____ for help, but decided it was better *(ask)* _____

40   41

the hotel personnel. He hoped the elevator would be empty.

    When he *(reach)* _____ the elevator, he *(push)* _____

42   43

the down button and *(wait)* _____. When it *(come)* _____,

44   45

Uncle Ernesto *(take)* _____ a deep breath and *(get)* _____ in

46   47

even though the elevator wasn't empty. The other people in the elevator *(surprise)*

_____ when they *(see)* _____ a man who *(wrap)*

48   49

_____ in a towel.

50

    Uncle Ernesto *(think)* _____ about *(try)* _____

51   52

(explain) _____ his problem, but unfortunately he *(know, not)*

53

_____ any Norwegian. He said, in English, "Door. Locked. No

54

key." A businessman in the elevator *(nod)* _____, but he *(smile, not)*

55

_____. Another man *(look)* _____ at Uncle

56   57

Ernesto and *(smile)* _____ broadly.

58

    After an eternity, the elevator *(reach)* _____ the ground floor.

59

Uncle Ernesto *(walk)* _____ straight to the front desk and *(look)*

60

_____ at the hotel manager helplessly. The hotel manager

61

(have to understand, not) _____

_____
                    62
any language *(figure)* _____ out the problem. My uncle
                                  63

(have to say, not) _____ a word. The manager
                                         64

(grab) _____ a key, *(take)* _____ my uncle by the
                    65   66

elbow, and *(lead)* _____ him back to the nearest elevator.
                          67

    My uncle *(embarrass, still)* _____ about
                                                      68

this incident. But he *(laugh)* _____ a lot when he *(tell)* _____
                                      69   70

the story.

☐ **EXERCISE 41. Review of verb forms: writing. (Chapters 1 → 13)**
    Directions: Write a composition about one of the most embarrassing experiences you have
    had in your life.

CHAPTER *14*
Noun Clauses

CONTENTS

14-1   NOUN CLAUSES: INTRODUCTION

s   **v**   **o**
 (a) I know ⌐*his address*.⌐
            (noun phrase)
	Verbs are often followed by objects. The object is usually a noun phrase.★
	 In (a): ***his address*** is a noun phrase;
	         his address is the object of the verb *know*.

s   **v**   **o**
 (b) I know ⌐*where he lives*.⌐
          (noun clause)
	Some verbs can be followed by noun clauses.★
	 In (b): ***where he lives*** is a noun clause;
	         where he lives is the object of the verb *know*.

o **s** **v** ⌐ **s** **v** ⌐ (c) I know *where **he lives***.	A noun clause has its own subject and verb. In (c): ***he*** is the subject of the noun clause; ***lives*** is the verb of the noun clause.
(d) I know ***where my book is***. (noun clause)	A noun clause can begin with a question word. (See Chart 14-2.)
(e) I don't know ***if Ed is married***. (noun clause)	A noun clause can begin with *if* or *whether*. (See Chart 14-4, p. 409.)
(f) I know ***that the world is round***. (noun clause)	A noun clause can begin with *that*. (See Chart 14-5, p. 414.)

★A **phrase** is a group of related words. It does not contain a subject and a verb.
 A **clause** is a group of related words. It contains a subject and a verb.

14-2 NOUN CLAUSES THAT BEGIN WITH A QUESTION WORD

These question words can be used to introduce a noun clause: *when, where, why, how, who, whom, what, which, whose*.

INFORMATION QUESTION	NOUN CLAUSE	Notice in the examples: Usual question word order is NOT used in a noun clause. *INCORRECT: I know where does he live.* *CORRECT: I know where he lives.*
(a) Where **does he live?** (c) When **did they leave?** (e) What **did she say?** (g) Why **is Tom** absent?	(b) I don't know *where* **he lives.** (d) Do you know *when* **they left?*** (f) Please tell me *what* **she said.** (h) I wonder *why* **Tom is** absent.	
(i) **Who came** to class? (k) **What happened?**	(j) I don't know **who came** *to class.* (l) Tell me **what happened.**	In (i) and (j): Question word order and noun clause word order are the same when the question word is used as a subject.

*A question mark is used at the end of this noun clause because the main subject and the verb of the sentence *(Do you know)* are in question word order.
     Example: *Do you know when they left?*
Do you know asks a question; *when they left* is a noun clause.

☐ **EXERCISE 1. Information questions and noun clauses. (Charts 5-2 and 14-2)**
    Directions: Are the given words (1) an information question or (2) a noun clause?
- Add "I don't know" and a period to make a sentence with a noun clause. OR
- Add a capital letter and a question mark if the given words are a question.

1. _____I don't know_____ why he left. *(noun clause)*

2. _____ W̶w̶hy did he leave? *(information question)*

3. _____ where she is living

4. _____ where is she living

5. _____ where did Paul go

6. _____ where Paul went

7. _____ what time the movie begins

8. _____ what time does the movie begin

9. _____ how old is Kate

10. _____ why Yoko is angry

11. _____ what happened

12. _____ who came to the party

13. _____ who(m) did you see at the party

14. _____ what did Sue say

15. _____ what Sue is talking about

□ **EXERCISE 2. Noun clauses that begin with a question word. (Chart 14-2)**

Directions: Complete the dialogues by changing Speaker A's questions to noun clauses.

1. A: Where does Jim go to school?

    B: I don't know ____where Jim goes____ to school.

2. A: Where did Natasha go yesterday?

    B: I don't know. Do you know _____ yesterday?

3. A: Why is Maria laughing?

    B: I don't know. Does anybody know _____ ?

4. A: Why is fire hot?

    B: I don't know _____ hot.

5. A: How much does a new Honda cost?

    B: Peter can tell you _____ .

6. A: Why is Mike always late?

    B: Don't ask me. I don't understand _____ late.

7. A: How long do birds live?

    B: I don't know _____ .

8. A: When was the first wheel invented?

    B: I don't know. Do you know

    _____

    _____

    _____ ?

9. A: How many hours does a
    light bulb burn?

    B: I don't know exactly _____

    _____ .

10. A: Where did Emily buy her computer?

    B: I don't know _____ her computer.

11. A: Who lives next door to Kate?

    B: I don't know _____ next door to Kate.

12. A: Who(m) did Julie talk to?

    B: I don't know _____ to.

☐ EXERCISE 3. Information questions and noun clauses. (Charts 5-2 and 14-2)
Directions: Ask and answer questions. Only the leader's book is open. Work as a class or in groups.
Speaker A: Ask a question, using the cue.
Speaker B: Answer the question, beginning with either *"I don't know . . ."* OR *"I think . . ."* followed by a noun clause.

Example: Ask (. . .) where (. . .) lives.
LEADER TO A: Marco, ask Ingrid where Mustafa lives.
  SPEAKER A: Ingrid, where does Mustafa live?
  SPEAKER B: I don't know where Mustafa lives. OR I think that Mustafa lives in Reed Hall.

1. Ask (. . .) where (. . .) ate breakfast this morning.
2. Ask (. . .) what (. . .)'s favorite color is.
3. Ask (. . .) when (. . .) got up this morning.
4. Ask (. . .) why (. . .) isn't sitting in his/her usual seat today.
5. Ask (. . .) how (. . .) got to class today.
6. Ask (. . .) what kind of watch (. . .) has.
7. Ask (. . .) why (. . .) didn't come to class yesterday.
8. Ask (. . .) where (. . .) went after class yesterday.

☐ EXERCISE 4. Information questions and noun clauses. (Charts 5-2 and 14-2)
Directions: Complete the sentences with the words in parentheses.

1. A: Where *(Susan, eat)* ___did Susan eat___ lunch yesterday?

   B: I don't know where *(she, eat)* ___she ate___ lunch yesterday.

2. A: Do you know where *(Jason, work)* _____?

   B: Who?

   A: Jason. Where *(he, work)* _____?

   B: I don't know.

3. A: Excuse me.

   B: Yes. How can I help you?

   A: How much *(that camera, cost)* _____?

   B: You want to know how much *(this camera, cost)* _____,
   is that right?

   A: No, not that one. The one next to it.

4. A: How far *(you, can run)* _____ without stopping?

   B: I have no idea. I don't know how far *(I, can run)* _____
   without stopping. I've never tried.

5. A: Where *(you, see)* _____ the ad for the computer sale last week?

   B: I don't remember where *(I, see)* _____ it. One of the local papers, I think.

6. A: Ann was out late last night, wasn't she? When *(she, get)* _____ in?

   B: Why do you want to know what time *(she, get)* _____ home?

   A: Just curious.

7. A: What time *(it, is)* _____ ?

   B: I don't know. I'll ask Sara. Sara, do you know what time *(it, is)* _____ ?

   C: Almost four-thirty.

8. A: *(who, invent)* _____ the first refrigerator?

   B: I don't know *(who, invent)* _____ the first refrigerator. Do you?

9. A: Mom, why *(some people, be)* _____ cruel to other people?

   B: Honey, I don't really understand why *(some people, be)* _____ cruel to others. It's difficult to explain.

10. A: I don't care about the future. All I care about is today.

    B: Oh? Well, answer this question for me. Where *(you, spend)* _____ _____ the rest of your life?

    A: What do you mean?

    B: I mean it's important to pay attention to the future. That's where *(you, spend)* _____ the rest of your life.

14-3 NOUN CLAUSES WITH *WHO, WHAT, WHOSE + BE*

QUESTION	NOUN CLAUSE	
(a) Who **is** **that boy**? V S	(b) Tell me *who* **that boy** **is**. S V	A noun or pronoun that follows main verb **be** in a question comes in front of **be** in a noun clause, as in (b) and (d).
(c) Whose pen **is** **this**? V S	(d) Tell me *whose pen* **this** **is**. S V	
(e) **Who** **is** in the office? S V	(f) Tell me **who** **is** in the office. S V	A prepositional phrase (e.g., *in the office*) does not come in front of **be** in a noun clause, as in (f) and (h).
(g) **Whose pen** **is** on the desk? S V	(h) Tell me **whose pen** **is** on the desk. S V	

☐ **EXERCISE 5. Noun clauses with WHO, WHAT, WHOSE + BE. (Chart 14-3)**
    Directions: <u>Underline</u> and identify the subject and verb of Speaker A's question. Complete
    Speaker B's noun clause.

                        V   S

1. A: Who <u>is</u> <u>that woman</u>?

   B: I don't know _____ *who that woman is* _____ .

                S   V

2. A: <u>Who</u> <u>is</u> on the phone?

   B: I don't know _____ *who is on the phone* _____ .

3. A: What is a crow?

   B: I don't know _____ .

4. A: What is in that bag?

   B: I don't know _____ .

5. A: Whose cat is in the driveway?

   B: I don't know _____ .

6. A: Whose car is that?

   B: I don't know _____ .

7. A: What is a violin?

   B: I don't know _____ .

   C: It's a musical instrument that has strings.

8. A: Who is in the doctor's office?

   B: I don't know _____ .

9. A: Whose hammer is this?

   B: I don't know _____ . Hey, Hank, do you know

     _____ ?

   C: It's Ralph's.

10. A: Who is Bob's doctor?

   B: I don't know _____

     _____ .

11. A: What's at the end of a rainbow?

   B: What did you say, Susie?

   A: I want to know _____

     _____ .

☐ EXERCISE 6. Noun clauses. (Charts 14-2 and 14-3)
Directions: Work in pairs.
Speaker A: Read the question. Your book is open.
Speaker B: Change the question to a noun clause. Begin your reponse with *"I don't know . . . ."* Your book is closed.

Example: Where does (. . .) live?
SPEAKER A *(book open):*   Where does Anita live?
SPEAKER B *(book closed):*   I don't know where Anita lives.

Switch roles.

1. Where did (. . .) go yesterday?
2. How old is (. . .)?
3. Where does (. . .) eat lunch?
4. What is (. . .)'s last name?
5. What time does (. . .) usually get up?
6. When did (. . .) get home last night?
7. What time did (. . .) go to bed last night?
8. Who is (. . .)'s best friend?
9. Who did (. . .) call last night?

10. How long has (. . .) been living here?
11. Who wrote *(Tales of the South Pacific)?*
12. What happened in Alaska yesterday?
13. What did (. . .) do yesterday?
14. Who is that girl?
15. Who are those people?
16. What kind of tree is that?
17. Whose (backpack) is that?
18. Whose (gloves) are those?

☐ EXERCISE 7. Information questions and noun clauses. (Charts 5-2, 14-2, and 14-3)
Directions: Ask information questions and respond using noun clauses.
Speaker A: Using the given question word, ask any question that you are sure Speaker B cannot answer. (You don't have to know the answer to the question.)
Speaker B: Respond to the question by saying *"I don't know . . . ."* followed by a noun clause. Then you can guess at an answer if you wish.

Example: when
SPEAKER A: When was the first book printed?
SPEAKER B: I don't know when the first book was printed. Probably three or four hundred years ago.

1. where	3. how far	5. what time	7. when	9. what
2. who	4. what kind	6. whose	8. why	

14-4   NOUN CLAUSES THAT BEGIN WITH *IF* OR *WHETHER*

YES/NO QUESTION	NOUN CLAUSE	When a yes/no question is changed to a noun clause, *if* is usually used to introduce the clause.★
(a) Is Eric at home?	(b) I don't know *if Eric is at home*.	
(c) Does the bus stop here?	(d) Do you know *if the bus stops here?*	
(e) Did Alice go to Chicago?	(f) I wonder *if Alice went to Chicago*.	

(g) I don't know *if Eric is at home **or not**.	When *if* introduces a noun clause, the expression *or not* sometimes comes at the end of the clause, as in (g).
(h) I don't know ***whether*** Eric is at home *(or not)*.	In (h): ***whether*** has the same meaning as *if*.

★See Chart 14-11, p. 425, for the use of *if* with ***ask*** in reported speech.

□ **EXERCISE 8. Noun clauses that begin with IF or WHETHER. (Chart 14-4)**
    Directions: Change the yes/no question to a noun clause.

1. YES/NO QUESTION: Is Susan here today?

    NOUN CLAUSE: Can you tell me ___if (whether) Susan is here today___?

2. YES/NO QUESTION: Will Mr. Pips be at the meeting?

    NOUN CLAUSE: Do you know _____?

3. YES/NO QUESTION: Did Paulo go to work yesterday?

    NOUN CLAUSE: I wonder _____.

4. YES/NO QUESTION: Is Barcelona a coastal town?

    NOUN CLAUSE: I can't remember _____.

5. YES/NO QUESTION: Do you still have Yung Soo's address?

    NOUN CLAUSE: I don't know _____.

□ **EXERCISE 9. Noun clauses that begin with IF or WHETHER. (Chart 14-4)**
    Directions: Complete the dialogues by completing the noun clauses. Use *if* to introduce
    the noun clause.

1. A: Are you tired?

   B: Why do you want to know ___if I am___ tired?

   A: You look tired. I'm worried about you.

2. A: Are you going to be in your office later today?

   B: What? Sorry. I didn't hear you.

   A: I need to know _____ in your office later
      today.

3. A: Do all birds have feathers?

   B: Well, I don't really know for sure _____
      feathers, but I suppose they do.

4. A: Did Rosa take my dictionary off my desk?

   B: Who?

   A: Rosa. I want to know _____ my dictionary off my desk.

5. A: Can Uncle Pete babysit tonight?

   B: Sorry. I wasn't listening. I was thinking about something else.

   A: Have you talked to Uncle Pete? We need to know _____
      _____ tonight.

6. A: Does Al have a flashlight in his car?

B: I'll ask him. Hey, Al! Al! Fred wants to know _____ a

flashlight in your car.

C: Yeah, I do. Why?

7. A: Should I take my umbrella?

B: How am I supposed to know _____ your

umbrella? I'm not a weather forecaster.

A: You're kind of grumpy today, aren't you?

☐ EXERCISE 10. Noun clauses. (Charts 14-2 → 14-4)

Directions: Change the questions to noun clauses.

1. *Will it rain tomorrow?* I wonder . . . *if it will rain tomorrow.*

2. *What time is it?* I wonder . . . .

3. *What is an amphibian?* Do you know . . . .

4. *Is a frog an amphibian?* Can you tell me . . . .

5. *What's on TV tonight?* I wonder . . . .

6. *What is the speed of sound?* Do you know . . . .

7. *Does sound travel faster than light?* Do you know . . . .

8. *Are dogs colorblind?* Do you know . . . .

9. *Why is the sky blue?* Annie wants to know . . . .

10. *Do insects have ears?* Annie also wants to know . . . .

11. *Have beings from outer space ever visited the earth?*

I wonder . . . .

12. *How do dolphins communicate with each other?*

Do scientists know . . . .

13. *Can people communicate with dolphins?*

I wonder . . . .

□ **EXERCISE 11. Noun clauses.** (Charts 14-2 → 14-4)

Directions: Practice using noun clauses.

Speaker A: Ask the given question. Your book is open.
Speaker B: Restate A's question, beginning with *"You want to know . . . ."* and ask if that is right. Your book is closed.
Speaker A: Tell B if that is right.
Speaker B: Answer the question.

Example: Is (. . .) at the bank?

SPEAKER A *(book open):*   Is Gina at the bank?
SPEAKER B *(book closed):* You want to know if Gina is at the bank. Is that right?
SPEAKER A *(book open):*   Yes, that's right.
SPEAKER B *(book closed):* I don't know if Gina is at the bank. OR
                            No, Gina isn't at the bank. She's here in class. OR
                            Yes, she is. Gina is at the bank.

Switch roles.

1. Does (. . .) have a bicycle?

2. What time does class end?

3. Can (. . .) sing?

4. What does "delicious" mean?

5. Whose books are those?

6. Is (. . .) married?

7. Where did (. . .) go last night?

8. Does (. . .) have a job?

9. Who is that person?

10. Is there a pay phone in this building?

11. Why is (. . .) absent today?

12. Whose pen is that?

13. How much does a new refrigerator cost?

14. Does (. . .) speak *(name of a language)*?

15. What kind of wristwatch does (. . .) have?

16. Is (. . .) planning to take another English course?

17. Who is the mayor of *(name this city/town)*?

18. Who is in charge of the English classes at this school?

□ **EXERCISE 12. Noun clauses.** (Charts 14-2 → 14-4)

Directions: Answer the questions using the words in **boldface**. Give two or three different answers. Work in groups or as a class.

Example: What do you know?
            where
            → SPEAKER A: I know ***where*** Madagascar is located.
              SPEAKER B: I know ***where*** (. . .)'s dictionary is.
              SPEAKER C: I know ***where*** my parents got married.

QUESTION 1: What do you know?
   a. ***where***
   b. ***what***
   c. ***why***
   d. ***who***
   e. ***whose***

QUESTION 2: What do you NOT know?
   a. ***where***
   b. ***if***
   c. ***why***
   d. ***who***

QUESTION 3: What do you want to know?
  a. *if*
  b. *when*
  c. *what*
  d. *who*

QUESTION 4: What do you wonder?
  a. *why*
  b. *if*
  c. *what*
  d. *who*
  e. *how*
  f. *whether*

☐ EXERCISE 13. Noun clauses. (Charts 14-1 → 14-4)
Directions: What are some of the things you wonder about? Consider the given topics. Create sentences using *"I wonder . . . (why, when, how, if, whether, etc.)."* Work in groups or as a class.

Example: fish
  → *I wonder how many fish there are in the world.*
  I wonder how many different kinds of fish there are in the world.
  I wonder how long fish have lived on earth.
  I wonder whether fish can communicate with each other.
  I wonder if fish in fish tanks are happy.
  Etc.

1. birds
2. the earth
3. *(name of a person you know)*
4. events in the future

5. electricity
6. dinosaurs
7. *(topic of your own choosing)*

☐ EXERCISE 14. Noun clauses and questions. (Charts 5-2 and 14-1 → 14-4)
Directions: Create questions and answer them using noun clauses. Work in pairs.
Speaker A: Ask a question. Use the suggestions below. Try to ask a question that Speaker B can't answer.
Speaker B: Answer the question if you can. If you can't, say *"I don't know . . ."* followed by a noun clause. Then you can guess at the answer if you wish.

Example: location of X★
SPEAKER A: Where is Mr. Fong's briefcase right now?
SPEAKER B: Under his desk. OR I don't know where his briefcase is. I suppose he left it at home today.

Switch roles.

1. location of X
2. cost of X
3. owner of X
4. reason for X
5. person who did X
6. country X is from

7. meaning of X
8. time of X
9. amount of X
10. year that X happened
11. type of X
12. distance from X to Y

★"X" simply indicates that the questioner should supply her/his own ideas.

14-5 NOUN CLAUSES THAT BEGIN WITH *THAT*

S **V** **O** (a) ⌐I⌐ ⌐think⌐ ⌐*that Mr. Jones is a good teacher.*⌐ (b) I hope **that** *you can come to the game.* (c) Mary realizes **that** *she should study harder.* (d) I dreamed **that** *I was on the top of a mountain.*	A noun clause can be introduced by the word **that**. In (a): *that Mr. Jones is a good teacher* is a noun clause. It is the object of the verb *think*. *That*-clauses are frequently used as the objects of verbs that express mental activity. (See the list below.)
(e) *I think* **that** *Mr. Jones is a good teacher.* (f) *I think* Ø *Mr. Jones is a good teacher.*	The word **that** is often omitted, especially in speaking. (e) and (f) have the same meaning.

COMMON VERBS FOLLOWED BY *THAT*-CLAUSES[*]

assume that	*feel that*	*learn that*	*read that*
believe that	*hear that*	*notice that*	*say that*
discover that	*hope that*	*predict that*	*suppose that*
dream that	*know that*	*prove that*	*think that*

[*]The verbs in the above list are those that are emphasized in the exercises. Some other common verbs that can be followed by *that*-clauses are:

agree that	*fear that*	*imagine that*	*realize that*	*reveal that*
conclude that	*figure out that*	*indicate that*	*recall that*	*show that*
decide that	*find out that*	*observe that*	*recognize that*	*suspect that*
demonstrate that	*forget that*	*presume that*	*regret that*	*teach that*
doubt that	*guess that*	*pretend that*	*remember that*	*understand that*

☐ **EXERCISE 15. THAT-clauses. (Chart 14-5)**

Directions: Add the word **that** in the appropriate place to mark the beginning of a noun clause.

1. I think ∧ *that* most people have kind hearts.

2. Last night I dreamed I was at my aunt's house.

3. I believe we need to protect endangered species of animals.

4. I know Matt walks to school every day. I assume he doesn't have a bicycle.

5. Did you notice Ji Ming wasn't in class yesterday? I hope he's okay.

6. I trust Linda. I believe what she said. I believe she told the truth.

7. In yesterday's newspaper, I read half of the people in the world have never used a telephone of any kind in their entire lives.

8. The population of New York City is extraordinarily diverse. Did you know forty percent of the people who live in New York City are foreign born? Many people believe these immigrants are revitalizing the city.

9. A: Do you think a monster really exists in Loch Ness in Scotland?

   B: I don't know. Look at this story in the newspaper. It says some investigators say they can prove the Loch Ness Monster exists.

   A: You shouldn't always believe what you read in the newspapers.

□ EXERCISE 16. THAT-clauses. (Chart 14-5)
　　　Directions: Complete the sentences with your own words. Omit the word ***that*** if you wish.

1. I believe that . . . .
2. I assume that . . . .
3. Do you realize that . . . ?
4. I can prove that . . . .
5. I predict that . . . .
6. I've heard that . . . .
7. I suppose that . . . .
8. Have you ever noticed that . . . ?
9. Last night I dreamed that . . . .
10. Do you think that . . . ?
11. I've discovered that . . . .
12. Did you know that . . . ?

14-6 OTHER USES OF *THAT*-CLAUSES

(a) **I'm sure that** the bus stops here. (b) **I'm glad that** you're feeling better today. (c) **I'm sorry that** I missed class yesterday. (d) I **was disappointed that** the peace conference failed.	*That*-clauses can follow certain expressions with **be** + *adjective* or **be** + *past participle*. The word ***that*** can be omitted with no change in meaning: 　　*I'm sure Ø the bus stops here.*
(e) **It is true that** the world is round. (f) **It is a fact that** the world is round.	Two common expressions followed by *that*-clauses are: 　　*It is true (that) . . . .* 　　*It is a fact (that) . . . .*

COMMON EXPRESSIONS FOLLOWED BY *THAT*-CLAUSES*

be afraid that	*be disappointed that*	*be sorry that*	*It is true that*
be aware that	*be glad that*	*be sure that*	*It is a fact that*
be certain that	*be happy that*	*be surprised that*	
be convinced that	*be pleased that*	*be worried that*	

*The above list contains expressions emphasized in the exercises. Some other common expressions with **be** that are frequently followed by *that*-clauses are:

be amazed that	*be delighted that*	*be impressed that*	*be sad that*
be angry that	*be fortunate that*	*be lucky that*	*be shocked that*
be ashamed that	*be furious that*	*be positive that*	*be terrified that*
be astounded that	*be horrified that*	*be proud that*	*be thrilled that*

☐ EXERCISE 17. THAT-clauses. (Charts 14-5 and 14-6)

Directions: Add the word ***that*** wherever possible.

1. A: Welcome. We're glad _∧ ^that^ you could come.

   B: Thank you. I'm happy to be here.

2. A: Thank you so much for your gift.

   B: I'm so pleased you like it.

3. A: I wonder why Tom was promoted to general manager instead of Ann.

   B: So do I. I'm surprised Ann didn't get the job. I think she is more qualified.

4. A: Are you afraid another nuclear disaster like the one at Chernobyl might occur?

   B: Yes. I'm convinced it can happen again.

5. A: Are you aware you have to pass the English test to get into the university?

   B: Yes, but I'm not worried about it. I'm certain I'll do well on it.

6. A: I'm disappointed my son quit his job. I realize young people must follow their own paths, but I'm worried my son's path isn't going to lead him to a rewarding career.

   B: Don't forget he's grown up now and responsible for himself. I think he'll be fine. You shouldn't worry about him. He knows what he's doing.

7. It is a fact some ancient Egyptian cats wore earrings.

8. Are you aware dinosaurs lived on earth for one hundred and twenty-five million (125,000,000) years? Is it true human beings have lived on earth for only four million (4,000,000) years?

9. A: Is it a fact blue whales are the largest creatures on earth?

   B: Yes. In fact, I believe they are the largest creatures that have ever lived on earth.

☐ EXERCISE 18. THAT-clauses. (Charts 14-5 and 14-6)

Directions: Read each dialogue. Then use the expressions in parentheses to explain what the people are talking about.

DIALOGUE 1.   ALICIA: I really like my English teacher.

   BONNIE: Great! That's wonderful. It's important to have a good English teacher.

(think that, be delighted that)

→ *Alicia thinks that her English teacher is very good.*
Bonnie is delighted that Alicia likes her English teacher.
Bonnie thinks that it's important to have a good English teacher.

DIALOGUE 2.   MRS. DAY: How do you feel, honey? You might have the flu.

             BOBBY: I'm okay, Mom. Honest. I don't have the flu.

(be worried that, be sure that)

DIALOGUE 3.   KIM: Did you really fail your chemistry course? How is that possible?

          TINA: I didn't study hard enough. I was too busy having fun with my friends. I feel terrible about it.

(be surprised that, be disappointed that)

DIALOGUE 4.   DAVID: Mike! Hello! It's nice to see you.

         MIKE: It's nice to be here. Thank you for inviting me.

(be glad/happy/pleased that)

DIALOGUE 5.   FRED: Susan has left. Look. Her closet is empty. Her suitcases are gone. She won't be back. I just know it!

       ERICA: She'll be back.

(be afraid that, be upset that, be sure that)

DIALOGUE 6.   JOHN: I heard you were in jail. I couldn't believe it!

         ED: Neither could I! I was arrested for robbing a house on my block. Can you believe that? It was a case of mistaken identity. I didn't have to stay in jail long.

(be shocked that, be relieved that)

☐ **EXERCISE 19. THAT-clauses. (Charts 14-5 and 14-6)**

Directions: Complete the sentences. Use any appropriate verb form in the ***that***-clause. (Notice the various verb forms used in the example.) Omit ***that*** if you wish.

Example: I'm glad that . . . .

     → *the weather is nice today.*

     Sam is going to finish school.

     I can speak English.

1. I'm pleased that . . . .
2. I'm sure that . . . .
3. I'm surprised that . . . .
4. Are you certain that . . . ?
5. I'm very happy that . . . .
6. I'm sorry that . . . .
7. I'm not sorry that . . . .
8. I'm afraid that . . . .*
9. Are you aware that . . . ?
10. I'm disappointed that . . . .
11. I'm convinced that . . . .
12. Is it true that . . . .
13. It is a fact that . . . .
14. It's not true that . . . .

_____

*Sometimes **be afraid** expresses fear:

   I don't want to go near that dog. I'm afraid that it will bite me.

Sometimes **be afraid** expresses polite regret:

   I'm afraid you have the wrong number. = I'm sorry, but I think you have the wrong number.

   I'm afraid I can't come to your party. = I'm sorry, but I can't come to your party.

☐ **EXERCISE 20. THAT-clauses. (Charts 14-5 and 14-6)**

Directions: What are your views on the following topics? Introduce your opinion with an expression from the given list, then state your opinion in a *that*-clause. Discuss your opinions in groups, as a class, or in writing.

Example: guns

→ *I believe that ordinary people shouldn't have guns in their homes.*

I think anyone should be able to have any kind of gun.

I have concluded that countries in which it is easy to get a gun have a higher rate of murder than other countries do.

am certain that	believe that	hope that
am convinced that	can prove that	predict that
am sure that	have concluded that	think that

1. smoking (cigarettes, cigars, pipes)

2. a controversy at your school (perhaps something that has been on the front pages of a student newspaper)

3. a recent political event in the world (something that has been on the front pages of the newspaper)

4. the importance of protecting the environment

5. freedom of the press vs. government-controlled news

6. solutions to world hunger

14-7 SUBSTITUTING *SO* FOR A *THAT*-CLAUSE IN CONVERSATIONAL RESPONSES

(a) A: Is Ana from Peru? 　　B: **I think so.** *(so = that Ana is from Peru)* (b) A: Does Judy live in Dallas? 　　B: **I believe so.** *(so = that Judy lives in Dallas)* (c) A: Did you pass the test? 　　B: **I hope so.** *(so = that I passed the test)*	***Think***, ***believe***, and ***hope*** are frequently followed by ***so*** in conversational English in response to a yes/no question. They are alternatives to *yes*, *no*, or *I don't know*. ***So*** replaces a *that*-clause. *INCORRECT: I think so that Ana is from Peru.*
(d) A: Is Jack married? 　　B: **I *don't* think so.** / **I *don't* believe so.**	Negative usage of ***think so*** and ***believe so***: 　*do not think so / do not believe so*
(e) A: Did you fail the test? 　　B: **I hope *not*.**	Negative usage of ***hope*** in conversational responses: *hope not.* In (e): *I hope not = I hope I didn't fail the test.* *INCORRECT: I don't hope so.*
(f) A: Do you want to come with us? 　　B: Oh, I don't know. **I guess *so*.**	Other common conversational responses: 　*I guess so. I guess not.* 　*I suppose so. I suppose not.*

□ **EXERCISE 21. Substituting SO for a THAT-clause.** (Chart 14-7)

Directions: Restate Speaker B's answers to Speaker A's questions by using a *that*-clause.

1. A: Is Karen going to be home tonight?
   B: I think so. → *I think that Karen is going to be home tonight.*

2. A: Are we going to have a test
   in grammar tomorrow?
   B: I don't believe so.

3. A: Will Margo be at the conference
   in March?
   B: I hope so.

4. A: Can cats swim?
   B: I believe so.

5. A: Do gorillas have tails?
   B: I don't think so.

6. A: Will Janet be at Omar's wedding?
   B: I suppose so.

7. A: Will your flight be canceled because
   of the bad weather in Copenhagen?
   B: I hope not.

□ **EXERCISE 22. Substituting SO for a THAT-clause.** (Chart 14-7)

Directions: Answer the questions by using ***think so*** or ***believe so*** if you are not sure, or
yes or ***no*** if you are sure. Work in pairs or as a class.

Example:
SPEAKER A *(book open):* Does this book have more than 500 pages?
SPEAKER B: *(book closed):* I think / believe so. OR
I don't think / don't believe so. OR
Yes, it does. / No, it doesn't.

1. Are we going to have a grammar quiz tomorrow?
2. Do spiders have noses?
3. Do spiders have eyes?
4. Is there a fire extinguisher in this building?
5. Is Toronto farther north than New York City?
6. Does the word "patient" have more than one meaning?
7. Don't look at your watch. Is it *(supply a time)* yet?
8. Is next Tuesday the *(supply a date)*?

(Switch roles if working in pairs.)

9. Does the word "dozen" have more than one meaning?
10. Is your left foot bigger than your right foot?
11. Do gorillas eat meat?
12. Is Bangkok farther from the equator than Mexico City?
13. Can I buy a window fan at *(name of a local store)*?
14. Do any English words begin with the letter "x"?
15. Do you know what a noun clause is?
16. Is (. . .) getting married soon?

14-8 QUOTED SPEECH

Sometimes we want to quote a speaker's words—to write a speaker's exact words. Exact quotations are used in many kinds of writing, such as newspaper articles, stories and novels, and academic papers. When we quote a speaker's words, we use quotation marks.

(a) **SPEAKERS' EXACT WORDS** Jane: Cats are fun to watch. Mike: Yes, I agree. They're graceful and playful. Do you own a cat?	(b) **QUOTING THE SPEAKERS' WORDS** Jane said, **"**Cats are fun to watch.**"** Mike said, **"Y**es, I agree. They're graceful and playful. Do you own a cat?**"**

(c) **HOW TO WRITE QUOTATIONS** 1. Add a comma after *said.* ★ ————————→ Jane said, 2. Add quotation marks. ★★ ————————→ Jane said, " 3. Capitalize the first word of the quotation. ——→ Jane said, "Cats 4. Write the quotation. Add a final period. ——→ Jane said, "Cats are fun to watch. 5. Add quotation marks **after** the period. ——→ Jane said, "Cats are fun to watch."	

(d) Mike said, "Yes, I agree. They're graceful and playful. Do you own a cat?" (e) *INCORRECT: Mike said, "Yes, I agree." "They're graceful and playful." "Do you own a cat?"*	When there are two (or more) sentences in a quotation, put the quotation marks at the beginning and end of the whole quote, as in (d). Do not put quotation marks around each sentence. As with a period, put the quotation marks after a question mark at the end of a quote.

(f) "Cats are fun to watch," Jane said. (g) "Do you own a cat?" Mike asked.	In (f): Notice that a comma (not a period) is used at the end of the quoted **sentence** when *Jane said* comes after the quote. In (g): Notice that a question mark (not a comma) is used at the end of the quoted **question**.

*Other common verbs besides *say* that introduce questions: *admit, announce, answer, ask, complain, explain, inquire, report, reply, shout, state, write.*

**Quotation marks are called "inverted commas" in British English.

☐ **EXERCISE 23. Quoted speech. (Chart 14-8)**

Directions: Write sentences in which you quote the speaker's exact words. Use **said** or **asked**. Punctuate carefully.

1. ANN: My sister is a student.
   → Ann said, "My sister is a student." OR "My sister is a student," Ann said.

2. ANN: Is your brother a student?

3. RITA: We're hungry.

4. RITA: We're hungry. Are you hungry too?★★★

★★★*Rita said* can come
    (1) at the beginning of the quote: ***Rita said,*** *"I'm tired. I'm going to bed."*
    (2) in the middle of the quote: *"I'm tired,"* ***Rita said***. *"I'm going to bed."*
    (3) at the end of the quote: *"I'm tired. I'm going to bed,"* ***Rita said***.

5. RITA: We're hungry. Are you hungry too? Let's eat.

6. JOHN F. KENNEDY: Ask not what your country can do for you. Ask what you can do for your country.

7. THE FOX: I'm going to eat you.*
   THE RABBIT: You have to catch me first!

☐ **EXERCISE 24. Quoted speech. (Chart 14-8)**
   Directions: Practice punctuating quoted speech. Notice that a new paragraph signals a change in speakers.

```
Both of your parents are deaf, aren't they I asked Roberto.

Yes, they are he replied

I'm looking for someone who knows sign language I said.  Do
you know sign language I asked.

He said of course I do.  I've been using sign language with
my parents since I was a baby.  It's a beautiful and expressive
language.  I often prefer it to spoken language.

A deaf student is going to visit our class next Monday.
Could you interpret for her I asked.

I'd be delighted to he answered.  I'm looking forward to
meeting her.  Can you tell me why she is coming?

She's interested in seeing what we do in our English classes
I said.
```

---

*In fables, animals are frequently given the ability to speak.

Directions: Practice writing quoted speech. Only the teacher's book is open.

1. Write exactly what I say. Identify that I said it. Punctuate carefully.

   a. (Say one short sentence—e.g., *The weather is nice today.*)

   b. (Say two short sentences—e.g., *The weather is nice today. It's warm.*)

   c. (Say two short sentences and one question—e.g., *The weather is nice today. It's warm. Do you like warm weather?*)

2. Write exactly what your classmates say.

   a. (. . .), please say one short sentence.

   b. (. . .), please ask one short question.

   c. (. . .), please say one short sentence and ask one short question.

3. (. . .) and I are going to have a short conversation. Everyone should write exactly what we say.

4. Pair up with another student. Have a brief conversation. Then write your conversation using quoted speech.

☐ EXERCISE 26. Quoted speech. (Chart 14-8)

Directions: Write a composition. Choose one of the following topics.

Topics:
1. Write a fable from your country in which animals speak. Use quotation marks.
2. Write a children's story that you learned when you were young. When the characters in your story speak, use quotation marks.
3. Make up a children's story. When the characters in your story speak, use quotation marks.
4. Make up any kind of story. When the characters in your story speak, use quotation marks.
5. Write a joke in which at least two people are talking to each other. Use quotation marks when the people are speaking.
6. Make up an interview you would like to have with a famous person. Use your imagination. Write the imaginary interview using quotation marks.

14-9 QUOTED SPEECH vs. REPORTED SPEECH

QUOTED SPEECH (a) Ann said, *"I'm* hungry." (b) Tom said, *"I need* my pen."	**Quoted speech** = giving a speaker's exact words. Quotation marks are used.★
REPORTED SPEECH (c) Ann said (that) *she was* hungry. (d) Tom said (that) *he needed* his pen.	**Reported speech** = giving the idea of a speaker's words. Not all of the exact words are used; pronouns and verb forms may change. Quotation marks are NOT used.★

★*Quoted speech* is also called "direct speech." *Reported speech* is also called "indirect speech."

□ EXERCISE 27. Reported speech: pronoun usage. (Chart 14-9)

   Directions: Change the pronouns from the quoted speech to reported speech.

   1. Mr. Smith said, "I need help with my luggage."

      → Mr. Smith said that ____he____ needed help with ____his____ luggage.

   2. Mrs. Peacock said, "I am going to visit my brother."

      → Mrs. Peacock said that _____ was going to visit _____ brother.

   3. Sue and Tom said, "We don't like our new apartment."

      → Sue and Tom said that _____ didn't like _____ new apartment.

   4. Joe said to me, "I will call you."

      → Joe said _____ would call _____ .

   5. Paul said to me, "I'll meet you at your house after I finish my work at my house."

      → Paul said that _____ would meet _____ at _____
      house after _____ finished _____ work at _____
      house.

14-10 VERB FORMS IN REPORTED SPEECH

(a) QUOTED: Joe said, "I *feel* good." (b) REPORTED: Joe said he *felt* good. (c) QUOTED: Sue said, "I *am* happy." (d) REPORTED: Sue said she *was* happy.	In formal English, if the reporting verb (e.g., *said*) is in the past, the verb in the noun clause is often also in a past form, as in (b) and (d).

—Ann said, "I am hungry."
(e) A: What did Ann just say? I didn't hear her.
  B: She said she *is* hungry.
(f) A: What did Ann say when she got home last night?
  B: She said she *was* hungry.
	In informal English, often the verb in the noun clause is not changed to a past form, especially when words are reported *soon after* they are said, as in (e).
	
	In *later reporting*, however, or in formal English, a past verb is commonly used, as in (f).

(g) Ann *says* (that) she *is* hungry.	If the reporting verb is present tense (e.g., *says*), no change is made in the noun clause verb.

QUOTED SPEECH	REPORTED SPEECH *formal or later reporting*	REPORTED SPEECH *informal or immediate reporting*
He said, "I *work* hard."	He said he *worked* hard.	He said he *works* hard.
He said, "I *am working* hard."	He said he *was working* hard.	He said he *is working* hard.
He said, "I *worked* hard."	He said he *had worked* hard.	He said he *worked* hard.
He said, "I *have worked* hard."	He said he *had worked* hard.	He said he *has worked* hard.
He said, "I *am going to work* hard."	He said he *was going to work* hard.	He said he *is going to work* hard.
He said, "I *will work* hard."	He said he *would work* hard.	He said he *will work* hard.
He said, "I *can work* hard."	He said he *could work* hard.	He said he *can work* hard.

□ EXERCISE 28. Reported speech: formal verb forms. (Chart 14-10)

Directions: Complete the reported speech sentences. Use formal verb forms.

1. Sara said, "I need some help."

→ Sara said (that) she ___needed___ some help.

2. Linda said, "I'm meeting David for dinner."

→ Linda said (that) she _____ David for dinner.

3. Ms. Bell said, "I have studied in Cairo."

→ Ms. Bell said (that) she _____ in Cairo.

4. Bill said, "I forgot to pay my electric bill."

→ Bill said (that) he _____ to pay his electric bill.

5. Barbara said, "I am going to fly to Hawaii for my vacation."

→ Barbara said (that) she _____ to Hawaii for her vacation.

6. I said, "I'll carry the box up the stairs."

→ I said (that) I _____ the box up the stairs.

7. Taufik said to me, "I can teach you to drive."

→ Taufik said (that) he _____ me to drive.

□ EXERCISE 29. Quoted vs. reported speech. (Charts 14-9 and 14-10)

Directions: Change the quoted speech to reported speech. Change the verb in quoted speech to a past form in reported speech if possible.

1. Jim said, "I'm sleepy."
→ *Jim said (that) he was sleepy.*

2. Sally said, "I don't like chocolate."

3. Mary said, "I'm planning to take a trip with my family."

4. Tom said, "I have already eaten lunch."

5. Kate said, "I called my doctor."

6. Mr. Rice said, "I'm going to go to Chicago."

7. Eric said to me, "I will come to your house at ten."

8. Jane said, "I can't afford to buy a new car."

9. Ann says, "I can't afford to buy a new car."

10. Ms. Topp said to me, "I want to see you in my office after your meeting with your supervisor."

14-11 COMMON REPORTING VERBS: *TELL, ASK, ANSWER/REPLY*

(a) Ann *said* that she was hungry. (b) Ann *told me* that she was hungry. (c) Ann *told Tom* that she was hungry. INCORRECT: Ann told that she was hungry INCORRECT: Ann said me that she was hungry.	A main verb that introduces reported speech is called a "reporting verb." *Say* is the most common reporting verb★ and is usually followed immediately by a noun clause, as in (a). *Tell* is also commonly used. Note that *told* is followed by *me* in (b) and by *Tom* in (c). *Tell* needs to be followed immediately by a (pro)noun object and then by a noun clause.
(d) QUOTED: Sue said (to me), "Are you tired?" REPORTED: Sue *asked (me) if* I was tired. (e) Sue *wanted to know if* I was tired. Sue *wondered if* I was tired. Sue *inquired whether or not* I was tired.	*Asked*, not *said*, is used to report questions. Questions are also reported by using *want to know*, *wonder*, and *inquire*.
(f) QUOTED: I said (to Ann), "I am not tired." REPORTED: I *answered/replied* that I wasn't tired.	The verbs *answer* and *reply* are often used to report replies.

*Other common reporting verbs: Ann **announced, commented, complained, explained, remarked, stated** that she was hungry.*

□ EXERCISE 30. SAY vs. TELL vs. ASK. (Chart 14-11)
   Directions: Complete the sentences with *said, told,* or *asked*.

1. Karen _____told_____ me that she would be here at one o'clock.

2. Tom _____said_____ that he was going to get here around two.

3. Mary _____asked_____ me what time I would arrive.

4. Jack _____ that I had a message.

5. Jack _____ me that someone had called me around ten-thirty.

6. I _____ Jack if he knew the caller's name.

7. I had a short conversation with Alice yesterday. I _____ her that I would help her move into her new apartment next week. She _____ that she would welcome the help. She _____ me if I had a truck or knew anyone who had a truck. I _____ her Jason had a truck. She _____ she would call him.

8. My uncle in Chicago called and _____ that he was organizing a surprise party for my aunt's 60th birthday. He _____ me if I could come to Chicago for the party. I _____ him that I would be happy to come. I _____ when it was. He _____ it was the last weekend in August.

☐ EXERCISE 31. SAY vs. TELL vs. ASK. (Chart 14-11)
Directions: Use **said, told,** and **asked** in reported speech. Work in groups or as a class.
Speaker A: Choose a sentence at random from the list and whisper it to B.
Speaker B: Report what Speaker A said. Use either informal or formal verb forms in the
noun clause, as you prefer.★

Example:
SPEAKER A: I need to talk to you after class. *(whispered to B)*
SPEAKER B: Ali told me/said he needed to talk to me after class. *(reported aloud)*

I'll call you tomorrow.	Are you going to be at home tonight?
Can you hear what I'm saying?	Have you ever met *(name of a person)*?
✓I need to talk to you after class.	What are you going to do after class today?
I'm getting hungry.	I'll meet you after class for a cup of coffee.
I walked to school this morning	I'm not going to be in class tomorrow.
Your pronunciation is very good.	Have you seen *(name of a current movie)*?
What kind of food do you like best?	I've already seen *(name of a current movie)*.
Is *(name of a person)* married?	Can you speak *(name of a language)*?
How long have you been married?	Do you know how to cook *(name of a dish)*?
Do you think it's going to rain?	Are you going to take another English class?

☐ EXERCISE 32. Noun clauses and questions. (Charts 5-2, 14-2 → 14-4, and 14-11)
Directions: Create questions, then report them using noun clauses.
Student A: Write five questions you want to ask Student B about his/her life or opinions.
Sign your name. Hand the questions to Student B.
Student B: Report what Student A wants to know. Make your report orally to the class
(or to a smaller group) or in writing. Provide the information if you can or
want to.

Example:
Student A's list of questions:
1. Where were you born?
2. What is your favorite color?
3. What do you think about the recent election in your country?
4. Who do you admire most in the world?

Student B's report:
1. (Student A) wants to know where I was born. I was born in (Caracas).
2. He/She asked me what my favorite color is/was. Blue, I guess.
3. He/She wants to know what I think about the recent election in my country. I'm
very pleased about the election. The new leader will be good for my country.
4. He/She wants to know who I admire most in the world. I'll have to think about
that. Probably my parents.

★In everyday spoken English, native speakers sometimes change noun clause verbs to past forms, and sometimes they
don't. In an informal reporting situation such as in this exercise, either informal/immediate reporting or formal/later
reporting tenses are appropriate.

☐ **EXERCISE 33. Reported vs. quoted speech. (Charts 14-9 → 14-11)**

Directions: Change the reported speech to quoted speech. Begin a new paragraph each time the speaker changes. Pay special attention to pronouns, verb forms, and word order.

Example: This morning my mother asked me if I had gotten enough sleep last night. I told her that I was fine. I explained that I didn't need a lot of sleep. She told me that I needed to take better care of myself.

WRITTEN: This morning my mother said, "Did you get enough sleep last night?"

"I'm fine," I replied. "I don't need a lot of sleep."

She said, "You need to take better care of yourself."

1. In the middle of class yesterday, my friend tapped me on the shoulder and asked me what time it was. I told her it was two-thirty.

2. I met Mr. Redford at the reception for international students. He asked me where I was from. I told him I was from Argentina.

3. When I was putting on my hat and coat, Robert asked me where I was going. I told him that I had a date with Anna. He wanted to know what we were going to do. I told him that we were going to a movie.

☐ **EXERCISE 34. Reported speech. (Charts 14-9 → 14-11)**

Directions: In a written report, change the quoted speech to reported speech. Use formal sequence of tenses.

Example: QUOTED: "What are you doing?" Mr. Singh asked me.

"I'm doing a grammar exercise," I told him.

REPORTED: Mr. Singh asked me what I was doing. I told him (that) I was doing a grammar exercise.

QUOTED CONVERSATION ONE:

"Where's Bill?" Susan asked me.

"He's in the lunch room," I replied.

"When will he be back in his office?" she wanted to know.

I said, "He'll be back around two."

QUOTED CONVERSATION TWO:

"Can you help me clean the hall closet?" Mrs. Ball asked her husband.

"I'm really busy," he told his wife.

"What are you doing?" she wanted to know.

"I'm fixing the zipper on my winter jacket," he replied.

Then she asked him, "Will you have some time to help me after you fix the zipper?"

He said, "I can't because I have to watch a really important ball game on TV."

With a note of exasperation in her voice, Mrs. Ball finally said, "I'll clean the closet myself."

□ EXERCISE 35. Reported speech. (Charts 14-9 → 14-11)
Directions: Complete the written report based on what the people in the picture say. Use the formal sequence of tenses.

AT THE RESTAURANT

WHAT ARE YOU GOING TO HAVE?

THEN WHY DID YOU COME?

NOTHING. I'M NOT HUNGRY. I'VE ALREADY EATEN.

I NEED TO TALK TO YOU ABOUT A PROBLEM I'M HAVING AT WORK.

    One day Susan and Paul were at a restaurant. Susan picked up her menu and looked at it. Paul left his menu on the table. Susan asked Paul _____**what he was going to**_____

_____**have**_____ . He said _____ anything because

he _____ . He _____ already _____ .

Susan was surprised. She asked him why _____ . He told her

_____ .

□ EXERCISE 36. Reported speech. (Charts 14-9 → 14-11)
Directions: Work in pairs. Each pair should create a short dialogue (five to ten sentences) based on one of the given situations. Each pair will then present their dialogue to the class. After the dialogue, the class will report what was said.

Sample situation: Have a conversation about going to the zoo.
Sample dialogue:
ANN: Would you like to go to the zoo tomorrow?
BOB: I can't. I have to study.
ANN: That's too bad. Are you sure you can't go? It will take only a few hours.
BOB: Well, maybe I can study in the morning and then go to the zoo in the afternoon.
ANN: Great!

Sample report:
    Ann asked Bob if he wanted to go to the zoo tomorrow. Bob said that he couldn't go because he had to study. Ann finally persuaded him to go. She said that it would take only a few hours. Bob decided that he could study in the morning and go to the zoo in the afternoon.

(Notice in the sample report: The writer gives the idea of the speakers' words without necessarily using the speakers' exact words.)

1. Have a conversation in which one of you invites the other to a party.

2. One of you is a teenager, and the other is a parent. The teenager is having problems at school and is seeking advice and encouragement.

3. The two of you are a married couple. One of you is reminding the other about the things s/he should or has to do today.

4. Have a conversation in which one of you persuades the other to begin a health program by taking up a new kind of exercise (jogging, walking, tennis, etc.).
   Beginning of the dialogue:
   > A: I need to get some physical exercise.
   > B: Why don't you take up . . . ?
   > A: No, I don't want to do that.

5. One of you is fourteen years old, and the other is the parent. The fourteen-year-old wants to stay out late tonight. What will the parent say?

6. One of you is a store detective, and the other is a shoplifter. The store detective has just seen the shoplifter take something.

7. One of you is a stubborn, old-fashioned, uneducated person who thinks the world is flat. The other tries to convince the stubborn one that the world is round.

☐ EXERCISE 37. Error analysis: noun clauses. (Chapter 14)
   Directions: Correct the errors.

1. My friend knows where do I live.

2. I don't know what is your e-mail address?

3. I think so that Mr. Lee is out of town.

4. Can you tell me that where Victor is living now?

5. I asked my uncle what kind of movies does he like.

6. I think, that my English has improved a lot.

7. Is true that people are basically the same everywhere in the world.

8. A man came to my door last week. I don't know who is he.

9. I want to know does Pedro have a laptop computer.

10. They have no children, but their dog understands what do they say.

11. Sam and I talked about his classes. He told that he don't like his algebra class.

12. A woman came into the room and ask me Where is your brother?

13. I felt very relieved when the doctor said, you will be fine. It's nothing serious.

14. I can understand what do I read in the newspaper, but if someone speaks the same

sentences to me, I can't understand what is he saying.

15. My mother asked me that: "When you will be home,,?

☐ EXERCISE 38. Noun clauses and questions. (Charts 5-2 and 14-1 → 14-4)
Directions: Do you agree or disagree with the given quote? What do you think about the role of technology in children's education? Discuss in groups or as a class. Write a summary of your views.

"Technology brings into the classroom new capabilities and possibilities in a child's learning environment. However, the most important factor in whether an educational setting is effective for a child is the teacher. The second most critical factor in a child's educational success is the child's home. Technology is far down the list of things that really make a difference, but it can make a difference."

— *John Newsom, Director of Instructional Technology*
Saratoga School District

APPENDIX *1*
Phrasal Verbs

CONTENTS

☐ EXERCISE 1. Preview: phrasal verbs. (Appendix 1)
Directions: Complete the sentences with the given words. The words may be used more than once.

away	*back*	*off*	*on*	*up*

1. The children's toys are all over the floor during the day, but before they go to bed, they always **put** their toys _____away_____.

2. In the winter, I never go outside without a coat. Before I go out, I always **put** _____ my coat.

3. I took a book from the shelf and then returned it to the exact same place. In other words, when I was finished looking at the book, I **put** it _____ where I found it.

4. Sometimes I postpone doing my homework in the evening and watch TV or talk on the phone instead. I probably should do my homework first, but sometimes I **put** it _____ and do it later.

5. I am not a late sleeper. I **get** _____ early almost every day.

6. I usually take the bus to work. I **get** _____ the bus near my apartment and **get** _____ just a block from my office.

7. We're leaving on May 1. We'll return May 7. As soon as we **get** _____ from our trip on the 7th, we'll call you.

8. When I entered the dark room, I **turned** _____ the lights. When I left, I **turned** them _____ because it's important to save electricity.

A1-1 PHRASAL VERBS: INTRODUCTION

(a) We **put off** our trip. We'll go next month instead of this month. *(put off = postpone)* (b) Jimmy, **put on** your coat before you go outdoors. *(put on = place clothes on one's body)* (c) Someone left the scissors on the table. They didn't belong there. I **put** them **away**. *(put away = put something in its usual or proper place)* (d) After I used the dictionary, I **put** it **back** on the shelf. *(put back = return something to its original place)*	In (a): *put off* = a phrasal verb. A phrasal verb = a verb and a particle that together have a special meaning. For example, *put off* means "postpone." A particle = a "small word" (e.g., *off, on, away back*) that is used in a phrasal verb. Note that the phrasal verbs with *put* in (a), (b), (c), and (d) all have different meanings.

SEPARABLE	

(e) We *put* **off** *our* **trip**. = (vb + **particle** + NOUN)
 	
(f) We *put our* **trip off**. = (vb + NOUN + **particle**)
 	
(g) We *put* **it off**. = (vb + PRONOUN + **particle**)
	Some phrasal verbs are **separable**: a NOUN OBJECT can either
	  (1) follow the particle, as in (e), OR
	  (2) come between (separate) the verb and the particle, as in (f).
	If a phrasal verb is separable, a PRONOUN OBJECT comes between the verb and the particle, as in (g).
	  INCORRECT: We put off it.

NONSEPARABLE	

(h) I *ran* **into** Bob. = (vb + **particle** + NOUN)
(i) I *ran* **into** him. = (vb + **particle** + PRONOUN)
	If a phrasal verb is **nonseparable**, a NOUN or PRONOUN always follows (never precedes) the particle, as in (h) and (i).
	  INCORRECT: I ran Bob into.
	  INCORRECT: I ran him into.

☐ **EXERCISE 2. Phrasal verbs: separable vs. nonseparable. (Charts A1-1 and A1-4)**
    Directions: If the phrasal verb is separable, mark SEPARABLE. If it is not separable, mark NONSEPARABLE.

1. CORRECT: I *turned* the light *on.*
   CORRECT: I *turned on* the light.
                               turn on =   ☒ SEPARABLE   ☐ NONSEPARABLE

2. CORRECT: I *ran into* Mary.
   (INCORRECT: I *ran* Mary *into.*)
                               run into =   ☐ SEPARABLE   ☒ NONSEPARABLE

3. CORRECT: Joe *looked up* the definition.
   CORRECT: Joe *looked* the definition *up.*
                               look up =   ☐ SEPARABLE   ☐ NONSEPARABLE

4. CORRECT: I *got off* the bus.
   (INCORRECT: I *got* the bus *off.*)
                               get off =   ☐ SEPARABLE   ☐ NONSEPARABLE

5. CORRECT: I *took off* my coat.
   CORRECT: I *took* my coat *off.*
                               take off =   ☐ SEPARABLE   ☐ NONSEPARABLE

6. CORRECT: I *got in* the car and left.
   (INCORRECT: I *got* the car *in* and left.)
                                 get in =   ☐ SEPARABLE   ☐ NONSEPARABLE

7. CORRECT: I *figured out* the answer.   figure out =   ☐ SEPARABLE
    CORRECT: I *figured* the answer *out*.   ☐ NONSEPARABLE

8. CORRECT: I *turned* the radio *off*.   turn off =   ☐ SEPARABLE
    CORRECT: I *turned off* the radio.   ☐ NONSEPARABLE

☐ EXERCISE 3. Identifying phrasal verbs. (Chart A1-1)
    Directions: <u>Underline</u> the second part of the phrasal verb in each sentence.

    1. I *figured* the answer <u>out</u>.
    2. The teacher *called* <u>on</u> me in class.
    3. I *made* up a story about my childhood.
    4. I feel okay now. I *got* over my cold last week.
    5. The students *handed* their papers in at the end of the test.
    6. I *woke* my roommate up when I got home.
    7. I *picked* up a book and started to read.
    8. I *turned* the radio on to listen to some music.
    9. When I don't know how to spell a word, I *look* it up in the dictionary.
    10. I opened the telephone directory and *looked* up the number of a plumber.
    11. I *put* my book down and *turned* off the light.

☐ EXERCISE 4. Phrasal verbs: separable vs. nonseparable. (Chart A1-1)
    Directions: Complete the sentences with pronouns and particles. If the phrasal verb is separable, circle SEP. If it is nonseparable, circle NONSEP.

    1. I *got over* my cold. → I got _____ over it _____.   SEP   (NONSEP)

    2. I *made up* the story. → I made _____ it up _____.   (SEP)   NONSEP

    3. I *put off* my homework. → I put _____.   SEP   NONSEP

    4. I *wrote down* the numbers. → I wrote _____.   SEP   NONSEP

    5. I *ran into* Robert. → I ran _____.   SEP   NONSEP

    6. I *figured* the answer *out*. → I figured _____. SEP   NONSEP

    7. I *took off* my shoes. → I took _____.   SEP   NONSEP

    8. I *got over* my cold. → I got _____.   SEP   NONSEP

    9. I *turned off* the lights. → I turned _____.   SEP   NONSEP

    10. I *threw away* the newspaper. → I threw _____.   SEP   NONSEP

Group A: Phrasal Verbs (separable)*		
Verb	**Definition**	**Example**
figure out	find the solution to a problem	I *figured out* the answer.
hand in	give homework, papers, etc., to a teacher	We *handed in* our homework.
hand out	give something to this person, then to that person, then to another person, etc.	The teacher *handed out* the test papers.
look up	look for information in a dictionary, a telephone directory, an encyclopedia, etc.	I *looked* a word *up* in the dictionary.
make up	invent (a story)	Children like to *make up* stories.
pick up	lift	Tom *picked up* the baby.
put down	stop holding or carrying	I *put down* the heavy packages.
put off	postpone	We *put off* our trip until next summer.
put on	place clothes on one's body	I *put on* my coat before I left.
take off	remove clothes from one's body	I *took off* my coat when I arrived.
throw away ⎫ . . . . put in the trash, discard		I *threw away* my old notebooks.
throw out ⎭		I *threw out* my old notebooks.
turn off	stop a machine or a light	I *turned off* the lights and went to bed.
turn on	start a machine or a light	I *turned on* the light so I could read.
wake up	stop sleeping	My wife *woke* me *up* at six.
write down	write a note on a piece of paper	I *wrote* his phone number *down*.

*Appendix 1 presents phrasal verbs in small groups to be learned and practiced one group at a time. A complete reference list can be found on pp. 449–452.

☐ EXERCISE 5. Phrasal verbs. (Group A)
  Directions: Complete the sentences with the given particles.

away	*down*	*in*	*off*	*on*	*out*	*up*

1. Before I left home this morning, I put _____on_____ my coat.

2. When I got to class this morning, I took my coat _____.

3. The students handed their homework _____.

4. Johnny made _____ a story. He didn't tell the truth.

5. The weather was bad, so we put _____ the picnic until next week.

6. Alice looked a word _____ in her dictionary.

7. Alice wrote the definition _____.

8. My roommate is messy. He never picks _____ his clothes.

9. The teacher handed the test papers _____ at the beginning of the class period.

10. A strange noise woke _____ the children in the middle of the night.

11. When some friends came to visit, Chris stopped watching TV. He turned the television set _____.

12. It was dark when I got home last night, so I turned the lights _____.

13. Peggy finally figured _____ the answer to the arithmetic problem.

14. When I was walking through the airport, my arms got tired. So I put my suitcases _____ for a minute and rested.

15. I threw _____ yesterday's newspaper.

□ EXERCISE 6. Phrasal verbs. (Group A)
   Directions: Complete the sentences with pronouns and particles.

1. A: Did you postpone your trip to Puerto Rico?
   B: Yes, we did. We put _____it off_____ until next summer.

2. A: Is Pat's phone number 322-4454 or 322-4455?
   B: I don't remember. You'd better look _____. The telephone directory is in the kitchen.

3. A: Is Mary asleep?
   B: Yes. I'd better wake _____. She has a class at nine.

4. A: Do you want to keep these newspapers?
   B: No. Throw _____.

5. A: I'm hot. This sweater is too heavy.
   B: Why don't you take _____?

6. A: Is that story true?
   B: No. I made _____.

7. A: When does the teacher want our compositions?
   B: We have to hand _____ tomorrow.

8. A: I made an appointment with Dr. Armstrong for three o'clock next Thursday.
   B: You'd better write _____ so you won't forget.

9. A: Do you know the answer to this problem?
   B: No. I can't figure _____.

10. A: Johnny, you're too heavy for me to carry. I have to put _____.
    B: Okay, Mommy.

11. A: Oh, dear. I dropped my pen. Could you pick _____ for me?
    B: Sure.

12. A: How does this tape recorder work?
    B: Push this button to turn _____, and push that button to turn _____.

13. A: I have some papers for the class. Ali, would you please hand _____ for me?
    B: I'd be happy to.

14. A: Timmy, here's your hat. Put _____ before you go out. It's cold outside.
    B: Okay, Dad.

Group B: Phrasal Verbs (nonseparable)		
Verb	**Definition**	**Example**
call on	ask (someone) to speak in class	The teacher *called on* Ali.
come from	originate	Where do these bananas *come from?*
get over	recover from an illness or a shock	Sue *got over* her cold and returned to work.
get off	leave ⎱ a bus/airplane/train/subway	I *got off* the bus at Maple Street.
get on	enter ⎰	I *got on* the bus at Pine Street.
get in	enter ⎱ a car, a taxi	I *got in* the taxi at the airport.
get out of	leave ⎰	I *got out of* the taxi at the hotel.
look into	investigate	Someone needs to *look into* this problem.
run into	meet by chance	I *ran into* Peter at the market.

□ EXERCISE 7. Phrasal verbs. (Group B)
   Directions: Complete the sentences with particles.

   1. When I raised my hand in class, the teacher called ___on___ me.

   2. While I was walking down the street, I ran _____ an old friend.

   3. Fred feels okay today. He got _____ his cold.

   4. Last week I flew from Chicago to Miami. I got _____ the plane in Chicago. I got _____ the plane in Miami.

   5. Sally took a taxi to the airport. She got _____ the taxi in front of her apartment building. She got _____ the taxi at the airport.

   6. I take the bus to school every day. I get _____ the bus at the corner of First Street and Sunset Boulevard. I get _____ the bus just a block away from the classroom building.

   7. Mr. Zabidi will look _____ renting a car for his weekend trip.

   8. Where do snow leopards come _____?

□ EXERCISE 8. Review: phrasal verbs. (Groups A and B)
   Directions: Complete the sentences with particles and pronouns.

   1. I had the flu, but I got _____over it_____ a couple of days ago.

   2. I was wearing gloves. I took _____ before I shook hands with Mr. Lee.

   3. Stacy needed to find the date India became independent. She looked _____ on the computer and wrote _____ in her notebook.

   4. I tried to solve the math problem, but I couldn't figure _____.

   5. It looked like rain, so I got my raincoat from the closet and put _____ before I left the apartment.

   6. A: Have you seen Dan this morning?
      B: Not this morning. I ran _____ at the movie last night.

7. A: Why do you look so worried?

 B: I don't have my homework. My mother threw _____ with the trash this morning. If Ms. Anthony calls _____ in class to answer homework questions, I'll have to tell her what happened.

 A: She'll never believe your story. She'll think you made _____.

8. A: Miss Smith, our supply room is out of pencils again. Why are we always running out of pencils? What is the problem?

 B: I don't know, sir. I'll look _____ right away.

☐ EXERCISE 9. Review: phrasal verbs. (Groups A and B)
Directions: Work in pairs.
Speaker A: Read the cue. Your book is open.
Speaker B: Finish Speaker A's sentence. Your book is closed.

Example:
SPEAKER A *(book open):* Yesterday I cleaned my closet. I found an old pair of shoes that I don't wear anymore. I didn't keep the shoes. I threw . . . .
SPEAKER B *(book closed):* . . . them away/out.

1. The teacher gave us some important information in class yesterday. I didn't want to forget it, so I wrote . . . .
2. When I raised my hand in class, the teacher called . . . .
3. I was carrying a suitcase, but it was too heavy, so I put . . . .
4. I didn't know the meaning of a word, so I looked . . . .
5. I haven't finished my work. I'll do it later. I'm going to put . . . .
6. The lights were off in the dark room, so I turned . . . .
7. (. . .) isn't wearing his/her hat right now. When s/he got to class, s/he took . . . .
8. My pen just fell on the floor. Could you please pick . . . ?

Switch roles.

9. I saw (. . .) at a concert last night. I was surprised when I ran . . . .
10. When you finish using a stove, you should always be careful to turn . . . .
11. When I finished my test, I handed . . . .
12. Is (. . .) sleeping?! Would you please wake . . . ?
13. What's the answer to this problem? Have you figured . . . ?
14. I don't need this piece of paper anymore. I'm going to throw . . . .
15. I had the flu last week, but now I'm okay. I got . . . .
16. I told a story that wasn't true. I made . . . .

Switch roles.

17. Name some means of transportation that you get on.
18. Name some that you get in.
19. Name some that you get off.

Switch roles.

20. Name some that you get out of.

21. Name some things that you turn on.

22. Name some things that you turn off.

Group C: Phrasal Verbs (separable)		
Verb	**Definition**	**Example**
ask out	ask (someone) to go on a date	Tom *asked* Mary *out*. They went to a movie.
call back	return a telephone call	I'll *call* you *back* tomorrow.
call off	cancel	We *called off* the picnic due to bad weather.
call up	make a telephone call	I *called up* my friend in New York.
give back	return something to someone	I borrowed Al's pen, then I *gave* it *back*.
hang up	hang on a hanger or a hook	I *hung* my coat *up* in the closet.
pay back	return borrowed money to someone	Thanks for the loan. I'll *pay* you *back* soon.
put away	put something in its usual or proper place	I *put* the clean dishes *away*.
put back	return something to its original place	I *put* my papers *back* into my briefcase.
put out	extinguish (stop) a fire, a cigarette	We *put out* the campfire before we left.
shut off	stop a machine or light, turn off	I *shut off* my printer before I left the office.
try on	put on clothing to see if it fits	I *tried on* several pairs of shoes.
turn down	decrease the volume	Sue *turned down* the music. It was too loud.
turn up	increase the volume	Al *turned up* the radio. He likes loud music.

☐ EXERCISE 10. Phrasal verbs. (Group C)

Directions: Complete the sentences with pronouns and particles.

1. A: Could you lend me a couple of bucks?

   B: Sure.

   A: Thanks. I'll pay _____you back_____ tomorrow.

2. A: The radio is too loud. Could you please turn _____?

   B: Sure.

3. A: I can't hear the TV. Could you please turn _____?

   B: I'd be glad to.

4. A: Have you heard from Jack lately?

   B: No. I think I'll call _____ tonight and see how he is.★

5. A: Someone's at the door. Can I call _____?

   B: Sure.

6. A: Where's my coat?

   B: I hung _____.

————————

★There is no difference in meaning between *I'll call him tonight* and *I'll call him up tonight*.

7. A: Did you leave the water on?

   B: No. I shut _____ when I finished washing my hands.

8. A: May I borrow your calculator? I'll give _____ to you tomorrow.

   B: Sure. Keep it as long as you need it.

9. A: You can't smoke that cigarette in the auditorium. You'd better put

   _____ before we go in.

   B: Okay.

10. A: Do you have any plans for Saturday night?

    B: Yes. I have a date. Jim Olsen asked _____.

11. A: Did you take my eraser off my desk?

    B: Yes, but I put _____ on your desk when I was finished.

    A: Oh? It's not here.

    B: Look under your notebook.

    A: Ah. There it is. Thanks.

12. A: Your toys are all over the floor, kids. Before you go to bed, be sure to

    put _____.

    B: Okay, Daddy.

13. A: Did you go to Kathy's party last night?

    B: She didn't have the party. She called _____.

14. A: This is a nice-looking coat. Why don't you try _____?

    B: How much does it cost?

15. A: That's Annie's toy, Tommy. Give _____ to her.

    B: No!

☐ EXERCISE 11. Review: phrasal verbs. (Groups A, B, and C)

Directions: Complete the sentences with pronouns and particles. Work in pairs, in groups, or as a class.

Example:
SPEAKER A *(book open):* I wanted to be sure to remember (Anna)'s phone number, so I
                        wrote . . . .
SPEAKER B *(book closed):* . . . it down.

1. I can't hear the tape. Could you please turn . . . ?
2. I dropped my book. Could you please pick . . . ?
3. This is a hard problem. I can't figure . . . .
4. I bought these shoes a few days ago. Before I bought them, I tried . . . .
5. Where's your homework? Did you hand . . . ?
6. (. . .) asked (. . .) to go to a movie with him. He asked . . . .
7. We postponed the picnic. We put . . . .
8. I didn't know the meaning of a word, so I looked . . . .

9. We don't need that light. Would you please turn . . . ?

10. My coat was too warm to wear inside, so I took . . . .

(Switch roles if working in pairs.)

11. That music is too loud. Could you please turn . . . ?

12. These papers are for the class. Could you please hand . . . ?

13. (. . .) was going to have a party, but s/he canceled it. S/he called . . . .

14. My coat is in the closet. I hung . . . .

15. The story I told wasn't true. I made . . . .

16. I was cold. So I reached for my sweater and put . . . .

17. (. . .) fell asleep in class, so I woke . . . .

18. I was finished with the tools, so I put . . . .

19. I don't need these papers, so I'm going to throw . . . .

20. Let's listen to the radio. Would you please turn . . . ?

Group D: Phrasal Verbs (separable)		
Verb	**Definition**	**Example**
cross out	draw a line through	I *crossed out* the misspelled word.
fill in	complete by writing in a blank space	We *fill in* blanks in grammar exercises.
fill out	write information on a form	I *filled out* a job application.
fill up	fill completely with gas, water, coffee, etc.	We *filled up* the gas tank.
find out	discover information	I *found out* where he lives.
have on	wear	She *has* a blue blouse *on*.
look over	examine carefully	*Look over* your paper for errors before you hand it in.
point out	call attention to	The teacher *pointed out* a misspelling.
print out	create a paper copy from a computer	I finished the letter and *printed* it *out*.
tear down	destroy a building	They *tore down* the old house and built a new one.
tear out (of)	remove (paper) by tearing	I *tore* a page *out of* a magazine.
tear up	tear into small pieces	I *tore up* the secret note.
turn around / **turn back**	change to the opposite direction	After a mile, we *turned around/back*.
turn over	turn the top side to the bottom	I *turned* the paper *over* and wrote on the back.

☐ EXERCISE 12. Phrasal verbs. (Group D)
Directions: Complete the phrasal verbs.

1. There was no name on the front of the paper, so I turned it __*over*__ and looked on the back.

2. My wife pointed _____ an interesting article in the newspaper.

3. Before you submit the job application, look it _____ carefully to make sure you've filled it _____ correctly.

4. A: Good news! I've been accepted at the University of Florida.

   B: Great. When did you find _____?

   A: I got a letter in the mail today.

5. A: My roommate moved last week. Before he left, he filled _____ a change-of-address card at the post office, but I'm still getting some of his mail. What should I do?

   B: Cross _____ the old address on a letter and write in his new one. Also write "please forward" on the letter. You don't have to use another stamp.

6. How much does it cost to fill _____ your gas tank?

7. We're doing an exercise. We're filling _____ blanks with prepositions.

8. When I went to Dr. Green's office for the first time, I had to fill _____ a long form about my health history.

9. I made a mistake on the check I was writing, so I tore it _____ and wrote another.

10. An old building was in the way of the new highway through the city, so they tore the old building _____.

11. Sam has his new suit _____ today. He looks very handsome.

12. My employer asked for the latest sales figures, so I went to my computer and quickly printed _____ a new report.

13. I think we're going in the wrong direction. Let's turn _____.

☐ **EXERCISE 13. Phrasal verbs. (Group D)**
Directions: Work in pairs, in groups, or as a class.

Example:
SPEAKER A *(book open):* When your cup is empty, you fill it . . . .
SPEAKER B *(book closed):* . . . up.

1. I made a mistake, so I crossed it . . . .
2. When you read your composition carefully for mistakes, you look it . . . .
3. When you're done writing something on the computer and you want a hard copy, you print it . . . .
4. You look in reference books when you want to find something . . . .
5. If you want to remove a page from your notebook, you tear it . . . .
6. If you destroy an old building, you tear it . . . .
7. If you tear something into many small pieces, you tear it . . . .

(Switch roles if working in pairs.)
8. If you want to see the back of a piece of paper, you turn it . . . .
9. If you discover you are walking in the wrong direction, you turn . . . .
10. If you put water in a glass to the very top, you fill it . . . .

11. If you give information on an application form, you fill it . . . .

12. When you write words in a blank, you fill the blank . . . .

13. When you're wearing something, we say that you have it . . . .

14. When there's something the teacher wants to make sure we notice, she points it . . . .

Group E: Phrasal Verbs (separable)		
Verb	**Definition**	**Example**
blow out	extinguish (a match, a candle)	He *blew* the candles *out*.
bring back	return	She *brought* my books *back* to me.
bring up	(1) raise (children)	The Lees *brought up* six children.
	(2) mention, start to talk about	He *brought* the news *up* in conversation.
cheer up	make happier	The good news *cheered* me *up*.
clean up	make neat and clean	I *cleaned up* my apartment.
give away	donate, get rid of by giving	I didn't sell my old bike. I *gave* it *away*.
help out	assist (someone)	Could you please *help* me *out*?
lay off	stop employment	The company *laid off* 100 workers.
leave on	(1) not turn off (a light, a machine)	Please *leave* the light *on*.
	(2) not take off (clothing)	I *left* my coat *on* at the movie theater.
take back	return	She *took* a book *back* to the library.
take out	invite out and pay	He *took* Mary *out*. They went to a movie.
talk over	discuss	We *talked* the problem *over*.
think over	consider	I *thought* the problem *over*.
work out	solve	We *worked* the problem *out*.

☐ EXERCISE 14. Phrasal verbs. (Group E)
Directions: Complete the sentences.

1. When I am sad, my friends can always cheer me ____up____ .

2. These are bad economic times. Businesses are laying _____ hundreds of workers.

3. After I lit the candles, I blew _____ the match.

4. Jack and Ann are having some problems in their marriage, but they are trying hard to work them _____ .

5. When they have a problem, they always try to talk it _____ to make sure they are communicating with each other.

6. A: I'm leaving. Should I turn the TV off?

   B: No. Please leave it _____ .

7. Saturday night I took my parents _____ to a fancy restaurant.

8. After dinner, Michael helped me clean _____ the kitchen.

9. I was brought _____ in the South.

10. You're welcome to borrow my tools, but when you finish, please be sure to bring them _____ .

11. Don't forget to take the video _____ to the store today.

12. I didn't take off my hat when I came inside. I left it _____.

13. I hate to bring this problem _____, but we need to talk about it.

14. A: Are you going to accept the job offer?

    B: I don't know. I'm still thinking it _____.

15. I can't sell this old sofa. I guess I'll give it _____. Someone will be able to use it.

16. My parents usually help me _____ with a little money when I'm having trouble paying my bills.

☐ EXERCISE 15. Phrasal verbs. (Group E)

Directions: Work in pairs, in groups, or as a class.

Example:
SPEAKER A *(book open):* If I am sad, you will try to cheer me . . . .
SPEAKER B *(book closed):* . . . up.

1. You need to return that book to the library. You need to take it . . . .

2. I lost my job. The company I'm working for laid me . . . .

3. If you don't need the light from a candle anymore, you blow it . . . .

4. If we need to discuss something, we need to talk it . . . .

5. You walked into a cold building. Instead of taking your coat off, you left it . . . .

6. If you give your old clothes to charity, you give them . . . .

7. When we have a problem to solve, we need to work it . . . .

8. If I lend you something, I want you to return it to me. I want you to bring it . . . .

(Switch roles if working in pairs.)

9. Parents feed, educate, and love their children. They bring their children . . . .

10. When I finish using my computer, I don't turn it off each time. Instead, I often leave it . . . .

11. Someone offered you a job. Before you give an answer, you need some time to think it . . . .

12. When you take guests to a restaurant and pay the bill, you take them . . . .

13. If you introduce a topic into a conversation, you bring it . . . .

14. If you make a mess, you need to clean it . . . .

15. You rented a video. When you were finished with it, you took it . . . .

16. When friends need our assistance, we offer to help them . . . .

A1-2 PHRASAL VERBS: INTRANSITIVE

(a) The machine *broke down*. (b) Please *come in*. (c) I *fell down*.	Some phrasal verbs are intransitive; i.e., they are not followed by an object.

Group F: Phrasal Verbs (intransitive)		
Verb	**Definition**	**Example**
break down	stop functioning properly	My car *broke down* on the highway.
break out	happen suddenly	War *broke out* between the two countries.
break up	separate, end a relationship	Ann and Tom *broke up*.
come in	enter a room or building	May I *come in?*
dress up	put on nice clothes	People usually *dress up* for weddings.
eat out	eat outside of one's home	Would you like to *eat out* tonight?
fall down	fall to the ground	I *fell down* and hurt myself.
get up	get out of bed in the morning	What time did you *get up* this morning?
give up	quit doing something or quit trying	I can't do it. I *give up*.
go on	continue	Let's not stop. Let's *go on*.
go out	not stay home	Jane *went out* with her friends last night.
grow up	become an adult	Jack *grew up* in Sweden.
hang up	end a telephone conversation	When we finished talking, I *hung up*.
move in (**to**)	start living in a new home	Some people *moved in* next door to me.
move out (**of**)	stop living at a place	My roommate is *moving out*.
show up	come, appear	Jack *showed up* late for the meeting.
sit back	put one's back against a chair back	*Sit back* and relax. I'll get you a drink.
sit down	go from standing to sitting	Please *sit down*.
speak up	speak louder	I can't hear you. You'll have to *speak up*.
stand up	go from sitting to standing	I *stood up* and walked to the door.
start over	begin again	I lost count, so I *started over*.
stay up	not go to bed	I *stayed up* late last night.
take off	ascend in an airplane	The plane *took off* 30 minutes late.

☐ EXERCISE 16. Phrasal verbs. (Group F)

Directions: Complete the sentences.

1. A: Are you comfortable?

   B: Yes. This is a very comfortable chair.

   A: Good. Now just sit __back__ and take it easy. There's nothing to worry about.

2. A: I'm exhausted. I can't go _____. I have to stop and rest.

   B: Let's sit in the shade of that tree. I'll get you some water.

3. A: I don't feel like cooking tonight. Let's eat _____.

   B: Okay. Where do you want to go?

4. A: Are you going to get dressed _____ for the symphony tonight?

   B: Yes. I think so. You?

5. A: What time do you usually get _____ in the morning?

   B: Around seven.

6. A: Knock, knock. Hello? Is anyone here? Professor Cook?

   B: Ah, Miss Sweeney. Hello. Come _____, come _____. Here, have a seat. Please sit _____.

7. A: I couldn't print out my composition.

   B: Why not?

   A: My printer broke _____.

8. A: Are you going to bed soon?

   B: No. I think I'll stay _____ for a while and read.

9. A: When I saw a pregnant woman on the crowded bus, I stood _____ and gave her my seat.

   B: Good for you. That's very considerate.

10. A: I don't feel like staying home. Let's go _____ this evening. I'm bored.

    B: How about going to a movie?

    A: Great! Let's go!

11. A: A riot broke _____ after the soccer finals.

    B: I find it hard to believe that people riot over a sports event.

12. A: Are you all right? What happened?

    B: I tripped on the rug and fell _____.

    A: Let me help you up.

13. A: Shall we begin the meeting without Ms. Lane?

    B: Yes. She'll probably show _____ soon, but we can begin without her.

14. A: When are Bill and Gloria getting married?

    B: They're not. They broke _____.

15. A: Don't forget that Grandma is a little hard of hearing.

    B: I won't. I'll be sure to speak _____ when I'm talking to her.

16. There's an empty apartment next to mine. My neighbors moved _____. Why don't you move _____? It'd be fun to live next door to each other.

17. A: It's been fun talking to you, but I need to hang _____ now.

    B: Okay. Let's talk again tomorrow.

18. I can't solve this math problem. I give _____.

19. Dan had trouble figuring out what to say in his letter to his girlfriend. He had to start _____ three times.

20. My flight was supposed to leave at 6:30, but the plane didn't take _____ until nearly 8:00.

□ EXERCISE 17. Phrasal verbs. (Group F)

Directions: Work in pairs, in groups, or as a class.

Example:
SPEAKER A *(book open)*: Don't stop. I'm enjoying your story. Please go . . . .
SPEAKER B *(book closed)*: . . . on.

1. If I'm sitting and then get to my feet, I stand . . . .

2. If you don't feel like staying at home, you go . . . .

3. When you put on nice clothes for a special affair, you dress . . . .

4. If you're not tired at night, instead of going to bed you stay . . . .

5. When you play soccer, sometimes you fall . . . .

6. When a fax machine stops working, you say that it broke . . . .

7. You walk to a chair, and then you sit . . . .

Switch roles.

8. If you relax into the chair, you sit . . . .

9. If two people end a relationship, they break . . . .

10. After you stop sleeping in the morning, you get . . . .

11. If you continue to do something and don't stop, you go . . . .

12. If a war begins, you say that it broke . . . .

13. If I invite you to enter my house, I say, "Please come . . . ."

14. If you eat at a restaurant instead of at home, you eat . . . .

15. If you ask someone to speak more loudly, you ask them to speak . . . .

16. When someone arrives for a meeting, you say that he or she shows . . . .

17. When you decide a problem is impossible to solve, you give . . . .

18. An airplane increases its speed on the runway, and then it takes . . . .

A1-3 THREE-WORD PHRASAL VERBS

	Some two-word verbs (e.g., ***drop in***) can become three-word verbs (e.g., ***drop in on***).
(a) Last night some friends ***dropped in***.	In (a): ***drop in*** is not followed by an object. It is an intransitive phrasal verb (i.e., it is not followed by an object).
(b) Let's ***drop in on*** Alice this afternoon.	In (b): ***drop in on*** is a three-word phrasal verb. Three-word phrasal verbs are transitive (they are followed by objects).
(c) We *dropped in on* ***her*** last week.	In (c): Three-word phrasal verbs are nonseparable (the noun or pronoun follows the phrasal verb).

Group G: Phrasal Verbs (three-word)		
Verb	**Definition**	**Example**
drop in (on)	visit without calling first or without an invitation	We *dropped in on* my aunt.
drop out (of)	stop attending (school)	Beth *dropped out of* graduate school.
fool around (with)	have fun while wasting time	My son likes to *fool around with* his friends on the weekends.
get along (with)	have a good relationship with	I *get along* well *with* my roommate.
get back (from)	return from (a trip)	When did you *get back from* Hawaii?
get through (with)	finish	I *got through with* my work before noon.
grow up (in)	become an adult	Hamid *grew up in* Sweden.
look out (for)	be careful	*Look out for* that car!
run out (of)	finish the supply of (something)	We *ran out of* gas.
sign up (for)	put one's own name on a list	Did you *sign up for* the school trip?
watch out (for)	be careful	*Watch out for* that car!

☐ EXERCISE 18. Phrasal verbs. (Group G)
   Directions: Complete the phrasal verbs.

   1. Look ___out___ ! There's a car coming!

   2. Look ___out___ ___for___ that car!

   3. Where did you grow _____?

   4. I grew _____ _____ Springfield.

   5. I couldn't finish the examination. I ran _____ _____ time.

   6. A: What did you do yesterday?

      B: Nothing much. I just fooled _____.

   7. A: Hi, Chris! What's up? I haven't seen you in a long time. Where have you been?

      B: I went to California last week to visit my brother.

      A: Oh? When did you get _____ _____ California?

      B: Just yesterday.

   8. A: Where's Jack? He hasn't been in class for at least two weeks.

      B: He dropped _____ _____ school.

   9. A: Watch _____ _____ that truck!

      B: What truck?

   10. A: What time do you expect to get _____ _____ your homework?

       B: In about an hour, as soon as I finish reading this chapter.

   11. A: I haven't seen the Grants for a long time. Let's drop _____ _____ them this evening.

       B: We'd better call first. They may not like unexpected company.

12. A: I want to change my room in the dorm.

B: Why?

A: I don't get _____ _____ my roommate.

13. A: I signed _____ _____ Mrs. Grant's art class.

B: You're lucky. I tried to sign _____ too, but it was full.

Group H: Phrasal Verbs (three-word)		
Verb	Definition	Example
come along (**with**) .... accompany		Do you want to *come along with* us?
come over (**to**) .... visit the speaker's place		Some friends are *coming over* tonight.
cut out (**of**) .... remove with scissors or knife		I *cut* an article *out of* today's paper.
find out (**about**) .... discover information about		When did you *find out about* the problem?
get together (**with**) .... join, meet		Let's *get together* after work today.
go back (**to**) .... return to a place		I *went back to* work after my illness.
go over (**to**) .... (1) approach		I *went over to* the window.
(2) visit another's home		Let's *go over to* Jim's tonight.
hang around (**with**) } .... spend undirected, idle time		John likes to *hang around* the coffee shop.
hang out (**with**) }		Kids like to *hang out with* each other.
keep away (**from**) .... not give to		*Keep* matches *away from* children.
set out (**for**) .... begin a trip		We *set out for* our destination at dawn.
sit around (**with**) .... sit and do nothing		You can't just *sit around.* Do something.

☐ EXERCISE 19. Phrasal verbs. (Group H)
Directions: Complete the sentences.

1. A: Are you busy tonight?

B: No.

A: Would you like to come ____along____ ____with____ us to the movie?

2. A: I need to talk to you. When can we get _____?

B: How about tomorrow morning?

3. My teenage daughter is lazy. All she wants to do is hang _____ _____ her friends.

4. I saw a young child who was all alone. He was crying. I went _____ _____ him and asked if I could help.

5. How did you find _____ _____ the change in the schedule?

6. It's a long trip. We'd better set _____ early.

7. Keep that cat _____ _____ me! I'm allergic.

8. Do you want to come _____ tonight? We could watch a movie or something.

9. There was a funny cartoon in the newspaper. I cut it _____ for my aunt.

10. A: I was born in Viet Nam, but I haven't been there for many years.

 B: Do you expect to go _____ _____ Viet Nam again someday?

 A: Yes.

11. A: What did you do at your aunt's?

 B: Not much. We just sat _____ and talked about the relatives who weren't there.

A1-4 PHRASAL VERBS: A REFERENCE LIST*

A **ask out** . . . . *ask (someone) to go on a date*

B **blow out** . . . . *extinguish (a match, a candle)*
 break down . . . . *stop functioning properly*
 break out . . . . *happen suddenly*
 break up . . . . *separate, end a relationship*
 bring back . . . . *return*
 bring up . . . . *(1) raise (children)*
 (2) mention, start to talk about

C **call back** . . . . *return a telephone call*
 call off . . . . *cancel*
 call on . . . . *ask (someone) to speak in class*
 call up . . . . *make a telephone call*
 cheer up . . . . *make happier*
 clean up . . . . *make neat and clean*
 come along (**with**) . . . . *accompany*
 come from . . . . *originate*
 come in . . . . *enter a room or building*
 come over (**to**) . . . . *visit the speaker's place*
 cross out . . . . *draw a line through*
 cut out (**of**) . . . . *remove with scissors or knife*

D **dress up** . . . . *put on nice clothes*
 drop in (**on**) . . . . *visit without calling first or without an invitation*
 drop out (**of**) . . . . *stop attending (school)*

E **eat out** . . . . *eat outside of one's home*

F **fall down** . . . . *fall to the ground*
 figure out . . . . *find the solution to a problem*

*For more information about phrasal verbs and their meanings, see dictionaries written especially for second language learners, such as the *Longman Advanced American Dictionary,* the *Longman Dictionary of Contemporary English,* the *Collins* COBUILD *English Learner's Dictionary,* or the *Oxford Advanced Learner's Dictionary.*

fill in . . . . *complete by writing in a blank space*

fill out . . . . *write information on a form*

fill up . . . . *fill completely with gas, water, coffee, etc.*

find out (about) . . . . *discover information*

fool around (with) . . . . *have fun while wasting time*

G   **get along (with)** . . . . *have a good relationship with*

    get back (from) . . . . *return from (a trip)*

    get in . . . . *enter a car, a taxi*

    get off . . . . *leave a bus/an airplane/a train/a subway*

    get on . . . . *enter a bus/an airplane/a train/a subway*

    get out of . . . . *leave a car, a taxi*

    get over . . . . *recover from an illness or a shock*

    get together (with) . . . . *join, meet*

    get through (with) . . . . *finish*

    get up . . . . *get out of bed in the morning*

    give away . . . . *donate, get rid of by giving*

    give back . . . . *return (something) to (someone)*

    give up . . . . *quit doing (something) or quit trying*

    go on . . . . *continue*

    go back (to) . . . . *return to a place*

    go out . . . . *not stay home*

    go over (to) . . . . (1) *approach*

        (2) *visit another's home*

    grow up (in) . . . . *become an adult*

H   **hand in** . . . . *give homework, test papers, etc., to a teacher*

    hand out . . . . *give (something) to this person, then to that person, then to*
        another person, etc.

    hang around/out (with) . . . . *spend undirected time*

    hang up . . . . (1) *hang on a hanger or a hook*

        (2) *end a telephone conversation*

    have on . . . . *wear*

    help out . . . . *assist (someone)*

K   **keep away (from)** . . . . *not give to*

    keep on . . . . *continue*

L   **lay off** . . . . *stop employment*

    leave on . . . . (1) *not turn off (a light, a machine)*

        (2) *not take off (clothing)*

    look into . . . . *investigate*

	look over	*examine carefully*
	look out (for)	*be careful*
	look up	*look for information in a dictionary, a telephone directory,n an encyclopedia, etc.*
M	**make up**	*invent (a story)*
	move in (to)	*start living in a new home*
	move out (of)	*stop living at a place*
P	**pay back**	*return borrowed money to (someone)*
	pick up	*lift*
	point out	*call attention to*
	print out	*create a paper copy from a computer*
	put away	*put (something) in its usual or proper place*
	put back	*return (something) to its original place*
	put down	*stop holding or carrying*
	put off	*postpone*
	put on	*put clothes on one's body*
	put out	*extinguish (stop) a fire, a cigarette*
R	**run into**	*meet by chance*
	run out (of)	*finish the supply of (something)*
S	**set out (for)**	*begin a trip*
	shut off	*stop a machine or a light, turn off*
	sign up (for)	*put one's name on a list*
	show up	*come, appear*
	sit around (with)	*sit and do nothing*
	sit back	*put one's back against a chair back*
	sit down	*go from standing to sitting*
	speak up	*speak louder*
	stand up	*go from sitting to standing*
	start over	*begin again*
	stay up	*not go to bed*
T	**take back**	*return*
	take off	*(1) remove clothes from one's body*
		(2) ascend in an airplane
	take out	*invite out and pay*
	talk over	*discuss*
	tear down	*destroy a building*
	tear out (of)	*remove (paper) by tearing*

tear up . . . . *tear into small pieces*

think over . . . . *consider*

throw away/out . . . . *put in the trash, discard*

try on . . . . *put on clothing to see if it fits*

turn around

turn back } . . . . *change to the opposite direction*

turn down . . . . *decrease the volume*

turn off . . . . *stop a machine or a light*

turn on . . . . *start a machine or a light*

turn over . . . . *turn the top side to the bottom*

turn up . . . . *increase the volume*

W **wake up** . . . . *stop sleeping*

watch out (for) . . . . *be careful*

work out . . . . *solve*

write down . . . . *write a note on a piece of paper*

APPENDIX 2
Preposition Combinations

CONTENTS	

A2-1 PREPOSITION COMBINATIONS: INTRODUCTION

adj + prep (a) Ali is **absent from** class today. verb + prep (b) This book **belongs to** me.	At, from, of, on, and to are examples of prepositions.* Prepositions are often combined with adjectives, as in (a), and verbs, as in (b).

*See Chart A2-2, p. 463, for a list of prepositions.

☐ EXERCISE 1. Preview: preposition combinations. (Chart A2-2)
   Directions: These sentences contain a sampling of the preposition combinations in this Appendix. Complete the sentences with prepositions. How many do you already know? Which ones do you still need to learn?

   1. Tom is devoted _____to_____ his family.

   2. I'm afraid I don't agree _____ you.

   3. I wasn't aware _____ the problem.

   4. I'm excited _____ the concert.

   5. Are you satisfied _____ your progress?

   6. She warned us _____ the coming storm.

   7. What's the matter _____ him?

   8. It doesn't matter _____ me.

   9. I got rid _____ my old bicycle.

   10. I don't approve _____ smoking in public.

   11. The solution is clear _____ me.

   12. Who is responsible _____ this?

   13. The hotel provides guests _____ towels.

   14. Protect your eyes _____ the sun.

   15. He filled my cup _____ hot tea.

Directions: The prepositions in the column on the left are the correct completions for the blanks. To test yourself and practice the preposition combinations, follow these steps:

(1) **Cover** the ANSWERS column with a piece of paper.

(2) Complete the SENTENCES.

(3) Then remove the paper and check your answers.

(4) Then **cover** both the ANSWERS and the SENTENCES to complete your own REFERENCE LIST.

(5) Again check your answers.

Preposition Combinations: Group A		
Answers	Sentences	Reference List
from	He was absent ___from___ work.	be absent ___from___ s.t.**
of	I'm afraid ___of___ rats.	be afraid ___of___ s.t./s.o.**
about	I'm angry ___about___ it.	be angry _____ s.t.
at / with	I'm angry _____ you.	be angry _____ s.o.
about	I'm curious _____ many things.	be curious _____ s.t./s.o.
to	This is equal _____ that.	be equal _____ s.t./s.o.
with	I'm familiar _____ that book.	be familiar _____ s.t./s.o.
of	The room is full _____ people.	be full _____ (people/things)
for	I'm happy _____ you.	be happy _____ s.o.
about	I'm happy _____ your good luck.	be happy _____ s.t.
to	He's kind _____ people and animals.	be kind _____ s.o.
to	She's always nice _____ me.	be nice _____ s.o.
to	Are you polite _____ strangers?	be polite _____ s.o.
for	I'm ready _____ my trip.	be ready _____ s.t.
for	She's thirsty _____ knowledge.	be thirsty _____ s.t.

**s.t. = "something"   s.o. = "someone"

☐ EXERCISE 2. Preposition combinations. (Group A)

Directions: Complete the sentences with prepositions.

1. Mr. Porter is nice ___to___ everyone.

2. Kathy was absent _____ class yesterday.

3. Are you ready _____ the test?

4. I'm angry _____ Greg.

5. Are you afraid _____ dogs?

6. Sometimes people aren't kind _____ animals.

7. One inch is equal _____ 2.54 centimeters.

8. I'm thirsty _____ a big glass of water.

9. Joe has good manners. He's always polite _____ everyone.

_____

*Appendix 2 presents preposition combinations in small groups to be learned and practiced one group at a time.

10. I'm not familiar _____ that book. Who wrote it?

11. Children ask "Why?" a lot. They are curious _____ everything.

12. Anna got a good job that pays well. I'm very happy _____ her.

13. Anna is very happy _____ getting a new job.

14. Jack's thermos bottle is full _____ coffee.

□ EXERCISE 3. Review: preposition combinations. (Group A)
Directions: Make up a review quiz for a classmate. On a separate piece of paper, write sentences with the preposition combinations in Group A, but omit the preposition. Leave a blank for a classmate to write in the correct preposition. When your classmate has finished the quiz you wrote, correct his or her answers.

Example: 1. Are you afraid _____ loud noises?
2. It's important to be nice _____ other people.
3. (Etc.)

□ SELF-STUDY PRACTICE. Group B.
Directions: The prepositions in the column on the left are the correct completions for the blanks. Follow the same steps you used for Group A on page 454.

	Preposition Combinations: Group B	
Answers	**Sentences**	**Reference List**
for	I admire you ____for____ your honesty.	**admire** s.o. ____for____ s.t.
for	He applied _____ a job.	**apply** _____ s.t.
with	I argued _____ my husband.	**argue** _____ s.o.
about / over	We argued _____ money.	**argue** _____ s.t.
in	My parents believe _____ me.	**believe** _____ s.o./s.t.
from	I borrowed a book _____ Oscar.	**borrow** s.t. _____ s.o.
with	I discussed the problem _____ Jane.	**discuss** s.t. _____ s.o.
with	Please help me _____ this.	**help** s.o. _____ s.t.
to	I introduced Sam _____ Helen.	**introduce** s.o. _____ s.o./s.t.
at	I laughed _____ the joke.	**laugh** _____ s.t./s.o.
for	I'm leaving _____ Rome next week.	**leave** _____ (a place)
at	Don't stare _____ me.	**stare** _____ s.o./s.t.

□ EXERCISE 4. Preposition combinations. (Group B)
Directions: Complete the sentences with prepositions.

1. I borrowed this dictionary _____ Pedro.

2. Could you please help me _____ these heavy suitcases?

3. Sue, I'd like to introduce you _____ Ed Jones.

4. You shouldn't stare _____ other people. It's not polite.

5. Do you believe _____ ghosts?

6. Are you laughing _____ my mistake?

7. I admire my father _____ his honesty and intelligence.

8. I argued _____ Anna _____ politics.

9. I discussed my educational plans _____ my parents.

10. I applied _____ admission to the University of Massachusetts.

11. We're leaving _____ Cairo next week.

12. Mrs. Wertz smiled _____ her grandchildren.

☐ SELF-STUDY PRACTICE. Group C.

Directions: The prepositions in the column on the left are the correct completions for the blanks. Follow the same steps you used for Group A on page 454.

Preposition Combinations: Group C		
Answers	**Sentences**	**Reference List**
of	I'm aware _____ the problem.	**be aware** _____ s.t./s.o.
for	Smoking is bad _____ you.	**be bad** _____ s.o./s.t.
to	The solution is clear _____ me.	**be clear** _____ s.o
about	Alex is crazy _____ football.	**be crazy** _____ s.t.
from	Jane is very different _____ me.	**be different** _____ s.o./s.t.
for	Venice is famous _____ its canals.	**be famous** _____ s.t.
to / with	She's friendly _____ everyone.	**be friendly** _____ s.o.
for	Fresh fruit is good _____ you.	**be good** _____ s.o.
for	I'm hungry _____ some chocolate.	**be hungry** _____ s.t.
in	I'm interested _____ art.	**be interested** _____ s.t.
about	I'm nervous _____ my test scores.	**be nervous** _____ s.t.
with	I'm patient _____ children.	**be patient** _____ s.o.
of	My parents are proud _____ me.	**be proud** _____ s.o./s.t.
for	Who's responsible _____ this?	**be responsible** _____ s.t./s.o.
about	I'm sad _____ losing my job.	**be sad** _____ s.t.
to	A canoe is similar _____ a kayak.	**be similar** _____ s.o./s.t.
of / about	I'm sure _____ the facts.	**be sure** _____ s.t.

☐ EXERCISE 5. Preposition combinations. (Group C)

Directions: Complete the sentences with prepositions.

1. I don't understand that sentence. It isn't clear _____ me.

2. Mark Twain is famous _____ his novels about life on the Mississippi River.

3. I'm hungry _____ some chocolate ice cream.

4. Our daughter graduated from the university. We're very proud _____ her.

5. A lot of sugar isn't good _____ you. It is bad _____ your teeth.

6. Who was responsible _____ the accident?

7. My coat is similar _____ yours, but different _____ Ben's.

8. Some people aren't friendly _____ strangers.

9. My daughter is crazy _____ horses. She is very interested _____ them.

10. Sara knows what she's talking about. She's sure _____ her facts.

11. Are you aware _____ the number of children who die each day throughout the world? According to one report, 40,000 children die each day, mostly due to malnutrition and lack of minimal medical care.

☐ SELF-STUDY PRACTICE. Group D.
Directions: The prepositions in the column on the left are the correct completions for the blanks. Follow the same steps you used for Group A on page 454.

Preposition Combinations: Group D		
Answers	**Sentences**	**Reference List**
with	I agree _____ you.	**agree** _____ s.o.
about	I agree with you _____ that.	**agree with** s.o. _____ s.t.
in	We arrived _____ Toronto at six.	**arrive** _____ (*a city/country*)
at	We arrived _____ the hotel.	**arrive** _____ (*a building/room*)
about	We all complain _____ the weather.	**complain** _____ s.t./s.o.
about	Sally complained to me _____ my dog.	**complain to** s.o. _____ s.t.
of	A book consists _____ printed pages.	**consist** _____ s.t.
with	I disagree _____ you.	**disagree** _____ s.o.
about	I disagree with you _____ that.	**disagree with** s.o. _____ s.t.
from	She graduated _____ Reed College.	**graduate** _____ (*a place*)
to	Ted invited me _____ a picnic.	**invite** s.o. _____ s.t.
to	We listened _____ some music.	**listen** _____ s.t./s.o.
for	Jack paid _____ my dinner.	**pay** _____ s.t.
to	I talked _____ Anna.	**talk** _____ s.o.
about	We talked _____ her problem.	**talk** _____ s.t.
on	A salesman waited _____ a customer.	**wait** _____ s.o.
for	We waited _____ the bus.	**wait** _____ s.t.

☐ EXERCISE 6. Preposition combinations. (Group D)
Directions: Complete the sentences with prepositions.

1. Tom paid _____ his airplane ticket in cash.

2. Joan graduated _____ high school two years ago.

3. I waited _____ the bus.

4. Jim is a waiter. He waits _____ customers at a restaurant.

5. I have a different opinion. I don't agree _____ you.

6. I arrived _____ this city last month.

7. I arrived _____ the airport around eight.

8. I listened _____ the news on TV last night.

9. This exercise consists _____ verbs that are followed by certain prepositions.

10. Jack invited me _____ his party.

11. I complained _____ the landlord _____ the leaky faucet in the kitchen.

12. Annie disagreed _____ her father about the amount of her weekly allowance.

13. Did you talk _____ Professor Adams _____ your grades?

☐ EXERCISE 7. Review: preposition combinations. (Groups A and B)
Directions: Complete the sentences with prepositions.

1. Dan is always nice _____ everyone.

2. A: How long do you need to keep the Spanish book you borrowed _____ me?

   B: I'd like to keep it until I'm ready _____ the exam next week.

3. A: Why weren't you more polite _____ Alan's friend?

   B: Because he kept staring _____ me all evening. He made me nervous.

4. A: We're going to beat you in the soccer game on Saturday.

   B: No way. Two of your players are equal _____ only one of ours.

   A: Oh yeah? We'll see.

5. Stop pouring! My cup is already full _____ coffee.

6. May I please borrow some money _____ you? I'm thirsty _____ an ice cream soda, and we're walking right by the ice cream shop.

7. A: Do you believe _____ astrology?

   B: I'm really not familiar _____ it.

8. A: Mike, I really admire you _____ your ability to remember names. Will you help me _____ the introductions?

   B: Sure. Ellen, let me introduce you _____ Pat, Andy, Debbie, Olga, Ramon, and Kate.

☐ EXERCISE 8. Review: preposition combinations. (Groups A, B, C, and D)
Directions: Complete the sentences with prepositions.

1. Everyone is talking _____ the explosion in the high school chemistry lab.

2. Carlos was absent _____ class six times last term.

3. Fruit consists mostly _____ water.

4. Our children are very polite _____ adults, but they argue _____ their playmates all the time.

5. Three centimeters is equal _____ approximately one and a half inches.

6. I'm not ready _____ my trip. I haven't packed yet.

7. I borrowed some clothes _____ my best friend.

8. Are you familiar _____ ancient Greek history?

9. I discussed my problem _____ my uncle.

10. Someday astronauts will travel _____ another solar system.

11. Jennifer arrived _____ this city last Tuesday.

12. Jack's plane arrived _____ the airport in Mexico City two hours ago.

13. I admire you _____ your ability to laugh _____ yourself when you make a silly mistake.

14. A: Why are you staring _____ the wall?

    B: I'm not. I'm thinking.

15. A: Are you two arguing _____ each other _____ your in-laws again?

    B: Do you know what his father did?

    C: Oh yeah? Listen _____ what her sister said.

    A: Shhh. I don't want to hear any of this. Stop complaining _____ me _____ your relatives. I don't agree _____ either of you.

☐ SELF-STUDY PRACTICE. Group E.

Directions: The prepositions in the column on the left are the correct completions for the blanks. Follow the same steps you used for Group A on page 454.

Preposition Combinations: Group E		
Answers	**Sentences**	**Reference List**
about	She asked me _____ my trip.	**ask** s.o. _____ s.t. (inquire)
for	She asked me _____ my advice.	**ask** s.o. _____ s.t. (request)
to	This book belongs _____ me.	**belong** _____ s.o.
about / of	I dreamed _____ my girlfriend.	**dream** _____ s.o./s.t.
about	Do you know anything _____ jazz?	**know** _____ s.t.
at	I'm looking _____ this page.	**look** _____ s.t./s.o.
for	I'm looking _____ my lost keys.	**look** _____ s.t./s.o. (search)
like	Anna looks _____ her sister.	**look** _____ s.o. (resemble)
to	I'm looking forward _____ vacation.	**look forward** _____ s.t.
to	Your opinion doesn't matter _____ me.	**matter** _____ s.o.
with	Something is the matter _____ the cat.	**be the matter** _____ s.t./s.o.
for	I'm searching _____ my lost keys.	**search** _____ s.t./s.o.
from	She separated the boys _____ the girls.	**separate** *(this)* _____ *(that)*
about / of	I warned them _____ the danger.	**warn** s.o. _____ s.t.

□ EXERCISE 9. Preposition combinations. (Group E)
   Directions: Complete the sentences with prepositions.

1. What's the matter _____ you? What's wrong?

2. We can go out for dinner, or we can eat at home. It doesn't matter _____ me.

3. To make this recipe, you have to separate the egg whites _____ the yolks.

4. I don't know anything _____ astrology.

5. I'm looking forward _____ my vacation next month.

6. Dennis dreamed _____ his girlfriend last night.

7. Right now I'm doing an exercise. I'm looking _____ my book.

8. Jim can't find his book. He's looking _____ it.

9. Jim is searching _____ his book.

10. I asked the waitress _____ another cup of coffee.

11. I asked Rebecca _____ her trip to Japan.

12. Does this pen belong _____ you?

13. The city was warned _____ the hurricane in advance.

□ SELF-STUDY PRACTICE. Group F.
   Directions: The prepositions in the column on the left are the correct completions for the blanks. Follow the same steps you used for Group A on page 454.

	Preposition Combinations: Group F	
Answers	**Sentences**	**Reference List**
to	I apologized _____ my friend.	**apologize** _____ s.o.
for	I apologized _____ my behavior.	**apologize** _____ s.t.
of	I don't approve _____ Al's behavior.	**approve** _____ s.t.
to / with	I compared this book _____ that book.	**compare** *(this)* _____ *(that)*★
on	I depend _____ my family.	**depend** _____ s.o./s.t.
of / from	He died _____ heart disease.	**die** _____ s.t.
from	The teacher excused me _____ class.	**excuse** s.o. _____ s.t.
for	I excused him _____ his mistake.	**excuse** s.o. _____ s.t. (forgive)
for	I forgave him _____ his mistake.	**forgive** s.o. _____ s.t.
of	I got rid _____ my old clothes.	**get rid** _____ s.t./s.o.
to	What happened _____ your car?	**happen** _____ s.t./s.o.
on	I insist _____ the truth.	**insist** _____ s.t.
from	I protected my eyes _____ the sun.	**protect** s.t./s.o. _____ s.t./s.o.
on	I am relying _____ you to help me.	**rely** _____ s.o./s.t.
of	Mr. Lee took care _____ the problem.	**take care** _____ s.t./s.o.
for	Thank you _____ your help.	**thank** s.o. _____ s.t.

★Also possible: *I compared this **and** that.* (***And*** is not a preposition. A parallel structure with ***and*** may follow ***compare.***)

☐ EXERCISE 10. Preposition combinations. (Group F)

Directions: Complete the sentences with prepositions.

1. I apologized _____ Ann _____ stepping on her toe.

2. I thanked Sam _____ helping me fix my car.

3. My grandfather doesn't approve _____ gambling.

4. Please forgive me _____ forgetting your birthday.

5. My friend insisted _____ taking me to the airport.

6. Please excuse me _____ being late.

7. Children depend _____ their parents for love and support.

8. In my composition, I compared this city _____ my hometown.

9. Umbrellas protect people _____ rain.

10. We're relying _____ Jason to help us move into our new apartment.

11. We had mice in the house, so we set some traps to get rid _____ them.

12. What happened _____ your finger? Did you cut it?

13. My boss excused me _____ the meeting when I became ill.

14. What did old Mr. Hill die _____?

☐ SELF-STUDY PRACTICE. Group G.

Directions: The prepositions in the column on the left are the correct completions for the blanks. Follow the same steps you used for Group A on page 454.

Preposition Combinations: Group G		
Answers	**Sentences**	**Reference List**
to	I'm accustomed _____ hot weather.	**be accustomed** _____ s.t.
to	I added a name _____ my address book.	**add** *(this)* _____ *(that)*
on	I'm concentrating _____ this exercise.	**concentrate** _____ s.t.
into	I divided the cookie _____ two pieces.	**divide** *(this)* _____ *(that)*
from	They escaped _____ prison.	**escape** _____ *(a place)*
about	I heard _____ the prison escape.	**hear** _____ s.t./s.o.
from	I heard about it _____ my cousin.	**hear about** s.t. _____ s.o.
from	The escapees hid _____ the police.	**hide** *(s.t.)* _____ s.o.
for	We're hoping _____ good weather.	**hope** _____ s.t.
by	I multiplied 8 _____ 2.	**multiply** *(this)* _____ *(that)*
to / with	I spoke _____ the teacher.	**speak to/with** _____ s.t.
about	We spoke to Dr. Carter _____ my problem.	**speak** _____ s.o.
about	I told the teacher _____ my problem.	**tell** s.o. _____ s.t.
from	I subtracted 7 _____ 16.	**subtract** *(this)* _____ *(that)*
about	I wonder _____ lots of curious things.	**wonder** _____ s.t.

□ EXERCISE 11. Preposition combinations. (Group G)
   Directions: Complete the sentences with prepositions.

   1. Shhh. I'm trying to concentrate _____ this math problem.

   2. How did the bank robbers escape _____ jail?

   3. Did you tell your parents _____ the dent in their new car?

   4. We're hoping _____ good weather tomorrow so we can go sailing.

   5. Did you hear _____ the earthquake in Turkey?

   6. I heard _____ my sister last week. She wrote me a letter.

   7. I spoke _____ Dr. Rice _____ my problem.

   8. I'm not accustomed _____ cold weather.

   9. When you divide 2 _____ 6, the answer is 3.

   10. When you subtract 1 _____ 6, the answer is 5.

   11. When you multiply 6 _____ 3, the answer is 18.★

   12. When you add 6 _____ 4, the answer is 10.★★

   13. George wondered _____ his team's chances of winning the tennis
       tournament.

   14. Sally hid her journal _____ her younger sister.

□ EXERCISE 12. Review: preposition combinations. (Groups E, F, and G)
   Directions: Complete the sentences with prepositions.

   1. He insisted _____ knowing the truth.

   2. I was wondering _____ that!

   3. What's the matter _____ you today?

   4. He hid the money _____ his wife.

   5. We separated the ducks _____ the chickens.

   6. I apologized _____ my boss _____ my mistake.

   7. We got rid _____ the cockroaches in our apartment.

   8. Who does this book belong _____?

   9. The prisoners escaped _____ their guards.

   10. What happened _____ you?

   11. I'm sorry. Please forgive me _____ my error.

   12. What did Mr. Grant die _____?

   13. Parents protect their children _____ harm.

   14. Shh. I'm trying to concentrate _____ my work.

   _____
   ★Also possible: *multiply 6 **times** 3*
   ★★Also possible: *add 6 **and** 4; add 6 **plus** 4*

15. I rely _____ my friends for their help.

16. I don't approve _____ his lifestyle.

17. The official warned us _____ the danger of traveling there.

18. Fresh vegetables are good _____ you.

19. We're looking forward _____ your visit.

20. Does it matter _____ you what time I call this evening?

A2-2 PREPOSITION COMBINATIONS: A REFERENCE LIST

A
be absent from
be accustomed to
   add *(this)* to *(that)*
be acquainted with
   admire *(someone)* for *(something)*
be afraid of
   agree with *(someone)* about *(something)*
be angry at / with *(someone)* about / over *(something)*
   apologize to *(someone)* for *(something)*
   apply for *(something)*
   approve of
   argue with *(someone)* about / over *(something)*
     arrive at *(a building / a room)*
     arrive in *(a city / a country)*
   ask *(someone)* about *(something)*
   ask *(someone)* for *(something)*
be aware of

B
be bad for
   believe in
   belong to
be bored with / by
   borrow *(something)* from *(someone)*

C
be clear to
   combine with
   compare *(this)* to / with *(that)*
   complain to *(someone)* about *(something)*
be composed of
   concentrate on
   consist of
be crazy about
be crowded with
be curious about

D
   depend on *(someone)* for *(something)*
be dependent on *(someone)* for *(something)*

be devoted to
   die of / from
be different from
   disagree with *(someone)* about *(something)*
be disappointed in
   discuss *(something)* with *(someone)*
   divide *(this)* into *(that)*
be divorced from
be done with
   dream about / of
   dream of

E
be engaged to
be equal to
   escape from *(a place)*
be excited about
   excuse *(someone)* for *(something)*
   excuse from
be exhausted from

F
be familiar with
be famous for
   feel about
   feel like
   fill *(something)* with
be finished with
   forgive *(someone)* for *(something)*
be friendly to / with
be frightened of / by
be full of

G
   get rid of
be gone from
be good for
   graduate from

H
   happen to
be happy about *(something)*

be happy for *(someone)*
hear about / of *(something)* from *(someone)*
help *(someone)* with *(something)*
hide *(something)* from *(someone)*
hope for
be hungry for

I
insist on
be interested in
introduce *(someone)* to *(someone)*
invite *(someone)* to *(something)*
be involved in

K
be kind to
know about

L
laugh at
leave for *(a place)*
listen to
look at
look for
look forward to
look like

M
be made of
be married to
matter to
be the matter with
multiply *(this)* by *(that)*

N
be nervous about
be nice to

O
be opposed to

P
pay for
be patient with
be pleased with / about
play with
point at
be polite to
prefer *(this)* to *(that)*
be prepared for

protect *(this)* from *(that)*
provide *(someone)* with
be proud of

Q
be qualified for

R
read about
be ready for
be related to
rely on
be responsible for

S
be sad about
be satisfied with
be scared of / by
search for
separate *(this)* from *(that)*
be similar to
speak to / with *(someone)* about *(something)*
stare at
subtract *(this)* from *(that)*
be sure of / about

T
take care of
talk about *(something)*
talk to / with *(someone)* about *(something)*
tell *(someone)* about *(something)*
be terrified of / by
thank *(someone)* for *(something)*
think about / of
be thirsty for
be tired from
be tired of
translate from *(one language)* to *(another)*

U
be used to

W
wait for
wait on
warn about / of
wonder about
be worried about

Index

A/an, 312–313, 326–327 *(Look on pages 312 through 313 and on pages 326 through 327.)*	The numbers following the words listed in the index refer to page numbers in the text.
Clauses defined, 343*fn.* *(Look at the footnote on page 343.)*	The letters *fn.* mean "footnote." Footnotes are at the bottom of a page or the bottom of a chart.

NOTES